The Truest Fairy Tale

For Alan, my brother,
who has always deserved better

We all believe fairy-tales, and live in them.

G.K. Chesterton, *Heretics*

Human nature simply cannot subsist without a hope and aim of some kind.

G.K. Chesterton, *Heretics*

Religion is exactly the thing which cannot be left out –
because it includes everything.

G.K. Chesterton, *Heretics*

The Truest Fairy Tale

A Religious Anthology of
G.K. Chesterton

Kevin L. Morris

The Lutterworth Press

The Lutterworth Press
P.O. Box 60
Cambridge
CB1 2NT

www.lutterworth.com
publishing@lutterworth.com

First Published in 2007

ISBN: 978 0 7188 3061 8

British Library Cataloguing in Publication Data
A catalogue record is available from the British Library

Contents

Foreword

by Professor Eamon Duffy

Gilbert Keith Chesterton was a one-man publishing phenomenon. More than ninety of his books appeared in his own (relatively short) lifetime – novels and short stories, travel-books, light essays, comic and serious verse, plays, literary criticism, social and economic theory, popular philosophy and religious apologetic – all generated in the course of an exhausting career as a debater, lecturer, and political activist, and as a magazine-editor and weekly columnist for a dozen London papers. He was also a talented comic draughtsman, illustrating his own and other men's books, and, at the end of his life, an accomplished radio broadcaster.

The millions of words he poured out made him a celebrity, who commanded four-figure lecture fees in Depression America, while his spectacular bulk, boozy *bonhomie* and theatrical appearance (slouch hat, pince-nez, cloak and swordstick) made him a cartoonist's godsend. The crime-novelist John Dixon Carr modelled a best-selling fictional detective, Dr Gideon Fell, round Chesterton's public persona. He was a hard man to ignore or forget, though not everyone liked what they saw. The diarist A.C. Benson, author of *Land of Hope and Glory*, and precisely the sort of establishment figure Chesterton loved to loathe, recalled him making an after-dinner speech at the Pepysean Feast at Magdalene College, Cambridge, and noted with fastidious horror the sweat which streamed under Chesterton's dress-shirt cuff as he talked, to sizzle off the end of his cigar.

Chesterton was a product of the turbulent last phase of the Victorian age. He was a child of Imperial Britain who was to become one of the fiercest critics of imperialism, a vehement opponent of the Boer War and author of an essay on Indian nationalism which decisively influenced Gandhi's thought and action. Born in 1874, he studied art at the Slade School during the era of Wilde, Beardsley and the *Yellow Book*, and he formed his deepest convictions in reaction against the decadent nihilism which he believed was sapping the culture of his time. Educated in a politically liberal Unitarian household, he struggled his way to a robust Christian faith which saw in the dogmatic and moral affirmations of mainstream Christianity an anchor in the rudderless drift of contemporary society. But he used his gift of aphorism and paradoxical inversion to present those traditional affirmations as the opposite of strait-jacketed convention. The 'Romance of Orthodoxy' was the distilled wisdom of the ages, as fresh and heady as champagne after the cloying absinthe of the Aesthetes or the joyless teetotalism of late-Victorian secular Puritanism.

He clothed these perceptions with the gift of memorable utterance. Every paragraph of Chesterton builds towards a ringing final sentence, every argument is clinched with an epigram. Reading him, one never forgets that, for all his rejection of Aestheticism, his literary taste was formed in the age of Stevenson and Wilde. This way of writing all too easily degenerates into laboured cleverness, and can be very tiresome. Reading Chesterton it is difficult at times not to sympathise with the early reviewer who declared that paradox and aphorism should flavour a salad like a sliver of onion; but 'Mr Chesterton's salad is all onion'. Nevertheless, in the midst of all this sometimes showy intellectual sharp-shooting, Chesterton scores an astonishing number of hits. When W.H. Auden edited an anthology of aphorisms for Faber and Faber, he included more extracts from Chesterton's work than from any other writer except Dr Johnson, Goethe and Nietzsche.

Chesterton's religious world-view was formulated very early in his career as a writer. It is implicit in his first sustained critique of the philosophical alternatives to Christianity on offer in Edwardian England, the rumbustious polemic *Heretics*, published in 1905. It was fully articulated three years later as a sparkling defence of historic Christianity, unquestionably his best and most constructive argumentative book, *Orthodoxy*. Thereafter, though he consolidated and revisited the themes set out in those two works, he added little that was entirely new. In 1925, however, he extended the scope of his critique of contemporary secularism in *The Everlasting Man*, a remarkable reply to H.G. Wells' *Outline of History*, characterized by a brilliantly iconoclastic scepticism about the assumptions underlying much early twentieth-century 'scientific' anthropology.

The consistency of Chesterton's religious and social convictions informs much of his best writing; but, combined with the relentless pressures on a jobbing journalist, it makes for an occasional sense of *déjà vu*. Anyone who reads him in bulk will recognise themes, tropes and even phrases reworked and reused from essay to essay, book to book. Most of his books were in fact compilations of recycled journalism, much of it in the form of whimsical excurses on apparently inconsequential topics – 'A piece of chalk', 'On lying in bed', 'On aids to golf', 'Cheese'. In fact, even his worst books are seldom without flashes of brilliance and unforgettable phrases; but the taste for essay-as-entertainment which shaped his staple production has passed, and only the rare enthusiast is likely to plough through these collections, whose very titles are a turn-off – *Tremendous*

Trifles, Fancies versus Fads, Generally Speaking, All Things Considered.

Chesterton was a prodigious worker, but a very lazy writer: a literary critic of genius, he habitually quoted from his prodigious memory, rarely entirely accurately, and he never checked a reference in his life. Even his best books are littered with contradictions and mistakes. In 1933 he was commissioned to write a short monograph on St Thomas Aquinas. He had perhaps read some Aquinas as a young man (his secretary Dorothy Collins claimed so, though there is little independent sign of it). Characteristically, he launched on the book and dictated more than half without notes or preparatory reading of any kind. He then told his secretary, 'I want you to go to London and get me some books.' When asked which books, he declared '*I* don't know'. She duly took advice, and supplied a bundle of appropriate secondary reading. Chesterton flipped through them, making no notes, though he doodled a cartoon of St Thomas in the margin opposite an anecdote which he subsequently elaborated. He then dictated the rest of the book. As a reviewer of genius, Chesterton had prodigious and rapid powers of assimilation, and he had evidently absorbed an understanding of some of the key elements of Thomism from knowledgeable friends like the Dominican Fr Vincent McNabb. Etienne Gilson, the greatest contemporary authority on St Thomas, more than once declared the resulting book the best ever written on its subject; but the claim is manifestly informed by hero-worship. Chesterton's treatment of Aquinas is almost entirely based on a few well-known anecdotes about the saint's life, and two or three salient ideas identified from secondary works by inferior but better-informed writers like the Jesuit Martin D'Arcy (fulsomely and embarrassingly deferred to in Chesterton's text). What makes the book remarkable is not its penetration to the heart of St Thomas so much as Chesterton's journalistic ability to spin a plausible and lively monograph out of such exiguous materials.

The books of Chesterton which survive *as books*, therefore, are few enough, though still more than most writers can hope for. The first two volumes of the Father Brown stories, certainly; perhaps also his disturbingly surreal fantasy novel, *The Man who was Thursday* (still in print as a Penguin paperback), his wonderfully insightful writings on Dickens, his short study of *The Victorian Age in Literature*, the collected verse, and, among the religious writings, *Orthodoxy* and *The Everlasting Man*. Though *Heretics* contains some of his wittiest and most telling polemic, many of the contemporaries he used as anvils on which to hammer out his thoughts – Joseph McCabe, G.W. Foote, Lowes Dickenson – have sunk into richly deserved obscurity, and in the process have blunted the sharpness and brilliance of his attack. Among the later works, *The Everlasting Man* stands out for its sustained intellectual power and focus.

Chesterton's reception into the Catholic Church in 1922 was a great personal happiness and the logical outcome of the convictions he had been defending all his adult life. One needs to be reminded that the author of *Heretics*, *Orthodoxy* and the best Father Brown stories was in fact an Anglican. But it cannot be said that this long-delayed conversion did very much for his writing. Chesterton the Catholic was too often prickly, waspish and excessively defensive. *The Thing*, a collection of essays on religious themes published in 1929, attempted to replicate for interwar England the moral and intellectual critique so sparklingly achieved for Edwardian England in *Heretics*. But *The Thing* is a self-consciously denominational and even sectarian book as *Heretics* was not, unattractively tribal, defending even the least lovely aspects of 1920s Catholicism against 'our enemies'. It was this sort of writing which stung George Orwell (never, it must be said, entirely free of old-fashioned anti-Catholic prejudice) to claim that, though Chesterton was a talented writer and 'according to his lights' a true friend to democracy, he had nevertheless chosen 'to suppress both his sensibilities and his intellectual honesty in the cause of Roman Catholic propaganda', so that 'during the last twenty years or so of his life, his entire output was in reality an endless repetition of the same thing. . . . Every book that he wrote, every paragraph, every sentence, every incident of every story, . . . had to demonstrate beyond possibility of mistake the superiority of the Catholic over the Protestant or the pagan.'

But if Chesterton is repetitive, and can be sectarian, Orwell was mistaken in dismissing the last twenty years of Chesterton's output. Even the worst of Chesterton's books show flashes of the old brilliance. He himself declared of the novels of Dickens that they 'are simply lengths cut from the flowing and mixed substance called Dickens – a substance of which any given length will be certain to contain a given portion of brilliant and of bad stuff. . . . The best of his work can be found in the worst of his works'. *Mutatis mutandis*, that applies as much to Chesterton himself as to Dickens: his verse apart, literary form was of less interest to Chesterton than the core ideas to which his writing so often returned. Kevin Morris's anthology does a great service in presenting the religious and philosophical thought of this prodigious but uneven genius in the aphoristic form in which in fact it was mostly conceived.

Eamon Duffy

Introduction

I
G.K. Chesterton's Religious Life

> The supreme adventure is being born.
> G.K. Chesterton, *Heretics*

> I for one have never left off playing,
> and I wish there were more time to play.
> G.K. Chesterton, *Autobiography*

In his own day G.K. Chesterton was a national institution, and a vivid image of him is still current: we can yet see his enormous dishevelled rotundity rolling down Fleet Street in his cape, with his black, broad-rimmed hat and pince-nez, a ham-fist hand swatting the air with his sword-stick, then quickly hailing a cab to take him the short distance to the 'Cheshire Cheese', a pub favoured by his literary cronies, where – 'til the witching hour – he would consume unwise quantities of beer and wine amidst a cloud of his own good cheer. We also think of his Fr. Brown detective stories, his Catholic apologetics, and the clutch of witticisms and lines of poetry in the quotation books. The image is true enough, so far as it goes: he was larger than life – charming, benign, fun-loving, a magical figure, and, some said, a saint. Once known simply as 'G.K.C.', much in demand as writer and speaker, adored by many of the literati, treasured by his friends and family, prized by Catholics as the great Catholic star of his time, he was relentlessly creative, witty, imaginative, insightful, fanciful, ebullient, child-like; the world – especially London – his playground. But there was more to him than that.

Gilbert Keith Chesterton (1874-1936) was one of the great stimulators of religious thought in the twentieth-century English-speaking world, and in his day was a popular writer of international repute. Yet though it matters that he was right as a Christian, it does not matter so much whether he was right or wrong as to detail: the point of reading Chesterton today is to be ideologically and intellectually stimulated, challenged and perhaps inspired and enlightened, rather than to be informed about facts or instructed in doctrinal details. This is certainly not to short-change his memory, because it was very much his view of himself, whom he always regarded as a journalist, who rarely made a fetish of facts or accuracy, whose role was to be an *agent provocateur* of ideas, a subverter of contemporary orthodoxies and heresies, a challenger of secular, liberal, materialist dogmas, prejudices, bigotries, habits of thought and narrownesses; to be a question mark against the efflorescence of off-the-wall pseudo-religions and phoney metaphysics, which so afflicted those days, when Christian life was thought to be collapsing. 'I am,' he averred, 'entirely on the side of the revolutionists. They are really right to be always suspecting human institutions; they are right not to put their trust in princes nor in any child of man.'[1]

It follows that in our own day of rampant materialism, burgeoning cults, 'New Ageism', of the intimidation of Christianity by political correctness and lobby groups pursuing sinister agendas under the guise of 'liberalism' and 'progress', of the 'commitment which is no commitment' to relativism and determinism, Chesterton still valuably challenges present-day fads, fancies, trends, heresies and orthodoxies. His doubts as much as his beliefs point us to the matter of where lies truth, what is real: 'real', 'reality', 'really' are words that recur in Chesterton like a speech impediment or mantra: 'religion is a rare and definite conviction of what this world of ours really is,' he insisted. It was because true religion was real that it had real effects on society. This meant, as he observed, that religion was the key to every age. For him, truth lay in a matrix of reason, common sense and imagination: if he could say, 'I believe in [Christianity] quite rationally upon the evidence', he also believed in the value of intuition and 'first principles' as much as did his mentor Cardinal Newman – 'only a man who knows nothing of reason talks of reasoning without strong, undisputed first principles' – and liked to think that God was a storyteller who was telling a fairy tale, in which we are the giants, the giant-slayers and the damsels in distress, all in quest of home and living happily ever after. He was well-placed to pose questions, for his own compulsive quest for truth had led him from a neo-Unitarian background, through agnosticism and socialism to a quasi-Enlightenment optimism, to Anglicanism, and ultimately to Roman Catholicism, his sharp insight allowing him a deep understanding of these varied sets of answers; these varied ideologies in turn giving him a broad, stereoscopic vision.

At the same time, he is constantly inviting us to be philosophers, to question the nature of principle, reality and belief, and with them why we feel, think and act as we do. His rhetoric breaks down the wall between matter, fact, the secular and the profane on the one hand, and spirit, belief, faith and the sacred on the other. The image of the bridge (Latin *pontifex*: 'priest', literally 'bridge-builder') was of particular importance to him. Then, as now, religion, and especially Christianity, was ridiculed as a defunct and demoralizing superstition, as dangerous, pernicious unreason; so he stressed that everybody, not just the Christian, lives by belief rather than knowledge, and that the beliefs of the proud, self-satisfied, secular, materialistic anti-Christian and non-Christian worlds are often more credulous, outrageous, damaging and dangerous than Christian beliefs; the secular world being littered with obsessive ideas, perverse superstitions, ludicrous idolatries and harmful heresies: 'those abuses which are supposed to belong specially to religion belong to all human institutions. They are not the sins of super-naturalism, but the sins of nature.'

In doing this, he even challenges everything which post-Enlightenment society treasures: individualism, liberalism, the concept of progress, democracy, freedom, toleration, socialism, capitalism, the welfare state, science and rationalism. He suggested that underlying all these modern systems, solutions and aspirations was a subtext of egoism, pride and lovelessness, the lust for status, wealth and power, which both rotted the individual and led society towards a culture of death, of *grand guignol* dressed in the motley of reason and decency, progress and liberality, where the welfare state was actually the 'Servile State', providing services in return for the yielding of liberty, with the enforcement of the will of the powerful and the manufacturing of consent merely taking a more subtle form than hitherto. He supposed that all the puffing of 'individualism' was reducible to the atomization of society, the isolating of the individual; that 'progress' and 'reason' were legerdemain, whereby people were being stripped of tradition and collective belief in order to render them vulnerable to the new 'high-priests'. In short, he was a Christian apologist attacking the covert poverty of modern thought.

But to question these things effectively he also had to criticize the milk-and-water Christianity which survived the Laodicean and latitud-inarian consensus of later Victorianism, when Christianity had been compromised and embarrassed by the advance of science, rationalism, capitalism and imperialism, and had conspired in the virtual victory of secularism and cultism over itself. He supposed that from the Reformation, Christianity had been not only weakened by division, but also set upon from within by the cancer of individualism and secularism, which had led to the decline of Christian faith in favour of egotistical, secular ways of thinking, which simply used Christianity as a 'successful brand name' with the power to elicit conformity, by which to make the heresy of materialism and new forms of power more readily digestible. Christianity had deliquesced into bourgeois capitalism, with all its attendant 'virtues' – thrift, self-help, the spirit of enterprise, and the like – which were really vices designed to venerate the god Mammon. Protestant Christianity especially was in league with the secular, even as it believed itself to be its greatest enemy: it had commonly become a badge of self-approval for the venal, individualist bourgeois, who, having got society's approval, now wanted God's.

It would be seriously mistaken, however, to see Chesterton simply as a tub-thumping, bigoted, narrow-minded Catholic, who merely replaced the power of society with the power of the Pope, and secular superstitions with Catholic ones. For him, true religious insight was a matter of sanity, reason and common sense, of what he called 'healthy hesitation and healthy complexity'. As well as seeing much that was good in other religions and denominations and the secular world – and how could he not, when for the majority of his life he was not a Roman Catholic, when his beloved parents had not been Catholics, when, for a while, he himself was not even a Christian, and when some of his best friends were not Christians? – he was keenly aware of the ambiguities of belief, of the overlap in the human mind between fact and fantasy, fairy tale and reality; of the undefined relationship between objective and subjective, truth and vision: was he awake, or was he dreaming? It is probably due to his acute sensitivity about this fundamental dilemma that while he sometimes assumed the persona of the arrogant Anglo-Catholic or Romanist dogmatist, he actually said relatively very little about the details of Catholic belief over the extent of his hundred-or-so-book literary career. Chesterton was a great believer in belief: belief was a creative gift, while non-belief solved nothing and achieved little; yet one of his beliefs was that it helped to have the best belief available. He knew, however, that knowledge was elusive, that one had, as it were, to live and feel one's way into one's grasp of truth: 'it seems a somewhat wild proposition,' he declared early in his career, 'to say that we can think we know anything, since knowledge implies certainty and sincerity. . . . Our knowledge is perpetually tricking and misleading us, [and] we do not know what we know, but only what we feel.'[2]

In a sense, he was an artist rather than a dogmatist, a storyteller, whose own life he regarded as a story; who regarded life in general as a story, because God was an artist, a storyteller. 'Romance,' he liked to think, 'is the deepest thing in life; romance is deeper than reality'; and though 'life may sometimes appear . . . as a book of metaphysics', 'life is always a novel'; 'our existence is . . . a story.'[3] As he said, 'the soul of a story is a personality'. Stories have a large measure of unpredictability, and not least their endings, which are only known when they are known. So he was telling stories even when not writing novels or short stories. For him, while Christianity was by far the truest truth available, it was also a story, even as the Gospel is a story; and existence is a never-ending story. It was this underpinning of mystery and inconclusiveness, of the consciousness of possible other endings, that informed his humility, which was for him not just a Christian doctrine, but the mode of his mind. His fascination with the Book of Job, with its intellectual open-endedness, alone indicates his idea of religion as an ultimately unresolved mystery. He knew that life and religion posed questions that were not always answered; that the mystery is truly solved only at the end, for death is the moment of truth.[1] He once went so far as to quip that the big difference between Christianity on the one hand, and 'the thousand transcendental schools of to-day' and all the ancient paganisms on the other, is that the latter were aristocratic in that they involved an initiation of comprehension for the élite of the cult, while in the former 'the Christian mysteries are so far democratic that nobody understands them at all.' And if life, man and existence were a story, it was one told about characters; it was a drama of time, place and action, and the engine of the art was spirit, or mind and heart, emotion and psychology; and he was perfectly well aware that religion was to do with mental need, with inner drives which were not susceptible to dissection by the materialist's scalpel, or even by the theologian's: what the theologian did was cast light upon the mystery, not solve it; and what the dogmatist did was provide the spot-marks by which to best direct the action of the stage drama.

Though he may now be regarded as an outdated eccentric, in the first third of the twentieth century Chesterton was perhaps the most prominent English literary-cum-religious figure. Born into a nominally Unitarian family in 1874, he became a Roman Catholic only in 1922, at the age of forty-eight, having been a convinced Anglo-Catholic for about sixteen years. He trained as an artist at the Slade School of Fine Arts (and was an accomplished caricaturist), but turned to journalism, his life's work, and married his Anglo-Catholic wife Frances in 1901, shortly after meeting the aggressively Roman Catholic historian and man of letters Hilaire Belloc, with whose name his own was to be henceforth associated. Though his brother Cecil, to whom he was devoted, became a Catholic, as well as friends such as the polymathic intellectual Maurice Baring, he resisted the logic of his own thought for many years; and he had been a Roman Catholic for just fourteen years when, in 1936, he died.

Crucial to understanding Chesterton's development is the fact that he enjoyed a very happy childhood, his love of life being instilled into him largely by his father. He came to see that as people grow out of childhood they lose much of their innate religious sensibility, and with it their sense of the magic of life, so that as they grow physically they shrink spiritually; and if Chesterton did not say 'adults are but children writ small', he could have. As a youth he became agnostic, sceptical, solipsistic, pessimistic and depressive to the point of – in his own word – 'madness'. He once referred to 'the old Agnosticism of my boyhood when my brother Cecil and my friend [Edmund Clerihew] Bentley almost worshipped old [Thomas Henry] Huxley like a god. . . . The other side often forgot that we began as free-thinkers as much as they did: and there was no earthly power but thinking to drive us on the way we went.'[5] At that time he came to see the world as divided between what he called 'pessimists' and 'optimists'; and for a while he fell into the former camp. He was disturbed by what he called 'the nihilism of the '90s', influenced, he thought, by such as Nietzsche and Schopenhauer; and the pessimist was associated with this movement, which had its roots in the atheistic, sceptical, critical rationalism which had taken such a hold in the 1870s, naming in the literary sphere Hardy, A.E. Housman, W.E. Henley and Swinburne amongst those who helped to create the pessimist ambience, the fashion of the pessimistic despising of good things as worthless and pointless. Optimists, as Chesterton supposed, tended to say, 'this is the best of all possible worlds', or at least that 'it is the best of all possible things that a world should be possible'; pessimists the reverse; optimists that things were getting better, that people were basically good; the pessimists that things were bad and going nowhere, that people were irredeemably bad. He saw 'Pessimism' as a pseudo-philosophical affliction of the ages, which at the time of the early Church was already preaching an anti-life doctrine. Pessimism did not consist in

> being tired of evil but in being tired of good. Despair does
> not lie in being weary of suffering, but in being weary of joy.
> It is when for some reason or other the good things in society
> no longer work that the society begins to decline; when its
> food does not feed, when its cures do not cure, when its
> blessings refuse to bless.[6]

Pessimism worried him especially, because it suggested that nothing had value.

He himself could not sustain the mental and spiritual anguish of such pessimism for long, and so decided to build for himself an ideology, an attitude to life, which would restore his childhood paradise. Like the alcoholic finally accepting he has a problem, he took the first essential step along the path to religion in recognizing that he had a profound need. At first, however, he thought that if the disease was pessimism, then philosophical 'Optimism' must be the remedy. This was 'the primary conviction that life is worth living and the world is worthy of our efforts for it'; but it had degenerated in present-day society into 'a sort of cheap cheeriness, at the back of which there is a curious sort of hollow unbelief in reality,' with no conception of the reality of evil. For him, Optimism was 'an attempt to hold on to religion by the thread of thanks for our creation; by the praise of existence and of created things.' Eventually he came to associate Optimism and Pessimism with the sins of presumption and despair: 'The heresies that have attacked human happiness in my time,' he observed,

> have all been variations either of presumption or of despair; which in the controversies of modern culture are called optimism and pessimism. And if I wanted to write an autobiography in a sentence, . . . I should say that my literary life has lasted from a time when men were losing happiness in despair to a time when they are losing it by presumption.[7]

Fairly soon, however, he realized that while Optimism coincided with fundamental features of his own disposition of the childhood years, it was ultimately insufficient and even vacuous, because it was rootless, only partially perceived present reality and looked to an unreal future perfection. He therefore continued his quest to find a combined attitude and belief which would answer his metaphysical and psychological anguish, and effectually restore his prelapsarian happiness.

He described his time in the wilderness:

> I was a pagan at the age of twelve, and a complete agnostic by the age of sixteen. . . . I certainly regarded [Christ] as a man. . . . I read the scientific and sceptical literature of my time. . . . I never read a line of Christian apologetics. I read as little as I can of them now. It was Huxley and Herbert Spencer and [Charles] Bradlaugh who brought me back to orthodox religion. They sowed in my mind my first wild doubts of doubt.[8]

At that period he 'assumed that the Catholic Church was a sort of ruined abbey, almost as deserted as Stonehenge'; while his family and friends were 'more concerned with the opening of the book of Darwin than the book of Daniel; and most of them regarded the Hebrew Scriptures as if they were Hittite sculptures.' The psychological strength he had taken from his father was no longer supported by his shifting ideological needs, so that his personality temporarily fractured. It is possible that one cause of his shrinking from religion was both personal and universal, in that he had a great fear of heights and falling, which he attributed to a deeper fear of helplessness before the divine will, which he posed in terms of 'the awful idea of immortality', wherein 'it is the infinity of the fall that freezes the spirit: it is the thought of not dying'; so that 'it is not death I fear, but hell; for hell must mean an infinity of falling.' It was while he was at the Slade School, in the earlier 1890s, at the age of about twenty, that he suddenly realized that he was, as he put it, 'becoming orthodox'.

Yet before he found orthodoxy, he had a strong suspicion that existence was religious: he had a fundamental intuition that the universe was spiritual more than material: 'it is *only* the spirituality of things that we are sure of. . . . I do not know on what principle the Universe is run, I know or feel that it is *good* or spiritual.'[9] 'Nothing,' he declared, 'is . . . so natural as supernaturalism.'[10] To his basic instinct for the wonder of existence he added a sympathy with socialistic ideals, a love of freedom, a valuing of Protestantism; but such things with which he thought he was in alliance let him down, and he came to realize that the idea of the centrality of God was the essential protection for all good things. He felt that all the atheisms were too simple a view of existence, while Christianity matched its complexity:

> Life is not an illogicality; yet it is a trap for logicians. It looks just a little more mathematical and regular than it is; its exactitude is obvious, but its inexactitude is hidden. . . . Everywhere in things there is this element of the quiet and incalculable. . . . Insight or inspiration is best tested by whether it guesses these hidden malformations or surprises. . . . This is exactly the claim which I have since come to propound for Christianity. . . . Its plan suits the secret irregularities, and expects the unexpected. It is simple about the simple truth; but it is stubborn about the subtle truth.[11]

He accepted Christianity because, he said, it revealed itself as 'a truth-telling thing', insisting on truths which do not at first appear credible, but turn out to be so; and being 'alone of all creeds . . . convincing where it is not attractive'. Also, 'it is only since I have known orthodoxy that I have known mental emancipation.' So he became an Anglican, but eventually moved on to Roman Catholicism because he came to believe the one to be the blurred image of the other, while Rome was the supreme Christian foe of all modern ideological degeneracies. As he indicated in his *Autobiography*, 'Mother Church' acted as a bridge back to his dead father, so that it was the key (the combined metaphor is his) which unlocked his inner child, enabling him once again to fully relish life. By 1908 he could say that with orthodoxy he had returned to 'my father's house. I end where I began – at the right end. I have entered at least the gate of all good philosophy. I have come into my second childhood.'

He would not have been the thinker he was, nor would he have displayed the ideological development that he did, had he not started from a point of nothingness, of realizing and accepting that he knew nothing. In 1906 he wrote an essay called 'A Fairy Tale', in which he recounted a recent personal epiphany, which he believed had universal application:

> I was sitting . . . on a heap of stones in the Isle of Thanet, when I remembered that I had forgotten. . . . My blood ran cold, and I knew at once that I was in fairyland. . . . A domestic and even prosaic landscape, like that of this flat corner of Kent, can be soaked in a supernaturalism all the more awful from being detached and alien from the landscape itself. Everything that stood up around me stood up shapeless and yet with some horrible hint of the human shape. . . . Everything was at once secretive and vigilant; even the heap of stones beneath me seemed to be all eyes. But all external oddities were secondary to, or perhaps only symbolic of, the sudden sense of a sacred and splendid ignorance that had fallen upon my soul; the enigma of being alive. Saints have not discovered the answer. Philosophers have not even discovered the riddle. But in that moment at least I remembered that I could not remember. . . . The essence of fairyland is this; that it is a country of which we do not know the laws. This is also a peculiarity of the universe in which we live. We do not know anything about the laws of nature; we do not even know whether they are laws.[12]

For him, this acknowledgement of total scepticism was a fundamental religious insight, and the starting point of 'remembering'.

Chesterton's response upon becoming a Christian was to defend Christianity, to become a literary crusader, bounding from his corner with both metaphysical fists flying, believing that if a thing was good it was worth fighting for, that if an ideal was adopted it had to be defended: 'the moment a man is something, he is essentially defying everything.' If one truly stood for something, offending others was inevitable: Jesus, who said he came to bring not peace but a sword – the sword of truth – was murdered partly because he gave offence. Chesterton confessed that

'that peculiar diplomatic and tactful art of saying that Catholicism is true, without suggesting for one moment that anti-Catholicism is false, is an art which I am too old a Rationalist to learn.' On the occasion of his reception into the Roman Catholic Church, he told his mother:

> I have thought about you, and all that I owe to you and my father, not only in the way of affection, but of the ideals of honour and freedom and charity and all other good things you always taught me: and I am not conscious of the smallest break or difference in those ideals; but only of a new and necessary way of fighting for them. I think . . . that the fight for the family and the free citizen and everything decent must now be waged by [the] one fighting form of Christianity.[13]

Having ached since childhood to be a knight in shining armour, he fought for Christianity as a true champion; none too carefully, but boldly and with good cheer. Shortly after his conversion to Rome, he wrote that the Church 'has recaptured the initiative and is conducting the counter-attack; . . . it is aggressive. It is this atmosphere of the aggressiveness of Catholicism that has thrown the old intellectuals on the defensive.'[14] He himself was part of that counter-attack.

Though he was, with Belloc and Ronald Knox, one of the three pillars of English Catholic wisdom in the first half of the twentieth century, Chesterton was unskilled at being a blindly conformist Catholic, just as he was poor at conforming to any other ideology or institution. For several years he shied from becoming a Roman Catholic; a friend witnessed that 'for a time he conceived the possibility of a Catholic accepting the authority of the Church without accepting the authority of Rome.' Following his conversion, George Bernard Shaw told him, 'I know that an officially Catholic Chesterton is an impossibility.'[15] Realising that people thought Catholics had no intellectual independence, he insisted that 'Catholics are much more and not less individualistic than other men in their general opinions': 'Catholics know the two or three transcendental truths on which they do agree; and take rather a pleasure in disagreeing on everything else.' In his radical politics, his originality, his florid vivacity, his individualist whimsy, he strained away from the tenor of the contemporary Catholic Church, which was very much absorbed with legalism, censoriousness and the power of Rome and its clergy. While it is true that his detective hero is a Catholic priest, Fr. Brown is an oddball, *sui generis*, whose forte is sensitive insight rather than theology. Similarly, it was Chesterton's personal paradox that he, a great individualist, preached conformity to Rome. His lifelong preoccupation with liberty was probably partly responsible for his long delay in becoming a Roman Catholic; although eventually he managed to convince himself that the Church stood for freedom more than any other institution or ideology of the time. He was always particularly suspicious of prigs and puritans, if only because he suspected they wanted to prohibit his beloved beer and cigars; and correlatively he supposed that 'our travels are interludes in comradeship and joy, which through God shall endure for ever. The inn does not point to the road; the road points to the inn. And all roads point at last to an ultimate inn, . . . and when we drink again it shall be from the great flagons in the tavern at the end of the world.'

Belloc, who knew Chesterton's mind as well as most, was surprised at his conversion, and commented at the time that 'faith is an act of will and as it seemed to me the whole of his mind was occupied in expressing his liking for and attraction towards a certain mood, not at all towards the acceptation of a certain Institution as defined and representing full reality in this world.'[16] Belloc's judgement was valid; but he missed the delicate 'mood', or psychology, which finally led him to feel that the Catholic Church best matched his personal needs. Chesterton had always felt the need for an ideology that would be universally relevant and applicable, while allowing for the individual, the local, the homely. Anglicanism had seemed to fit the bill, in so far as it was 'Catholic': i.e. 'universal'. But he was always uneasy about Henry VIII and the establishment of a local Catholicism – as opposed to a Catholicism which provided for the local – which had transmogrified so readily into Protestantism. He came to see Anglicanism as a muddle of compromises between men who did not believe a great deal. He rather cruelly characterized the State Church as 'a mere illogical interlude; in which God holds his authority from Caesar; instead of Caesar holding it from God.'

When he did belatedly become a Roman Catholic, he was not – and never had been – an avid practitioner of the Faith (rarely going to Communion, though more from humility than indifference), and seldom went into detail about Catholic authority or specifically and uniquely Catholic doctrine or practice. He did not, for example, analyze the 1917 revision of the Code of Canon Law – a major event in the world of Catholic discipline. Like most Catholics, while he explicitly accepted 'the whole package', he implicitly warmed to some parts of it, though not others, and so tended to emphasize the bits which seemed most important to him. Happily, these bits were generally ones to which a wide audience could relate; which conformed with his concern to convey Christian fundamentals. ('Almost every Englishman,' acknowledged the patriotic Chesterton, 'has his own separate form of Christianity.') He once referred to 'that excellent method which Cardinal Newman employed when he spoke of the "notes" of Catholicism.' In the same way, Chesterton explored the 'notes' of Catholicism, rather than their supporting technicalities.

Throughout his life he was sensitive to Rome's shortcomings, as well as to its cultural glory and its incomparable significance in presenting Christ to the world. 'The Saints,' he once remarked, 'were sometimes great men when the Popes were small men.' Obviously, for the forty-eight years when he was not a Catholic he had his reservations. For example, he then observed that

> against the Church of Pio Nono [Pope Pius IX] the main thing to be said was that it was simply and supremely cynical; that it was . . . founded . . . on the worldly counsel to leave life as it is; that it was not the inspirer of insane hopes, of reward and miracle, but the enemy, the cool and sceptical enemy, of hope of any kind of description.[17]

And, perhaps with a particular eye on Roman celibacy, he admitted, 'I have not myself any instinctive kinship with that enthusiasm for physical virginity, which has certainly been a note of historic Christianity.' In 1903 he observed that 'the stoic philosophy and the early church discussed woman as if she were an institution, and in many cases decided to abolish her.' He said that following his conversion, 'I sympathize with doubts and difficulties more than I did before. . . . It may be that I shall never again have such absolute assurance that the thing is true as I had when I made my last effort to deny it.' As a Catholic, he could still observe that 'undoubtedly some harm was done . . . when the Popes of the Renaissance filled Rome with trophies that might have marked the triumphs of the Caesars, and permitted the slander that the father of Christian man had usurped the title of King of Kings and forgotten his own actual title of Servant of Servants.' He knew, like any other educated, reasonable Catholic, that the historic Church had always needed reforming: Voltaire, he said, had been right to hate the 'horrors' of the Spanish Inquisition. He was very conscious of the saints, such as Teresa of Avila and St Francis of Assisi, as reformers of the Church. The men of the Enlightenment had had 'a just impatience with corrupt and cynical priests.'

Things could and did go wrong in the historic Church: even in his favourite High Middle Ages, for example, 'mediaeval sins hampered and corrupted mediaeval ideas'; and there were 'certain historic tendencies' which had 'hardened into habits in many great schools and authorities' in the Church, which St Francis of Assisi and St Thomas

Aquinas were destined to address as reformers. These 'tendencies' included the Augustinian and Anselmian schools, which had too much emphasized the soul to the neglect of the body, making them 'less orthodox in being more spiritual'. When he observed that the Church had always been subject to 'treason', he had in mind the treason of the Manichaean mentality, the puritanism that said the material world was evil. Another problem in the mediaeval Church was that some of the Scholastic theologians took 'everything that was worst in Scholasticism and made it worse. . . . They were a sort of rabid rationalists, who would have left no mysteries in the Faith at all.' He was well aware of what he called the 'harsher side' of mediaeval religion, 'what many would call [its] ferocity'. He admitted that the 'corruptions' of mediaeval theology 'often took the form of the most abominable abuses; because the corruption of the best is the worst.'

He was phlegmatic about the unchristianness of Catholics down the ages, because he realized that 'Christianity is not a creed for good men, but for men', who, like St Peter, tend to betray their ideals. He acknowledged that 'it is part of that high inconsistency which is the fate of the Christian faith in human hands, that no man knows when the higher side of it will really be uppermost, if only for an instant; and that the worst ages of the Church will not do or say something, as if by accident, that is worthy of the best.' He was also aware of – as he expressed it – 'that casual kind of Catholic that never remembers his religion until he is really in a hole.'

He did not always like the way the Church expressed faith: 'When we see the Roman churches of the Baroque period, especially of the later seventeenth and early eighteenth centuries, we naturally feel a revulsion against them, because of something overloaded in their magnificence and something garish in their very gaiety': it was glory turned to vainglory. He tells the story of St Dominic meeting the Pope, who points to his gorgeous papal palace and brags, 'Peter can no longer say "Silver and gold have I none" '; to which Dominic replies, 'No, and neither can he now say, "Rise and walk" '.[18]

He once associated the later-mediaeval papacy with 'dubious "drives" of the Charity Bazaar sort; not always producing (or receiving) perfect charity.' He even implicitly admitted that he was not completely temperamentally in tune with the Roman way: 'By every instinct of my being, by every tradition of my blood, I should prefer English liberty to Latin discipline'; and someone – like himself – becoming a Catholic 'must often face the dull and repulsive aspects of duty' in the Church: they 'must realise all the sides upon which the religion may seem sordid or humdrum or humiliating or harsh.' He was reluctant to visit Lourdes, and never liked the cult surrounding St Thérèse of Lisieux. As a Catholic, he admitted there were 'real rocks of offence' in the Church. It is this preparedness and ability to criticize his own ideological base which licenses him to criticize other denominations, other religions and secularisms.

This is not, however, to say that Chesterton was not happy as a Catholic: real people – like the Faith itself – are more complex than extremists would allow. In his *Autobiography* (chapter 4) he cheekily cocks a snook at his anti-Catholic society: 'So far,' he says,

> as a man may be proud of a religion rooted in humility, I am very proud of my religion; I am especially proud of those parts of it that are most commonly called superstition. I am proud of being fettered by antiquated dogmas . . . it is only the reasonable dogma that lives long enough to be called antiquated. I am very proud of what people call priestcraft . . . [and] Mariolatry . . . [and] the mysteries of the Trinity or the Mass; I am proud of believing in the Confessional; I am proud of believing in the Papacy.

Also, in some respects he even saw the Church through rose-tinted spectacles: though he denied being a 'medievalist' – in the sense of one who sees value only in mediaeval culture – he did tend to present mediaeval culture and religion – 'Catholic culture' – as the measure of all things; and he did tend to stress the merits of Catholicism in an exaggerated form: 'Catholic doctrine and discipline,' he says, 'may be walls; but they are the walls of a playground,' where children can 'fling themselves into every frantic game and make the place the noisiest of nurseries.' (Although, in a more prosaic mood he would probably have pleaded 'poetic license' over such expressions.) His sister-in-law observed that he 'was so impregnated with the supernatural power of the Church over her disciples, that he credited Catholics as such with an undue impeccability of motive and purpose in worldly affairs.'[19] This would certainly account for his giving some benefit of the doubt – though largely critical – to the Fascists of Catholic Spain and Italy. The priest who received him into the Catholic Church noted his awe of Catholic priests: 'he would carefully weigh their opinion however fatuous.' His child-like enthusiasm for Catholicism led him to perhaps unwarranted optimism about its present performance and immediate fate: the Catholic Church, he declared in 1925, was 'newer in spirit than the newest schools of thought'; a mother who 'grows younger as the world grows old', and more beautiful; and she was 'on the eve of new triumphs'. He was clear that Rome was the prime Church: 'the Roman Church is the Church and is not a sect . . . the Catholic Church stands alone. It does not merely belong to a class of Christian churches.' And, contrary to the common criticism that Catholicism was emotionalist, he insisted that it was 'the most rationalistic of all religions', alone 'accepting the action of the reason and the will.' He supposed poetically that 'if every human being lived a thousand years, every human being would end up either in utter pessimistic scepticism or in the Catholic creed;' implying that such was the richness of the Church's intellectual and spiritual stores that it would take a thousand years to properly appreciate her gifts.

Chesterton's charm and importance can be indicated by the comments of his contemporaries, such as George Bernard Shaw, who called him 'the sort of man that England can produce when she is doing her best.'[20] Walter de la Mare's epitaph was :

> Knight of the Holy Ghost, he goes his way
> Wisdom his motley, Truth his loving jest;
> The mills of Satan keep his lance in play,
> Pity and innocence his heart at rest.[21]

Catholics were, of course, admiring: Ronald Knox – the most prominent and respected English Catholic priest of that generation – commented: 'if you asked me who was the simplest person I have ever known I should mention the name of one of the cleverest men of our generation, Mr. G.K. Chesterton.' Knox said he would be remembered by Catholics as 'a man who fought always on the side of the angels, a great model, to the authors of all time, of two virtues in particular – innocence and humility.'[22] The journalist and publisher Douglas Jerrold said that he, along with Belloc and A.R. Orage, 'changed the current of public opinion and taught us to look beneath the surface and examine the foundations of old loyalties'; and that he, along with Shaw, Wells, Belloc, Bennett, Galsworthy and Conrad, was one of 'the great Edwardians'.[23] For the man of letters Douglas Woodruff, writing in 1942, Chesterton and Newman were 'the two chief apologists for Catholicism in the last hundred years in England.'[24]

The obituaries were predictably fulsome: his colleague Gregory MacDonald recalled that, though Chesterton eventually 'suffered as all great men may do by becoming a national institution', 'pre-War England knew better than post-War England the excitement of finding on any day of the year that its Plato had broken out with an original lecture, that its Shakespeare had shattered everything with a single song. . . . In the twentieth century he was one of the few free men.'[25] Another colleague and friend, W.R. Titterton, wrote:

> he had all his life acute and blissful awareness of the miracle

of common things. . . . he had a little world of beliefs from earliest childhood, which . . . were in fact fibre of his fibre and blood of his blood. This little world was a world of fairy-tales. He believed in fairies, first of all . . . because of his awareness of the miracle of Nature, but secondly because the law of fairyland chimed with the law of his soul.[26]

His Dominican friend Vincent McNabb compared him to Aquinas: 'with both men thought becomes consecration. . . . The finest quality about their mental work is not its truth, but its moral worth, its goodness – indeed its holiness.' Yet 'he himself was so much better than anything he wrote or did that his words and deeds were but symbols of the inner source of all he said or did.'

This constant abiding with what was highest in human thought and desire gave him that indescribable but unmistakable character of humility. . . . He was . . . not only the *servus servorum*, making all he met his masters whom in love he served, but [made] them all his teaching-masters from whom in gratitude he learned. . . . So knit were his mind and soul with God that his very laughter – so frequent and so infectious – had a quality almost liturgical. It seemed in its own human way a ritual worship of the Truth. . . . It was hard to speak with Gilbert Chesterton and not to think – *and think of God.*[27]

When McNabb had visited the unconscious, dying Chesterton he sang the *Salve Regina* over him, as he would have done for a fellow Dominican. His parting reverential act was to pick up from the bedside table Chesterton's pen – through which he had communicated so much goodness to the world – then bless and kiss it.

II

Chesterton's Religious Mind

> Let us, then, go upon a long journey and enter on a
> dreadful search. Let us, at least, dig and seek till we have
> discovered our own opinions.
>
> G.K. Chesterton, *Heretics*

> Cardinal Manning's portrait hangs now at the end of
> my room, as a symbol of a spiritual state which many
> would call my second childhood.
>
> G.K. Chesterton, *Autobiography*

Chesterton had a fundamentally religious mind; and Vincent McNabb
told him, "I think there never was a time when your heart was not a
catholic heart. You were an *'anima naturaliter catholica'*."[28] Most people
are divided, or are diverse wholes, and so was Chesterton to an unusual
degree: he loved life passionately; but he was also very dissatisfied with
it, so that both his nature and his mind drove him to think and talk
constantly about religion, ideals, principles, truth, morals, value and
reality. He said he began to write largely because of the pessimism of
the times; but that pessimism was also his own; and it was in accepting
his need that he could properly begin his quest for religion.

Chesterton deliberately set out to find and write the inner story of
his life and the cosmos, a story which would articulate his instinct for
goodness, wonder, meaning and value, while vanquishing the despair,
unbalance and morbidity of his youth; in the process promoting good
news for his corroding society. As a young man he had been, he said,
'trying to construct a healthier conception of cosmic life', and 'invented
a rudimentary . . . mystical theory . . . that even mere existence . . . was
extraordinary enough to be exciting'; and he realized that 'the object of
the artistic and spiritual life was to dig for this submerged sunrise of
wonder; so that a man sitting in a chair might suddenly understand that
he was actually alive, and be happy.' To find the satisfactory story, by
which a life could be lived and happiness inspired, a person had to hold
two modes in tension: he had to accept his ignorance, his need for
external help; and he needed dogmas, for he had to balance the personal
with the public, and dogma was a balance because it helped to prevent
the individual from being wild or eccentric, to draw him back to the
value of existence, to provide a sense of proportion and relationship.

Optimism was inadequate: though he never lost his conviction that 'primal things are mysterious and amazing', he wondered: 'if they were amazing, why did anybody have to remind us that they were amazing? Why was there . . . a sort of daily fight to appreciate the daylight?' Catholicism showed him that, without being as pessimistic as the Protestant, 'we were only partially or imperfectly the sons of God; not indeed wholly disinherited, but not wholly domesticated. In short, we suffered by the Fall or Original Sin.'

Yet single insights were not enough, and the Church gave him 'some vision of the thousand things that have to be interrelated and balanced in Catholic thought; justice as well as joy; liberty as well as light'; and the sense that the Church provided a harmonizing and steadying influence over all these questions.

Chesterton's duality is also there in the nature of his spirituality and world-view: his head was in the clouds, but his feet were also on the ground. He particularly liked the teachings of St Thomas Aquinas and St Francis of Assisi because they were rooted in common sense, while always aspiring heavenwards; they fully valued the material world, while being intensely spiritual. These were lifelong touchstones for Chesterton: the intellectual and spiritual benchmarks of Catholicism. And common sense was twin sister to reason, another touchstone. He said, 'I believe in the supernatural as a matter of intellect and reason, not as a matter of personal experience. I do not see ghosts; I only see their inherent probability.' His ordinary life was, he insisted, 'quite mystical enough for me.' Mysticism and philosophy had to have practical consequences, and religion had to be real: hence his mantra-like repetition of the word and its variants.

Yet if his spirituality was down-to-earth and rooted in the ordinary, it was no less intense or constant than that of any mystic. Belloc told him: you 'have the blessing of profound religious emotion.' An old friend recalled that 'he had an excessive calm of soul. He enjoyed a perpetual Eucharist, the Eucharist of desire. . . . Gilbert, busy always with the other world, was ministered to by angels like Our Lord.' As others see faces in the carpet, so he saw the glory of God even in the mundane, he saw the Sign of the Cross everywhere, and constantly made the Sign of the Cross: as he lit his cigar, or over a cup of coffee, when he entered a room or began to write. In a private note he exclaimed: 'If the arms of a man could be a fiery circle embracing the round world, I think I should be that man.' The 'chief idea of my life,' he declared, was that of 'taking things with gratitude, and not taking things for granted'; and by 'things' he meant existence. His powerful, relentless emphasis on humility is like a dig in the ribs to our own age of ego. The classic Christian virtue of humility was essential to maintaining the grateful stance: 'The only way to enjoy even a weed is to feel unworthy even of a weed.'

Arrogance defeated the sense of gratitude: it is a 'heresy that a human being has a *right* to dandelions; that in some extraordinary fashion we can demand the very pick of all the dandelions in the garden of Paradise; that we owe no thanks for them at all and need feel no wonder at them at all; and above all no wonder at being thought worthy to receive them.' Yet 'the real difficulty of man' was not in the enjoying of individual things, but 'to enjoy enjoyment. To keep the capacity of really liking what he likes; that is the practical problem which the philosopher has to solve.'

> The first thing the casual critic will say is 'What nonsense all this is; do you mean that a poet cannot be thankful for grass and wild flowers without connecting it with theology; let alone your theology?' To which I answer: 'Yes; I mean he cannot do it without connecting it with theology, unless he can do it without connecting it with thought. If he can manage to be thankful when there is nobody to be thankful to, and no good intentions to be thankful for, then he is simply taking refuge in being thoughtless in order to avoid being thankless.'[29]

With Chesterton this was not an affectation or mere verbiage: his teaching was authentic because it sprang directly from who he was, as the man of letters Desmond MacCarthy recalled:

> From youth onwards he had seen marvels wherever he looked. . . . Every law was itself as surprising as any exception to it could be. Naturally to such a mind miracles were expected incidents. . . . He was a greatly religious man. . . . what seems to have been the compulsive force that threw him at the feet of God was an emotion best described as gratitude; a gratitude which was at once an ecstasy of humility and the most triumphant and comprehensive emotion of which he was capable.[30]

This whole concept of gratitude was also not an affectation in the sense that Christianity is a religion of worship; and Christians worship because existence and life are matter for wonder, which elicits the response of gratitude.

Turn over the Chesterton coin, and one finds the element of vision, or dream, or fantasy, which is to do with the life of the imagination, rather than the practical world, which believed, he suggested, that 'imagination, especially mystical imagination, is dangerous to man's mental balance'. There is a thread of fantasy in virtually everything he thought and wrote. Like Coleridge, he believed that imagination was the creative, aesthetic cognitive force linking the spiritual with the material dimension, that the power of imagination invested myth, dreams, legends, fairy tales with truth and true meaning: 'For he on honey-dew hath fed,/ And drunk the milk of Paradise.' For him matter is magical, and existence pulses with the blood of Spirit: only a gossamer veil separates ordinary reality and fairy tale, matter and spirit, fact and fiction, the secular and the sacred, evil from good. Paradoxically, the Chesterton who had this perception in his marrow believed that all this depended on the individual's will: you have to make a choice to see vital magic or dull matter; and having made your faith choice you have to live by it, as the greatest gamble of life.

In an extraordinary echo of William James's pragmatist philosophy – the notion that a belief was valid if it had good consequences in the external world, that believing that life was worth living made it so – he said that the Catholic, schooled in the doctrine of will, would 'decide whether the universe shall be, for him, the best or the worst of all possible worlds.' William Blake – one of Chesterton's heroes – asks the Prophet Isaias in the *Marriage of Heaven and Hell*, 'Does a firm persuasion that a thing is so make it so?'; to which Isaias responds, 'all poets believe that it does.' This goes hand in glove with Blake's belief that – as Chesterton put it – 'the ideal is more actual than the real'. This notion in turn complements Chesterton's concept of having to work at finding truth and living the good life. It also supports his veneration for the artist as a collaborator with the divine creative energy: for Chesterton, the story-maker was semi-divine; like the God who made a story out of existence, the story of redemption for humanity, and the story of Chesterton's individual life. For him, life was God's story: 'life is a living story, with a great beginning and a great close; rooted in the primeval joy of God and finding its fruition in the final happiness of humanity.' It is difficult to avoid the conclusion that he saw man as the co-author of his redemption; or at least of the understanding by which redemption might be perceived, appreciated, accepted and enacted. Correlatively, in his own mind he was the co-author of his own Christian story, for in his ideological search he 'did try to be original; but I only succeeded in inventing all by myself an inferior copy of the existing traditions of civilized religion. . . . I did try to found a heresy of my own; and when I had put the last touches to it, I discovered that it was orthodoxy.'

Chesterton's particular quest was to recapture and underpin the magic of his childhood. When he finally decided to become a Catholic, he wrote to Ronald Knox:

> I am concerned about what has become of a little boy whose father showed him a toy theatre, and a schoolboy whom nobody ever heard of, with his brooding on doubts and dirt and daydreams . . . and all the morbid life of the lonely mind of a living person with whom I have lived. It is that story, that so often came near to ending badly, that I want to end well.[31]

Believing that a person has the creative power to modify their life's story, he was singularly successful at writing his childhood bliss back into his adult script. That he did this by religion was appropriate because he believed that childhood, or the child-like, the child within, was a spiritual idea, because the child has the gifts of wonder, the cognitive imagination and intuitive understanding, which get tarnished with the coming of adulthood. To put this another way, for Chesterton – in another inspiration from Romanticism – 'the Child' was the model of the core self – or soul – undiminished either by the corrosions and limitations of practical living or by the mechanistic factuality of modern thinking. It was the Child that was both the true begetter of stories – by which shape and meaning (both physical and metaphysical) are given to experience – and the part of the self closest to God. When atheists said religion was childish, he would have smiled at how fully they missed the point. He supposed that the anti-humanity of diabolism and black magic was characterized by a 'mystical hatred of the idea of childhood'; that witches were commonly believed to have specialized in 'preventing the birth of children'; while 'the Hebrew prophets were perpetually protesting against the Hebrew race relapsing into an idolatry that involved such a war upon children.' 'What was wonderful about childhood,' he recorded, 'is that anything in it was a wonder. It was not merely a world full of miracles; it was a miraculous world.' While people regard the child's imagination as a sort of dream, he said, 'I remember it rather as a man dreaming might remember the world where he was awake.'[32] He also liked the idea of the Child because it personified impotence, which he contrasted with 'the old Pagan gods, who were the personifications of power'. This was in turn important because he saw an evolution of paganism as the greatest rival to Christianity.

It can be seen, then, that the image of Chesterton as a blustering, raucous, mediaevalist papist is only a caricature of one aspect of his religious mind. David Lodge once caricatured him and Belloc as 'the propagandists and cheer-leaders of the Catholic ghetto, dedicated to proving that it was really the City of God.' While it is true that they did engage in polemics, regarded the Church as being more the City of God than was the City of London, or Fleet Street, or the Liberal Club, or even Hackney Churchmen, and certainly preferred the Pope as supreme governor of their Church to George V, or even to Locke or Darwin, Chesterton's fascination with fairy tales alone shows that his mind did not entirely run along the rut of the Catholic Penny Catechism.

At a time when most people made a point of not showing a benign interest in anyone else's religion, he welcomed the developing study of comparative religion, and judged that 'it is indeed an excellent improvement that sincerely religious people should respect each other.' As examples of his friendliness to other denominations, he said the Unitarians were 'never to be mentioned without a special respect for their distinguished intellectual dignity and high intellectual honour;' while for the Puritans, whom he so often criticized, he declared 'a vast respect and admiration'. For the Lollards, the godfathers of English Protestantism, he admitted he had 'very considerable sympathy', because 'they were often infamously treated; and they were sometimes intuitively right;' and 'in so far as they had a desire to purify Catholicism, they may often have been spiritually right.' In an age in which most people disdained anything but an anthropological interest in alien religions, he valued Judaism as the parent of Christianity, and Islam as 'an imitation of Christianity;' Confucianism and Buddhism he called 'great things;' while the ancient Jews 'preserved the primary religion of all mankind.' He called Judaism 'an intrinsically sympathetic thing'; and he could at least stir himself to speak of 'the solid if somewhat stagnant sanity of Islam,' of 'the stately, the stable and the reverent religion of Mahomet', as of 'the virility and equality of Islam'.

'God,' he acknowledged, 'has given all men a conscience and conscience can give all men a kind of peace.' He said, 'my idea of broadmindedness is to sympathise with so many of these separate spiritual atmospheres as possible; to respect or love the Buddhists of Tibet or the agnostics of Tooting for their many real virtues and capacities, but to have a philosophy which explains each of them in turn and does not merely generalise from one of them. This I have found in the Catholic philosophy.' He made sincere efforts to understand other people's points of view: 'true liberty,' he supposed, 'consists in being able to imagine the enemy'; while 'the free man is he who sees the errors as clearly as he sees the truth.' And he claimed that while 'everyone, of course, must see one cosmos as the true cosmos', he could 'see six or seven universes quite plain.' It is true, however, that his comments on other religions and denominations are valuable not so much for the accuracy of his understanding of them – because he tends to present them as summary abstractions – but more because they reflect on his own concept of right religion. For him, Catholicism itself did not consist in the poverty of prejudice, or in self-satisfied, self-diminishing arrogance, directed against Jews, Protestants, women or homosexuals, whatever the nature of his own transient feelings. Life was a whole, and existence a mystery: teasing non-Catholics was good fun; but you had to be humble about the world – including the non-Catholic world; you had to be a seeker at least as much as a knower.

He was all for inclusivity and understanding. As Dom Illtyd Trethowan commented, Chesterton was disposed to an 'intellectual *receiving*', and was 'the enemy of those who would shut us out from the fullness of life.'[33] Consequently, Chesterton insisted that he and the Church were not 'mediaeval', or mediaevalist – 'Catholicism is not mediaevalism' – not exclusivistically enclosed; that 'unless a man understands that Rome is a modern city, he does not understand that it is an eternal city.' He supposed that 'the Church uses every style and will soon be using quite new styles.' He liked to present the early Church as tolerant, and claimed that Catholicism was more inclusive than Protestantism. He accepted the idea of doctrinal development, which involves an open attitude: he was, after all, a keen student of John Henry Newman, one of whose chief works was on the development of Christian doctrine. It was, he claimed, the 'moderns' who overlooked the modernity – i.e. the development – of the Church, as they insisted on labelling it with the pejorative epithet 'mediaeval'. 'The old system [of Catholicism]', he said, 'preserved the only seed and secret of novelty. . . . Whenever Catholicism is driven out as an old thing, it always returns as a new thing;' and it has thoughts which 'breed'.[34] Just as Newman concluded that 'to live is to change, and to be perfect is to have changed often', so Chesterton remarked that 'living things must constantly be broken up and destroyed; it is only the dead things that can be left alone.'

"I am not a 'medievalist' but a Catholic," he insisted against his detractors; which is to say he thought in terms of Catholicism, the word meaning 'Universal'. It was universally true (both then and now), accounted for the life of everyone, and answered every basic dilemma; it fed his mind and soul, and answered his needs: one of which was to comprehend and deal with the universal problem of evil: Catholicism, he said, starts with the reality of evil, and is crucial to understanding its agenda, thereby providing emancipation from it. Though he was not a mediaevalist, he did have a particular respect for the mediaeval Church, especially that of the thirteenth century, particularly as embodied in St Francis of Assisi and St Thomas Aquinas. He believed that mediaeval European society, though not perfect, at its peak had been a model for

the development of Christian wholeness and integration, and he
lamented that 'there is now no creed accepted as embodying the common
sense of all Europe, as the Catholic creed was accepted as embodying
it in mediaeval times.' 'The very reason of medievalism,' he declared,
'was rooted in religion.' He saw Aquinas as the comforting home of a
theology of common sense and reason, which gave respectability to
being down-to-earth while being heaven-bound. He said that in later
years he had grown to feel as much affection, or even more, for Aquinas
as for Francis, for 'this man who unconsciously inhabited a large heart
and a large head, like one inheriting a large house, and exercised there
an equally generous if rather more absent-minded hospitality.' As
Aquinas was the intellectual reactor which resonated with his brain, so
Francis was the spiritual ether which bathed his soul. He was the mirror
of the God of love, and fundamental to his understanding of
Catholicism: he was 'the greatest and most glorious of mediaeval men',
who is 'still upholding the Church as Atlas upheld the world'; he 'has
truly established the Church.'

Chesterton regarded 'The Hound of Heaven', by Francis Thompson,
as 'the greatest religious poem of modern times and one of the greatest
of all times', and Thompson himself as 'a very Catholic Catholic.'
Thompson was a very Franciscan figure, devoted to Francis, and was,
like Francis, a freewheeling spirit, a spirit of liberty in the love of God.
Perhaps thinking of St Augustine's dictum, 'Love God and do what
you will,' Chesterton liked to think of Catholicism as having to do with
liberty – an unusual notion to most Catholics and non-Catholics alike.
He once said, 'Catholicism created English liberty; . . . the freedom has
remained exactly in so far as the Faith has remained.' He will have meant
this primarily in the sense that Catholics are liberated by their faith
from servitude both to evil and to lesser doctrines and their smaller
view of life. This notion of Catholic liberty worked with the Catholic
emphasis on the importance – which he himself emphasized – of will
as liberating the individual both from his baser self and the inferior
dogmas of society. The two fundamental reasons for a person becoming
a Catholic were, he said, 'that he believes it to be the solid objective
truth, which is true whether he likes it or not; and . . . that he seeks
liberation from his sins.'

Just as he needed liberation from darkness, he naturally believed
that the society which had damaged him also needed it. The saying is
attributed to Chesterton that 'when men cease to believe in God, they
will not believe in nothing, they will believe in anything' (which is rather
like Belloc's saying, that 'when men abandon the worship of God and
His Saints they take to worshipping themselves'). He saw society filled

with people who had abandoned (partially or completely) orthodox Christianity, and replaced it with an inferior belief, by which they lived as if it were a religion, though they scorned religion. For example, he said, 'the capitalist really depends on some religion of inequality. The capitalist must somehow distinguish himself from human kind; he must be obviously above it – or he would be obviously below it.' As the distilled essence of materialism, capital was an especially poisonous idolatry because of 'the alien and grotesque nature of the power of wealth, the fact that money has no roots, that it is not a natural and familiar power, but a sort of airy and evil magic calling monsters from the ends of the earth.'

Taking his lead from Scripture, he saw the rich as a spiritually stultifying metaphysical entity, a sort of collective black hole for souls, believing that 'the lives of the rich are at bottom so tame and uneventful [because] they can choose the events. They are dull because they are omnipotent. They fail to feel adventures because they can make the adventures.' 'Among the Very Rich,' he observed, 'you will never find a really generous man. . . . They may give their money away, but they will never give themselves away; they are egoistic, secretive, dry as old bones. To be smart enough to get all that money you must be dull enough to want it.' Their bible was Adam Smith, whose teaching he summarized as: 'God so made the world that He could achieve the good if men were sufficiently greedy for the goods.'

Similarly, he suggested that at the turn of the century 'Imperialism, or at least patriotism, was a substitute for religion. Men believed in the British Empire precisely because they had nothing else to believe in.' 'England,' he observed, 'is really ruled by priestcraft, but not by priests. We have in this country all that has ever been alleged against the evil side of religion; the peculiar class with privileges, the sacred words that are unpronounceable; the important things known only to the few. In fact we lack nothing except the religion.'[35] He neatly condemned all forms of social élitism when he observed that 'the objection to an aristocracy is that it is a priesthood without a god.' All secularisms were really quasi-religions, if only in the sense of being committedly anti-religious. This perception of British society as saturated with various heresies and idolatries made it seem less extravagant to become a Christian and a Catholic.

It was not, of course, just 'society' which needed rescuing; it was everybody, since the human heart was the victim of original sin, by which all its motives and actions, no matter how pure-seeming, are corrupted: even love, unassisted by God, could be corrupt: 'the worst tyrant,' he observed, 'is not the man who rules by fear; the worst tyrant

is he who rules by love and plays on it as on a harp.' And on the social
level, even the law should not be the idol it is, for even law is corrupt in
its innermost nature: 'mere law might fail at its highest test', as when it
crucified Christ: 'it was the whole point of the Christian revolution to
maintain that in this, good government was as bad as bad. Even good
government was not good enough to know God among the thieves.'
Even the extension of the franchise was a device designed to help the
Establishment maintain power over those whom they have injured. He
came to believe that liberation from the inferior within oneself and
society was better effected by Catholicism than Protestantism because
the latter had tended to conform to society's secular demands: Calvinists,
for example, had – as R.H. Tawney explained – left their theology behind,
and rendered Calvinism into a style of thinking and behaviour well
adapted to making money.

Chesterton was in revolt against the modern age, which he thought
was dominated by the rich and by scepticism. He suggested that the
rich made ordinary people vulnerable and manipulable by eroding their
beliefs. The definers of the age tended to use Christian ideas for self-
serving purposes: 'wait and see,' he said, 'whether the religion of the
Servile State is not in every case what I say: the encouragement of
small virtues supporting capitalism, the discouragement of the huge
virtues that defy it.' 'A great deal of modern liberality merely consists
of leaving out the creed and keeping the credulity.' 'Modern broad-
mindedness benefits the rich; and benefits nobody else': 'the religion
of the Servile State must have no dogmas or definitions' because 'they
fight; and they fight fair.' There was "the universal, unconscious
assumption that life and sex must live by the laws of 'business' or
industrialism, and not *vice versa*."

Society was a man-trap or a soul-stealer: 'the young today are
themselves the children of a whole generation of sceptics and
agnostics. . . . These young people do not know anything about historical
Christianity; they are [a] rather limited sort of people in a good many
ways. They have heard only the latest jargon of their own generation;
the last heresy that has rebelled against the last heresy but one.'[36]
Somebody had run off with the goalposts, the guidebook and the
compass, and had replaced them with partial insights, designed to trap
the blind. People had been weaned off their spiritual birthright, and
given stones for bread, so that 'very few modern people . . . have any
idea of what they are', and 'the modern world will accept no dogmas
upon any authority; but it will accept any dogmas upon no authority.'
Individualism was destroying the corporate faith, and setting individuals
adrift, to be prey to any passing fad or corporate tiger. There was a

correlative 'failure to grasp and enjoy the things commonly called convention and tradition; which are foods upon which all human creatures must feed frequently if they are to live.' Correlatively, there was a great 'division of labour' underway, by which each aspect of life was being sundered from that which gave meaning, in a grand process of atomization:

> The romance of ritual and coloured emblem has been taken over by that narrowest of all trades, modern art (the sort called art for art's sake), and men are in modern practice informed that they may use all symbols, so long as they mean nothing by them. The romance of conscience has been dried up into the science of ethics; which may well be called decency for decency's sake, decency unborn of cosmic energies and barren of artistic flower. The cry to the dim gods, cut off from ethics and cosmology, has become mere Psychical Research. Everything has been sundered from everything else, and everything has grown cold. . . . This world is all one wild divorce court.

'In England . . . the princes conquered the saints.'[37] He supposed that 'in our age every man has a cosmos of his own, and is therefore horribly alone.'

Even the sceptics who were partly responsible for this situation had lost sight of their roots: they 'no longer know what their own foundations are, and if they trace back all those noble and honourable prejudices to their really logical origin, I think in nine times out of ten they will find that they were rooted in the Christian Faith.' The arrogance of such scepticism militated against the humility needed for spiritual insight and self-understanding, and offered only vacuity before the mystery of life: 'one may understand the cosmos, but never the ego; the self is more distant than any star.' The powers of society were corroding this ability to remember the truth. He could be very apocalyptic about the metaphysical decay of society, believing that without Christianity there was a smell of death in the air: 'The Christian religion has died daily; its enemies have only died . . . the world fares worse without that religion than with it. The Church is dying as usual; but the modern world is dead; and cannot be raised save in the fashion of Lazarus.' By 1905 he believed that 'humanity stands at a solemn parting of the ways', because it is 'deserting the path of religion and entering upon the path of secularism': 'this is the drama of our time.' It seemed that in England people 'believe that the material circumstances, however black and twisted, are more important than the spiritual realities, however powerful and pure.' The issue was a spiritually sick collection of individuals in a meaningless world: 'Can you not see,' he urged,

> that fairy tales in their essence are quite solid and straight-forward; but that this everlasting fiction about modern life is in its nature essentially incredible? Folk-lore means that the soul is sane, but that the universe is wild and full of marvels. Realism means that the world is dull and full of routine, but that the soul is sick and screaming. The problem of the fairy tale is – what will a healthy man do with a fantastic world? The problem of the modern novel? – what will a madman do with a dull world? In the fairy tales the cosmos goes mad; but the hero does not go mad. In the modern novels the hero is mad before the book begins, and suffers from the harsh steadiness and cruel sanity of the cosmos.[38]

Since the later Victorian period science had been increasingly elevated above Christianity, for in science there was certainty, clarity, meaning, progress, truth and solutions to all problems. Yet Chesterton declared, 'the facts of science are unproved', and he was not talking merely of the Darwinian theory which so agitated him. It is indeed so that in science there is no 'knowledge', only hypotheses deduced from data, subject through falsification to refinement. "Even the greatest scientific dogmas are not final. We have just this moment agreed that the ideas of the physical universe, which are really and truly 'obsolete,' are the very ideas taught by physicists thirty years ago", he observed in 1930. 'The scientific facts, which were supposed to contradict the Faith in the nineteenth century, are nearly all of them regarded as unscientific fictions in the twentieth century. Even the materialists have fled from materialism; and those who lectured us about determinism in psychology are already talking about indeterminism in matter.' It was even 'false to say that the world has increased in clarity and intelligibility and logical completeness . . . the world has grown more bewildering, especially in the scientific spheres supposed to be ruled by law or explained by reason.' Worse, in his view, the secular mind, with its pseudo-religions, had become 'Relativist; declaring that the reason is itself relative and unreliable; declaring that Being is only Becoming or that all time is only a time of transition; saying in mathematics that two and two make five in the fixed stars, saying in metaphysics and in morals that there is a good beyond good and evil.' And, of course, science was as subject to the human drive to establish dogmatic orthodoxies, and to human corruption as anything else: 'It was science, it was the natural philosophy encouraged by the Encyclopaedists, which begat Zeppelins and mustard gas.' Undue faith in science – 'scientism' – was a target because it stood at the end of a long line of anti-Christian thinking issuing from the early Enlightenment, which believed that rationality was going to make things increasingly better, as 'superstitious' religion was increasingly consigned to the dustbin of history. It colluded with a philosophical 'progressivism', which often accompanied 'perfectibilism' – the notion that man could be, and was going to be, perfected by reason – and was complemented in Britain by the 'Whig interpretation of history', which said that British society was, by a deterministic law of nature, improving; and apparently confirmed by the determinism associated with the Darwinian doctrine of evolution. The rationalists had particularly pitched progress against Catholicism as the 'most superstitious' form of Christianity. (In 1865 the historian William Lecky had declared: 'Whatever is lost by Catholicism is gained by Rationalism; wherever the spirit of Rationalism recedes, the spirit of Catholicism advances.') To Chesterton, all this was itself a superstition, an occult imposition of an ideology of group self-approval on the facts of man, history and science. Hence his relentless disapproval of 'determinism', 'progressivism', 'scientism' and 'evolutionism': all 'isms' of the ego. Had he lived to witness the horrendous effects of the atheistic political pseudo-religions – all claiming to be predetermined, scientific or progressive – which afflicted the twentieth century – Stalinism, Hitlerism, Maoism and Pol Potism amongst them – he would doubtless have continued to argue upon similar lines, only with more anguish and anger.

The mental ambience which Chesterton stood against was represented and described by Julian Huxley, the grandson of T.H. Huxley, and, rather like him, an atheistic scientist, who dabbled in a pseudo-religion of 'evolutionary humanism' influenced by the doctrine of natural selection. Chesterton commented ironically that 'the evolutionary theists of the type of Mr. Bernard Shaw or Professor Julian Huxley . . . make a god themselves; and then somehow manage to adore it as the god that has made them.' In 1927 Huxley observed that Christian spokesmen

> lament . . . the extraordinary spread of mushroom faiths, crank beliefs, superstitions, new sects, and indeed new religions, of which the most important in numbers and influence are perhaps Christian Science and Spiritualism, although those which manage to combine what they are pleased to call New Thought with a flavour of Eastern religious thinking and philosophy, and also with some insistence upon vegetarianism or other unusual dietary, are serious rivals. . . . But by far the gravest change of

all is the abstention of a large part of the cultivated and disciplined thought of our time from all and sundry established or organized religions. . . . If there is one characteristic of our present age by which we may set it over against the Middle Ages, for example, or the Renaissance, it is the growth of scientific knowledge and scientific application. . . . Those struggles of the nineteenth century terminated by the leaders of religious thought climbing down from their fathers' untenable position and using the discoveries of science – so recently abominated – to buttress their own new-modified views. This climbing-down process, however, went so far that the position of the more liberal-minded Christians became vague and indeed equivocal.[39]

(Truly, there is nothing new under the sun.) This assessment substantially bears out both what Chesterton had said in 1908, that all were agreed that 'there is a collapse of the intellect as unmistakable as a falling house', and his 1910 prophecy that 'it is more likely that the future will be crazily and corruptly superstitious than that it will be merely rationalist.'

Very little changes, so that if Chesterton was relevant then, he is relevant now, when strange ideologies proliferate like rabbits; when the intellectual and cultural establishment tells us things are improving; and when it is increasingly difficult for western Christians to speak publicly about the Faith without fear of ridicule. In 1905 he remarked that 'now it is . . . bad taste to be an avowed Christian'; today it is just so, at least in Britain. The mental atmosphere of his own generation was like a rehearsal, or prevision, of today's, in virtually every detail, with its own political correctness – the tyranny of the fashions which have replaced the Christian idea – liberal license and the abolition of personal responsibility, the 'culture of death', the 'worship of children' and 'the worship of Youth' (as he called them); the tendency to criticize everything American and European (and therefore 'Christian'), while implicitly exonerating everyone in the Third World; New Ageism, superstitions, the narrow-minded and bigoted cultural imperialism of ascendant atheism, the ennervating entropy of relativist individualism, the idolatries of science and money, and the uncomprehending but vicious anti-Christianity. He saw that science, or the scientific, mechanistic, reductionist mentality, was working to achieve what has come to pass: a post-modernist chaos, a schizophrenia-like fracturing of the mind or understanding, where tradition, loyalty, soul, value, ideals and meaning are systematically ridiculed and effectually abolished, at least amongst the determining intellectual élite. The only difference between then and now is that the agendas of the cultural and intellectual élite have largely taken root amongst the populace, to conspire in the virtual overthrow of Christianity in Britain and Europe.

Chesterton's fundamental truths were very fundamental: that existence and human life are wonderful and valuable, and have meaning and purpose beyond the 'necessities' of matter, and that they can be comprehended, but only to a limited extent; and that in a religious sense, for only God could provide deep meaning and true purpose. If he were asked to give the essence of his message, he might have said something like this:

> To our small minds the world seems a terrible place: one of fear, chaos, pain and death; it *is* a fallen world, and we poor creatures are broken with it.
>
> Yet all that seems is but a dream. Out of primeval darkness, rock and gas, miracles have come forth. Though the materialist denies it, there are real dreams: there is mind, instinct with the desire to give and create; there are indeed meaning and mercy, beauty and a blessing, goodness and love, wholeness, holiness and spirit; there is forgivenness, grace and salvation, and light at the end. We have an absolute right to believe, no matter how scientists and atheists may try to bully us into being less than we are.
>
> Our feet *are* of clay, yet our hearts are with heaven. We are in exile now, but there is a home, glimpsed by the child's mind, to which we rightly aspire; and the light of its warm hearth flickers over this cold earth. If we open our minds and hearts, if we scrape off the debris of bitter experience and acrid failure, if we free ourselves from the self-absorbed, conditioned dreariness of the adult mind, and allow ourselves to be touched by what is greater than us, henceforth we shall awake and see by that light, and wonder and joy will fill us until we cry with laughter as we play in the house of the Lord.
>
> And though we *are* called to fight injustice, we cannot grab at reality, to possess it: rather we must wait upon it, patiently, attentively, and accept its unfolding as pure gift. And we have our Faith to guide us to the promised land, a faith which is the best way of telling about all of this.
>
> So let us hold hands, and set forth humbly upon our pilgrimage, passing the time with wonderful stories, with humour on our lips, and with mercy, tolerance, justice and compassion in our hearts; knowing that the way is darkly mysterious and mysteriously dangerous, but *believing* that life is worth living, that there is a homecoming, a glory and peace at the last.

III

Chesterton's Writings

It is not altogether our fault if a chasm has opened in
the community of beliefs and social traditions, which
can only be spanned by the far halloo of the buffoon.
G.K. Chesterton, 'An Apology for Buffoons', in
The Well and the Shallows

'Well,' added Father Brown, with a broad smile, 'that
fairy tale was the nearest thing to the real truth that has
been said today.'
G.K. Chesterton, 'The Hammer of God', in
The Innocence of Father Brown

Chesterton created the taste by which he was appreciated, and his
writings were a novelty which remained novel and in demand for decades.
His habitually speaking of religion in witty terms was very unfamiliar.
He dealt with the most trivial, absurd matters seriously, even
metaphysically, and treated the most serious matters playfully and
humorously. He was the joker in the pack of the literary and religious
scenes; but he was much more than a joker, for he had breadth of
knowledge and depth of understanding; and while he played the fool,
he was nobody's fool. He was a tremendous character both in life and
on the page, strongly reminiscent of his literary hero Dr. Johnson; and
was much loved by his friends and colleagues, being greatly respected
and appreciated not only by his fellow Catholics, but also by those who
belonged to other churches or none. Only a few of his opponents,
such as the historian G.G. Coulton and Dean William Inge, were
irreconcilable; while even H.G. Wells, who was unsympathetic to
Christianity, admitted that Chesterton had succeeded in endowing
Catholicism with 'a kind of boozy halo', and observed how 'when he is
there . . . the whole gathering is by a sort of radiation convivial.' Such
'radiation' flooded from his writing, his irrepressible amiability drawing
a wide readership. Though George Bernard Shaw had no sympathy with
his religious views, he always held him in warm affection.
    Chesterton could hold a huge circle of non-Catholic and non-
Christian friends, and appeal to a wide audience, because while he

assumed the public persona of a hefty clown, who banged the Christian and Catholic drum, he rarely comes across as sincerely doctrinaire or alienatingly dogmatic, and never bores with the details of his religion or confession, so that his audience instinctively understood that he was not so much preaching at them as inviting them into the playground of thought. He caught and kept the public eye by his instinct for arousing his reader's interest and his talent for entertaining. Non-Catholics read him because he was neither a prig, nor a puritan, nor a dogmatist, nor a bully. He projected his beliefs with playful humour, warm humanity, innate courtesy and good-heartedness, his mission being not to humiliate his opponents, but to invite them to suppose that they might be wrong. It is true, though, that in his Roman Catholic years he did become angrier – or perhaps more alarmed – and the fatigue encompassed by failing health and overwork took the shine from his humour and the edge off his intellectual blade.

He had very characteristic forms of expression and thought, which were well suited to the relative brevity entailed in journalism, but rather trying to the patience over extended literary stretches. Because he was always looking for the heart of the argument, the bedrock principle, he was concerned to simplify things; which is signalled by his relentless use of the words 'mere' and 'merely', meaning 'simple', 'pure', 'basic' or 'unadulterated' – as in C.S. Lewis's title, *Mere Christianity*. Yet such simplification was balanced by paradox, which is itself a simple statement of complexity.

His paradoxes were his rapier, with which he poked in the eye the more formal, rationalistic intellectuals of his day. He said, 'I am a Jacobite myself'; and paradox was the literary device by which he proclaimed his rebel spirit, his love of disconcerting the Establishment-minded by turning perception upside-down in a single sentence; and its economy of means was ideally suited to a journalist trying to convey challenging ideas in short spaces. 'The use of paradox,' he observed, 'is to awaken the mind.' It was profoundly appropriate because he was substantially speaking of Christianity, which is a paradoxical religion: it is paradoxical that the One God is Three; that 'whosoever shall seek to save his life shall lose it;' that 'many that are first shall be last;' that God became as men are, and that in Christ the all-powerful God was rendered a victim of power on the cross; that from suffering and death springs resurrection. He said that Christianity's 'paradoxes corresponded to the paradoxes of life,' and that God invented them, not him, so that he could refer to the 'great paradoxes by which men live,' paradox being 'built into the very foundations of human affairs'. 'Religion, by its very nature, consists of paradoxes. . . . All things grow more paradoxical as we approach the central truth.' Paradox was not his prime device simply because he was good at it, but because, as he said rather opaquely, it indicates 'a certain defiant joy which belongs to belief.'

Paradox expressed his devil-may-care attitude, and complemented his anti-intellectual tone, which itself co-existed with great faith in reason and common sense: he loved nonsense, while tending to laugh at academics in general and po-faced, self-righteous atheist intellectuals in particular. Nonsense was not only the 'best proof' of 'the abiding childhood of the world', but embodied 'the idea of *escape*, of escape into a world where things are not fixed horribly in an eternal appropriateness.' And it is better, he insisted, 'to speak wisdom foolishly, like the Saints, rather than to speak folly wisely, like the Dons.' He spoke of deserting 'the illusions of rationalism for the actualities of romance;' and supposed that 'the Puritans fell, through the damning fact that they had a complete theory of life, through the eternal paradox that a satisfactory explanation can never satisfy. . . . Reason is always a kind of brute force; those who appeal to the head rather than the heart . . . are necessarily men of violence. We speak of 'touching' a man's heart, but we can do nothing to his head but hit it.' Such whimsy was in itself paradoxical, for Chesterton also believed in defined intellectual and spiritual limits, and in the 'substantive' idea. For him, open-mindedness had its place, but the mind needed solid food: 'the object of opening the mind,' he supposed, 'as of opening the mouth, is to shut it again on something solid.'[40] He aimed to supply simple, nutritious, popular fare.

Such solidity met paradoxically with such whimsy in his appreciation of fairy tales; and in his writings one never feels far away from the world of legend. Fairy tales were stories with meaning, as the Gospel is a story with meaning. He thought George MacDonald – the Congregationalist preacher and poet, and writer of fairy tales – a great man, who 'did really believe that people were princesses and goblins and good fairies, and he dressed them up as ordinary men and women. The fairy-tale was the inside of the ordinary story and not the outside.' 'I believe in fairy-tales,' said Chesterton, 'in the sense that I marvel so much at what does exist that I am the readier to admit what might': 'Through all the noises of a town/ I hear the heart of fairyland.' Having their own logic, they were a world without miracle or superstition – 'nothing that recalls crystal-gazing and planchette'. There the earth is 'conceived as a place full of innumerable marvels,' and they contain 'the great lines of elementary laws and ideals as we see them nowhere else.' All acts, no matter how small, 'have in them some terrible value and are here bound up with the destiny of men.' 'The fairy tale warns us to be on our guard against the disguises of things and to regard every ugly and repellent exterior with a hopeful and divine suspicion.' And at the heart of the fairy tale is the morality of 'sympathy for the weak against the strong'. It is 'the history of man himself, at once the weakest and the strongest of the creatures.' He said that if he did not put his faith in the Gospel, he would put it in fairy tales, for they are a 'celebration of hope, surprise, courage, the fulfilment of contracts, and the natural relations of mankind'. And they speak of a fairyland that parallels the universe, because in neither are the laws of existence known: all seems to be magic and mystical.

To Chesterton, faith and fairy tales could not be inferior to 'facts' because of his profound vein of scepticism – 'everything,' as they say, 'is true but the facts.' His scepticism was there, for example, in his view of the facts of history: 'the past is always present,' he observed; 'yet it is not what was, but whatever seems to have been; for all the past is a part of faith.'

He once explained the rhetorical value of assuming the role of supreme sceptic, to show how scepticism undermined scepticism: while doubt had its legitimate place within the believer, it was good to test the professional doubter; to 'tell him to go on doubting . . . until at last, by some strange enlightenment, he may begin to doubt himself.' Dreams, visions, romances were food for the heart and soul: 'I have always found that it was the realists who were romancing – I have found . . . that the romances were generally real after all.' And why not, for 'the centre of every man's existence is a dream. Death, disease, insanity, are merely material accidents, like toothache or a twisted ankle. . . . Deeper than all these lies a man's vision of himself, as swaggering and sentimental as a penny novelette.'

So he could say that 'Little children ought to learn nothing but legends; they are the beginnings of all sound morals and manners;' that St Francis of Assisi gave 'the message from heaven; the story that is told out of the sky; the fairytale that is really true;' and that when a person decides to become a Catholic, 'you will find yourself among facts and not arguments, but facts as marvellous as fables; facts like those which the pagans pictured as a land of giants or an age of heroes; you will have returned to the age of the Epic.' In this sense, Catholicism was the greatest of the fairy tales. Loving paradox, and the way that paradox reflects upon the intractable complexities of life, he always relished the fact that life is both a fact which is a fiction and a fiction which is a fact: two dimensions inextricably connected in the fathomless complexities of the rather small human brain, which nevertheless reaches out to the stars. As Chesterton saw, the mind is a constant 'factional' dialogue (which is how fiction can mean so much to us): 'At the beginning and at the end of all life, learned and ignorant, there is the abiding truth that in the inmost theatre of the soul of man, with a scenery of bottomless infinities and appalling abstractions, there is always going forward one ancient mystery play in which there are only two characters.'

Chesterton's concept of the congruence between religion and art – he once said 'all art is religious' – and of the relationship between Christian story and myths, legends, romances and fairy tales, did not come out of nowhere. It is an echo of mediaeval hagiography, which was constituted of instructive and improving fables, presented as fact, but not necessarily read as literal truth, rather as allegorical truth; a feature of a culture which valued fantasy, or imagination, as well as reason in the depiction of truth.

He was also the descendant of the Romantic sensibility, which initially looked back to the ancient 'bards' as both poets and seers; which saw the poet as bringing fire from heaven, and which even developed a cult of the child as having a special wisdom in his innocence. In the Victorian period, writers such as Pugin and Ruskin conflated the aesthetic and metaphysical realms. To Chesterton the romantic, poetry, like religion, was of the world of imagination: 'Poetry is sane because it floats easily in an infinite sea; reason seeks to cross the infinite sea, and so make it finite. . . . The poet only asks to get his head into the heavens. It is the logician who seeks to get the heavens into his head. And it is his head that splits.' He saw imagination as the link between art and religion, because he valued imagination as the Romantics had: as a cognitive power, a power of insight into hidden realities, as well as the divine power of creativity. Hence he could observe that one of the constituents of religion is a 'tendency to break out into colours and symbols, to do wild and beautiful things with flowers or with garments'; then lament that this tendency had separated from religion and was now known as 'Art'. Conversely, St Francis of Assisi was 'primarily a poet', his poetic sensibility shown in his naming "the fire 'brother,' and the water 'sister'"; which is to say he had the power of imaginative cognition, of seeing life as an interrelated whole, of believing that there is a reciprocal relationship between mind and matter, informed by inherent meaning. Art itself was imbued with the potential for metaphysical exploration: 'the chalks in a box, or the paints in a paintbox . . . embrace in themselves an infinity of new possibilities. A cake of prussian blue contains all the sea stories in the world, . . . a cake of crimson is compounded of forgotten sunsets;' so there is 'this eternal metaphysical value in chalks and paints.' The meaning inherent in such metaphor, and in the interrelatedness of art and religion, meant that the universe had meaning, both spirit and matter. None of this, of course, is to say that for

Chesterton religion was no more than a story or a fairy tale: paganism was merely a mythology:

> this religion was not quite a religion. In other words, this religion was not quite a reality. It was the young world's riot with images and ideas like a young man's riot with wine or love-making; it was not so much immoral as irresponsible; it had no foresight of the final test of time. . . . Theology is thought. . . . Mythology was never thought.[41]

Religion had to be solidly about reality.

This mental framework determined the way he spoke to his readership. One does not look to Chesterton for academic, scholarly, objective, closely-reasoned, information-heavy analysis and theorizing. Instead we have a prophetical voice, couched in romantic, lyrical, poetic, metaphysical, paradoxical, epigrammatic, whimsical, conversational, humorous and always playful terms: a sort of anti-Nietzsche, who did not go mad. We do not read him as 'gospel', just as he did not read the Old Testament as literally true. His relentless playfulness is ultimately both an expression of his governing impulse to engender the playful spirit of childhood, and a tacit submission to his view that verbal language was wholly inadequate to the job of rendering the subtleties of the mind and spirit. There were, he judged, 'crimes that have never been condemned and virtues that have never been christened'; they were more honest who admitted they could not say what they meant, for 'language is not a scientific thing at all, but wholly an artistic thing', needing to be supplemented by other linguistic dimensions, such as gesture, colour, ritual, metaphor and symbol. 'Personally,' he once said, 'I am all for propaganda; and a great deal of what I write is deliberately propagandist. But even when it is not in the least propagandist, it will probably be full of the implications of my own religion; because that is what is meant by having a religion.' Christianity, he observed in the introduction to *The Everlasting Man*, suffered contempt from being too familiar, so that 'we must try at least to shake off the cloud of mere custom and see the thing as new'; 'I do propose to strike wherever possible this note of what is new and strange, and for that reason the style even on so serious a subject may sometimes be deliberately grotesque and fanciful.' He suggested that Christianity was not seen straight because of over-familiarity and a tradition of prejudice; that 'people would see the Christian story if it could only be told as a heathen story'; so that is what he tried to do. As he once observed: 'The preaching friar puts his sermon into popular language, the missionary fills his sermon with anecdotes and even jokes, because he is thinking of his mission and not of himself.' (In an essay called 'Heroic Wit' he suggested how wit could be used even in religious contexts.) 'Taking trouble,' he admitted, 'has certainly never been a particular weakness of mine.' He spoke of 'the meaningless affectation of impartiality. It is impossible for any man to state what he believes as if he did not believe it.' He who once referred to himself as 'a mere dot on the crowded horizon' took himself lightly, saying in his book *Orthodoxy* that he did not propose to make it one of 'ordinary Christian apologetics'; and admitting of *The Everlasting Man* – one of his most important religious statements – that it was meant as 'a popular criticism of popular fallacies'. In *A Short History of England*, he explicitly described the book as having no pretence to scholarship, but as having the merit of being 'a history from the standpoint of a member of the public'. He was, he confessed, 'an amateur, ignorant of all but human experience.' He always regarded himself as no more than a journalist, and always kept his writings in perspective. Raphael Davies, a monk friend, recalled how his study was littered with toys; and when he offered to clear it up, Chesterton replied: 'I don't mind what you do to those wretched papers, but you *must* leave me my toys!'[42]

He was a controversialist and rhetorician, who spoke suggestively rather than definitively, converted facts into ideas or ideals, exaggerated for effect, and habitually made 'lateral-thinking' connections between the unlike, indicating his meaning by painterly strokes rather than by mechanistic exposition. The urgency of his message was almost always expressed in terms of an emphatic, hyperbolic tone. In a sense, his skill with metaphor, analogy and symbol was making a virtue out of necessity because of the ultimate impossibility of describing God in rational terms: 'all descriptions of the creating and sustaining principle in things must be metaphorical, because they must be verbal.' Like his literary hero Charles Dickens, he was a caricaturist, and in reading him one has to adjust one's mental register accordingly. Additionally, he was always deeply drawn to simplicity, the simplicity of childhood: as he said, 'when men pause in the pursuit of happiness, seriously to picture happiness, they have always made what may be called a 'primitive' picture. Men rush towards complexity; but they yearn towards simplicity. They try to be kings; but they dream of being shepherds.' While he favoured the broad, hyperbolic statement because it was striking and challenging, and though he commonly spoke loosely as in conversation, like Wittgenstein he was aware that 'philosophy . . . is a fight against the fascination which forms of expression exert upon us;' so that in his war against anti-Christianity he often analyzed the verbal manipulations, illogicalities and *non sequiturs*, the 'forms of expression', of the modernists. He liked to think that 'the Catholic Church, as the guardian of all values, guards also the value of words', whose use was being so degraded in his day; so that 'it is a question of liberty from catchwords and headlines and hypnotic repetitions and all the plutocratic platitudes imposed on us by advertisement and journalism.' His literary clowning invited subtle thought. Epigrams can appear futile, but great teachers have often spoken in terms that do not appear to be of practical use. When Jesus said, 'Happy are the poor: they shall inherit the earth', he was not uttering something of immediate utility, but an idea which resonates in the heart for all time. Chesterton's prose could be as opaque as some of his poetry, so that the reader has to linger over his words and tease out the meaning. For example, in an essay called 'The Wheel' he uses the wheel as an image of an important paradox: the wheel 'humbly' descends to earth, then rises to heaven; which hints that humility is a precondition of progress and achievement; an idea which takes on more resonance in the light of, for example, Karl Popper's description of the necessity of intellectual humility for scientific advance. His opacity comes partly from his personal rhetoric, the personal 'language' of his thought, which was often implicit rather than explicit: one has to be aware of fundamental assumptions, such as the twin paradox that while the world is not merely material but miraculous, the secularists are not really atheists, but some sort of superstitious idolater.

Rather like Nietzsche, he was a long way from being an infallible prophet: one only has to consider his comments on Jews, suicide and feminism, his rather parochial Bellocian collocation of 'Europe and the Faith', and his failure to fully comprehend the poison within Fascism, to see that. Some of his positions were questionable: why, for example, did he oppose nationalization – 'it is wicked to nationalize' – when nationalization was the only modern process which could mirror the beneficent workings of the 'just monarch' he seems to have favoured? He seems to have resented hints of the nascent welfare state because those reforms were inspired by the Germany he detested. So one does not read Chesterton for infallibility (he himself denied that language could be infallible about ideas), but for his insights, his fresh angle of vision, his ability to provoke the reader to think by in effect presenting questions like grains of sand in the oyster. He was not a great educator because he was omniscient – he was not – but because his words tested the reader's own understanding and beliefs.

Despite his kindness, his tolerance, his generosity, his understanding, his common sense, his decency, had he been alive today he would have been cast into the pit by society's post-modernist pundits for his 'political incorrectness': his condemnation of the 'culture of death', his resistance to feminism and vegetarianism, his talk of 'pagans', 'heathens', 'heretics' and 'savages', his criticism of the liberal agenda, his willingness to criticize people who were neither European nor white nor Christian, his whole view of history – such as his notion of the Crusades as an essentially meritorious response to sustained Islamic aggression – and, most damningly of all, his brazen lack of shame about being a Christian – and a Catholic one at that. A staunch opponent of eugenics and contraception in his own day, he would doubtless today have equally strongly opposed euthanasia, the abortion culture, genetic engineering and foetal experimentation and exploitation. He would have enjoyed any offence he gave to the likes of *'Guardian* Man'. He suggested that there was in St Francis of Assisi 'something of a humorous sense of bewildering the worldly with the unexpected; something of the joy of carrying an enthusiastic conviction to a logical extreme': a something which was shared by Chesterton himself. His most notorious 'political incorrectness' was his alleged anti-Semitism, but this has been over-played. While he did say rude things about Jews, and believed there was a 'Jewish problem', basically he criticized rich, powerful and unscrupulous Jews, whom he saw as part of his real *bête noire*, which was the international capitalist plutocracy. In fact, having lifelong Jewish friends, he was sympathetic to Zionism, and deplored Nazi policies: as early as 1932 he rather extravagantly suggested he would 'probably die' defending German Jews; and he repeatedly criticized racism as an ideology, referring to 'this absurd deity of race'. He admitted that Jews had been 'ill-used' by Christians in his beloved Middle Ages, and called them 'a gifted and historic race', 'a sensitive and highly civilized people.' Denying that he 'did not like Jews', he attested that 'I have had Jews among my most intimate and faithful friends since my boyhood, and I hope to have them till I die.' (This is more than he would have said for Germans.)

From the beginning of the twentieth century, Chesterton was producing essays which grappled with the questions of meaning, relationship, faith and the sense of 'dis-ease' in society and sin in the individual, and he became famous very quickly, working for a range of periodicals, as well as writing books and lecturing. His first collection of essays, *The Defendant*, of 1901, contained several notable references to the religious world; but his first major work of a religious sort was *Heretics*, of 1905, which represented him finding his feet as an Anglican, and working out who his opponents might be. He displayed to the full how infectiously he relished writing about theology and the moral sensibility: he once said, 'books without morality in them are books that send one to sleep standing up.' The philosopher and psychologist William James wrote to his brother Henry, 'Do you know aught of G.K. Chesterton? I've just read his *Heretics*. A tremendously strong writer and true thinker.'[43] Its 'sequel' was *Orthodoxy*, of 1908, one of his major religious statements, which declared his sense of security in his faith and described the mental processes which brought him to mainstream Christianity. He explained that its main theme was the question of how we can 'continue to be at once astonished at the world and yet at home in it'. It was also a depiction of Christianity as 'the best root of energy and sound ethics', the use of reason simply not being enough for the maintenance of sanity and common sense. *Orthodoxy* was, he said, 'an account of my own growth in spiritual certainty.' One commentator judged of *Orthodoxy* that 'in the ten or twenty years following its publication its influence was incalculable', at the popular level representing 'a completely new approach to the proclamation of Christian truth. It wrested the initiative from the sceptics and presented the historic faith upon a note of triumphant challenge. That in itself was something quite new . . . a trumpet-call, . . . as exciting as a voyage of discovery.'[44] The historian Theodore Maynard wrote of *Orthodoxy* that 'it still seems to me a most extraordinary work and it sank deeply into my mind.' Chesterton, he testified, 'made a Catholic of me.'[45] As a young woman, Dorothy L. Sayers had been in two minds about continuing as a Christian, disliking parts of its ambience; but in *Orthodoxy* she found, she said, 'glimpses of this other Christianity, which was beautiful and adventurous and queerly full of honour': she was inspired by its vision of Christendom as a heavenly chariot which 'flies thundering through the ages, the dull heresies sprawling and prostrate, the wild truth reeling but erect.'[46] The Thomist scholar Etienne Gilson, who judged Chesterton to have been 'one of the deepest thinkers who ever existed', thought *Orthodoxy* 'the best piece of apologetic the century had produced', and regarded his book on Aquinas as 'the best book ever written on St. Thomas'.[47] Chesterton's writings influenced several Catholic organizations – especially socially-oriented ones – around the world.

Innumerable books, of essays, novels, short stories, literary criticism, history, verse, plays, travel and political discussion followed, including in 1917 one of his most popular works, *A Short History of England*. Much of the poetry had a religious dimension, while the slim volume called *The Queen of Seven Swords* (1926) is verse dedicated to Our Lady. It contains 'The Return of Eve', which the Catholic writer and publisher Frank Sheed called 'one of the greatest religious poems in the language'. Often his Father Brown detective stories carry a religious notion. Other principal religious works were: *St. Francis of Assisi* (1923), *The Everlasting Man* (1925), *The Catholic Church and Conversion* (1927), *St. Thomas Aquinas* (1933) (which experts have often recommended as an introduction to Aquinas) and the *Autobiography* (1936), as well as two books of Catholic essays:

The Thing (1929) and *The Well and the Shallows* (1935).

In the judgement of his friend and biographer Maisie Ward the St Francis book and *The Everlasting Man* were 'the highest expressions of Gilbert's mysticism'; although she also thought the publication of *Orthodoxy* 'a great event in the history of Christian thought'. *The Everlasting Man* is, indeed, a highly imaginative piece of combined speculative anthropology and Christology, arguing that humanity is unique and different within nature, and that Christ is unique and different within humanity. While the unsympathetic would always dismiss him as trivial, his writings have been highly valued: T.S. Eliot commented that Chesterton 'did more than any man of his time . . . to maintain the existence of the important minority [Catholicism being one] in the modern world.'[48] When, in the mid-1920s, the then atheistic C.S. Lewis was considering the claims of Christianity, he thought Chesterton 'the most sensible man alive'; he made 'such an immediate conquest of me.' He loved his particular humour, the type 'which is not in any way separable from the argument but is rather . . . the 'bloom' on dialectic itself.' And when he read *The Everlasting Man*, he 'for the first time saw the whole Christian outline of history set out in a form that seemed to me to make sense.'[49] In Graham Green's view,

> much of the difficulty of theology arises from the efforts of men who are not primarily writers to distinguish a quite simple idea with the utmost accuracy. He restated the original thought with the freshness, simplicity, and excitement of discovery. In fact, it was discovery: he unearthed the defined from beneath the definitions, and the reader wondered why the definitions had ever been thought necessary. *Orthodoxy*, *The Thing* and *The Everlasting Man* are among the great books of the age.

He also valued the *Autobiography*.[50] 'What a sense Chesterton gave one in youth of a great wind of Catholic truth that blew through the world scattering falsehood as so much dust,' recalled Maisie Ward.[51] Writing in 1933, the convert writer Arnold Lunn attested that 'we are in some danger to-day of underestimating our debt to Mr. Chesterton, and of forgetting the impact which his books made on the minds of young men who were infected by the fallacy of Victorian rationalism.'[52]

It does not matter that Chesterton was sometimes wrong, or only partly right: what matters is that he was imaginative, entertaining, stimulating, beneficent and insightful. And though his titles will never again be on the best-seller list, the mental and spiritual tone of his time echoes today, so that the essence of his thought and the vitality of his expression in responding to it still have instructive resonances and beguiling charm. If his vision of history was heavily mythologized, his insights into his own age were razor-sharp, his prophecies often uncannily true. Neither systematiser nor dogmatist, he was a very disorderly poetical philosopher and prophet, always making suggestive, provocative jumps from one idea, one category, to another, so that the reader has to respond imaginatively as well as rationally. If one accepts his idiosyncratic form of utterance, he remains a scintillating reminder of the eternal verities, and a creative poser of questions. His words succeed in stirring the jaded mind to look freshly at the world, to think for oneself, to think again, and to think hard. They tell us that he was aware that to aspire after the good, to search for meaning, to find freedom in truth, and to love life were noble things, salvific things, in which he was singularly gifted. He did his triumphant best to put aside his broken self, and to concentrate on breaking the bread of life and sharing it with as many as he well could, but particularly with those who were life's victims or rejects. Casting his bread on the water, it floated far, and so redeemed his inadequacies and gave a light to the world. His religion was life-affirming, beneficent and wonderfully provocative, and his ideas, views and sayings deserve to continue to be part of the Christian vocabulary.

· · · ·

The following selection of quotations is intended to represent Chesterton's core thinking on and feeling about metaphysics, religion, Christianity and anti-Christianity, and what he called 'orthodoxy'. It is justifiable to present such a collection of thoughts from different decades as a unity because his thinking was organic, cohesive and substantially stable. An attempt has been made to select those ideas which are of continuing interest or importance. Each quotation is as short as possible while maintaining the integrity of both the idea and the rhetorical thrust. Each is arranged sequentially under its appropriate heading, in the hope that what comes first will inform what follows, thereby resulting in a new synthesis of his view of the essence of the Faith. It is, I hope, a collection of pearls rescued from the extensive pebbled beach of his writings, and while the important context is obviously lost, it is equally true that such jewels are themselves normally lost, being buried under Chesterton's daunting mountain of words, and are here provided with a new setting. The index provides even readier access to his ideas, observations, inspirations and provocations. References to 'Ward *Gilbert Keith Chesterton*' are to Maisie Ward *Gilbert Keith Chesterton* (Sheed & Ward, 1944).

REFERENCES

(Place of publication London, and author G.K. Chesterton, unless otherwise stated.)

1. *Orthodoxy* (John Lane, 1927), ch. 7, p. 213. At the end of this quotation Chesterton is citing the version of Psalm 146.3 given in The Book of Common Prayer (where it appears as Psalm 146.2): cf. below, p. 204.
2. *Lunacy and Letters* (Sheed & Ward, 1958), pp. 50-1.
3. *Heretics* (John Lane, 1905), ch. 14, pp. 192, 193.
4. *The Common Man* (Sheed & Ward, 1950), p. 222.
5. Letter to H.G. Wells, cited Maisie Ward, *Gilbert Keith Chesterton* (Sheed & Ward, 1944), pp. 513-514.
6. *The Everlasting Man* (Hodder & Stoughton [1925]), Part 1, ch. 8, p. 173.
7. *All is Grist* (Methuen, 1931), pp. 61-2, *The Common Man*, p. 241; 'Where All Roads Lead', *Blackfriars* vol. III (Jan. 1923), pp. 559-60.
8. *Orthodoxy*, ch. 6, pp. 151, 152.
9. Letter of 1899, cited Ward, *Gilbert Keith Chesterton*, p. 104.
10. *Lunacy and Letters*, p. 30.
11. *Orthodoxy*, ch. 6, pp. 146, 147, 148.
12. *Lunacy and Letters*, pp. 103-5.
13. Maisie Ward, *Gilbert Keith Chesterton*, p. 397.
14. 'Where All Roads Lead', *Blackfriars* vol. III (Oct. 1922), p. 373.
15. W.R. Titterton, *G.K. Chesterton A Portrait* (Alexander Ouseley, 1936), p. 86; and Shaw letter of 16 Feb. 1923, cited Ward, *Gilbert Keith Chesterton*, p. 417.
16. *Letters from Hilaire Belloc*, ed. Robert Speaight (Hollis & Carter, 1958), p. 124.
17. *St. Francis of Assisi* (Hodder & Stoughton, n.d.), ch. 10, p. 174; *Robert Browning* (Macmillan, 1903), p. 43.
18. *St. Thomas Aquinas* (Hodder & Stoughton, 1933), ch. 1, p. 43; referencing King James Bible, Acts 3.6, John 5.8.
19. *Orthodoxy*, ch. 9, p. 267; Mrs. [Ada] Cecil Chesterton, *The Chestertons* (Chapman & Hall, 1941), p. 97.
20. George Bernard Shaw, *The Matter With Ireland* (Rupert Hart-Davis, 1962), p. 208.
21. Maisie Ward, *Gilbert Keith Chesterton*, p. 552.
22. *Occasional Sermons of Ronald A. Knox* (Burns & Oates, 1960), p. 98; *Great Catholics*, ed. Claude Williamson (Nicholson & Watson, 1938), p. 558.
23. Douglas Jerrold, *Georgian Adventure: The Autobiography of Douglas Jerrold* (Collins, 1938), pp. 97, 311.
24. *For Hilaire Belloc*, ed. Woodruff (Sheed & Ward, 1942), p. 37.
25. 'G.K. Chesterton', *The Month*, vol. CLXVIII (Aug. 1936), pp. 137, 140.
26. 'G.K. Chesterton: Great Catholic Apologist', *The Clergy Review*, vol. XII (July 1936), p. 4.
27. 'Gilbert Keith Chesterton', *Blackfriars*, vol. XVII (Aug. 1936), pp. 578-81.

28. Ferdinand Valentine, *Father Vincent McNabb, O.P.* (Burns & Oates, 1955), p. 271.

29. *Autobiography* (Hutchinson, 1936), pp. 330-33, 336.

30. 'G.K. Chesterton', *Sunday Times*, 23 Apr. 1944, p. 3.

31. Evelyn Waugh, *The Life of the Right Reverend Ronald Knox* (Chapman & Hall, 1959), p. 208.

32. *The Everlasting Man*, Part 1, ch. 6, p. 136; *Autobiography*, pp. 38, 107.

33. 'Chesterton as a Philosopher', *Downside Review*, vol. LIV (Oct. 1936), p. 492.

34. 'Where All Roads Lead', *Blackfriars*, vol. III (Nov. 1922), p. 466; ibid., (Dec. 1922), p. 493.

35. *Autobiography*, p. 145; *All Things Considered* (Methuen, 1925), p. 98.

36. *All I Survey* (Methuen, 1933), p. 151.

37. *George Bernard Shaw* (John Lane The Bodley Head, 1914), p. 184; *The Superstition of Divorce* (Chatto & Windus, 1920), p. 70; *What's Wrong With the World* (Cassell, 1910), pp. 121-2, 37.

38. *The Superstitions of the Sceptic* (I.D.K. Club Booklets, Cambridge, Heffer & Sons, 1925), p. 18; *Orthodoxy*, ch. 4, p. 95; 'Epilogue' in Jeremiah C. Harrington, *Catholicism, Capitalism or Communism* (St. Paul, The E.M. Lohmann Co., 1926), p. 445; *Heretics*, ch. 16, pp. 218, 219; *Tremendous Trifles* (Methuen, 1909), pp. 82, 97-8.

39. Julian Huxley, *Religion without Revelation* (Watts, 1941), pp. 31-2.

40. *The Defendant* (Dent, 1918), pp. 64, 65; *George Bernard Shaw*, p. 20; *A Miscellany of Men* (Methuen, 1926), p. 261; *Twelve Types* (Arthur L. Humphreys, 1902), p. 98; *Autobiography*, p. 224.

41. *Orthodoxy*, ch. 2, p. 27; *The Spice of Life* (Beaconsfield, 1964), p. 170; 'Francis' in *Twelve Types*; *The Coloured Lands* (Sheed & Ward, 1938), p. 121; *The Everlasting Man*, Part 1, ch. 8, pp. 180, 182.

42. Ralph Davies, 'Memories of G.K.C.', *Pax*, vol. 26, no. 178 (Aug. 1936), p. 115.

43. Letter of 1 Feb. 1906, *The Letters of William James*, ed. Henry James, 2 vols. in one, vol. II (1926), p. 241.

44. A.L. Maycock, *The Man Who Was Orthodox* (Dennis Dobson, 1963), pp. 57-8.

45. Theodore Maynard, 'My Easy Road to Rome', in *The Road to Damascus*, ed. John A. O'Brien (W.H. Allen, 1949), p. 86.

46. Barbara Reynolds, *Dorothy L. Sayers: Her Life and Soul* (Sceptre, 1998), pp. 57, 73-4; qu. from *Orthodoxy*, ch. 6.

47. Maisie Ward, *Gilbert Keith Chesterton*, pp. 525, 526.

48. T. S. Eliot, *The Tablet*, 20 June, 1936, p. 785.

49. C.S. Lewis, *Surprised by Joy* (Collins, 1967), pp. 153, 178.

50. Graham Greene, *Collected Essays* (Penguin Books, 1977), pp. 106, 107.

51. Maisie Ward, *Insurrection Versus Resurrection* (Sheed and Ward, 1937), p. 207.

52. Arnold Lunn, *Now I See* (Sheed and Ward, 1944), p. 51.

Part 1

Basic Religion

THE RELIGIOUS INSTINCT

This world is too small for the soul of man; and, since the end of Eden, the very sky is not large enough for lovers.

'If Don John of Austria had Married Mary Queen of Scots', in *The Common Man*

... that home behind home for which we are all homesick. The lost memory of it is the life at once of faith and of fairy-tale.

The New Jerusalem (1920), p. 40

Many have speculated on what they are really after; but what they are really after is still the same: those lost children who are themselves; lost in the deep gardens at dusk.

Robert Louis Stevenson, ch. 10

Alone of all creatures [man] is not self-sufficient, even while he is supreme. ... Why the lord of creation is a cripple ... is an open question; but some maintain that it is because he once had a bad fall.

Hearst's International, June 1922

Man is born with hope and courage indeed, but born outside that which he was meant to attain; ... there is a quest, a test, a trial by combat or pilgrimage of discovery; or, in other words, ... whatever else man is he is not sufficient to himself, either through peace or through despair.

Robert Louis Stevenson, ch. 6

Man is maimed as well as limited by arresting those upward gestures that are so natural to him. ... A self-contained and self-centred humanity would chill us in the same way as a self-contained and self-centred human being. For the spiritual hungers of humanity are never merely hungers for humanity.

'Utopias', in *G.K.C. As M.C.*

There will always be religions so long as certain primeval facts of life remain inexplicable and therefore religious. Such things as birth and death and dreams are at once so impenetrable and so provocative that to ask men to put them on one side, and have no hopes or theories about them, is like asking them not to look at a comet or not to look out the answer of a riddle. Around these elemental acrostics human hypothesis has circled and will always continue to circle.

'The Meaning of Dreams', in *Lunacy and Letters*

. . . the essential ground of all the religions, that we can only take a sample of the universe, and that that sample, even if it be a handful of dust (which is also a beautiful substance), will always assert the magic of itself, and hint at the magic of all things.

The Coloured Lands (1938), p. 122

For life the man of science . . . is still searching with a microscope. Life dwells alone in our very heart of hearts, life is one and virgin and unconjured, and sometimes in the watches of the night speaks in its own terrible harmony.

The Coloured Lands (1938), p. 83

THE NEED FOR RELIGION

Man has, . . . in the case of religion, perceived with a tolerable accuracy his own needs.

'January One', in *Lunacy and Letters*

It is felt by many . . . that ideas are dangerous things. . . . Ideas are dangerous, but the man to whom they are least dangerous is the man of ideas. He is acquainted with ideas, and moves among them like a lion-tamer. Ideas are dangerous, but the man to whom they are most dangerous is the man of no ideas. The man of no ideas will find the first idea fly to his head like wine to the head of a teetotaller. . . . It is precisely because an ideal is necessary to man that the man without ideals is in permanent danger of fanaticism. . . . Religious and philosophical beliefs are, indeed, as dangerous as fire, and nothing can take from them that beauty of danger. But there is only one way of really guarding ourselves against the excessive danger of them, and that is to be steeped in philosophy and soaked in religion.

Heretics, ch. 20

Man knows there is that within him that can never be valued too highly, as well as that within which can never be hated too much; and only a philosophy which emphasizes both, violently and simultaneously, can restore the balance to the brain.

'The Spirit of the Age in Literature',
in *Sidelights on New London and Newer York*

Human nature simply cannot subsist without a hope and aim of some kind; as the sanity of the Old Testament truly said, where there is no vision the people perisheth.[1]

Heretics, ch. 20

Take away the supernatural, and what remains is the unnatural. . . . The absence from modern life of . . . faith is largely due to a divorce from nature.

Heretics, ch. 6

Before any cosmic act of reform we must have a cosmic oath of allegiance. A man must be interested in life, then he could be disinterested in his views of it.

Orthodoxy, ch. 5

[Robert Louis] Stevenson . . . shook himself with a sort of impatient sanity; a shrug of scepticism about scepticism. His real distinction is that he had the sense to see that there is nothing to be done with Nothing. He saw that in that staggering universe it was absolutely necessary to stand somehow on something; and instead of falling about anyhow with all the other lunatics, he did seek for a ledge on which he could really stand. He did definitely and even dramatically refuse to go mad; or, what is very much worse, to remain futile.

Robert Louis Stevenson, ch. 4

The man who cannot lift his eyes to the sky, or bend his knee to the earth, is crippled and caught in a network of negations. It was Rossetti, I think, who said that the worst moment of the atheist was when he felt thankful and had nobody to thank. . . . But men are so made that something of drama and perils is commonly needed to awaken this wise amazement; and we require something of crisis to realize creation. We must see the sun and moon and all the seasons given back to man, as though he were raised from the dead. In more vulgar language, men need thrills to produce thanks, and have to be surprised into surprise. It is the whole aim of religion, of imagination, of poetry and the arts, to awaken that sense of something saved from nothing.

'On the King', in *Come to Think of It*

1. Proverbs 29.18.

There was a time when art and morals together were part of a great general view of life called philosophy or religion. The last appearance of that universal theory was the French Revolution, which defined the rights of man; the last appearance before that was the Christian morality which defined his obligations. But the supreme value of all religion has been this, and it is a value which a man can quite easily feel, even if he cannot admit any religious assumptions. The historic advantage of religion was that it made every part of a man's life, art and ethics and the rest, dependent upon a general view of life itself.

Daily News, 1 Aug. 1903

Unless we can make daybreak and daily bread and the creative secrets of labour interesting in themselves, there will fall on all our civilisation a fatigue which is the one disease from which civilisations do not recover. So died the great Pagan Civilisation; of bread and circuses and forgetfulness of the household gods.

The Listener, 31 Jan. 1934

It is a fundamental point of view, a philosophy or religion which is needed, and not any change in habit or social routine. The things we need most for immediate practical purposes are all abstractions. We need a right view of the human lot, a right view of the human society; and if we were living eagerly and angrily in the enthusiasm of those things, we should, *ipso facto*, be living simply in the genuine and spiritual sense. Desire and danger make every one simple. . . . "Take no thought what ye shall eat or what ye shall drink, or wherewithal ye shall be clothed. For after all these things do the Gentiles seek. But seek first the kingdom of God and His righteousness, and all these things shall be added unto you."[1] Those amazing words are not only extraordinarily good, practical politics; they are also superlatively good hygiene. The one supreme way of making all those processes go right, the processes of health, and strength, and grace, and beauty, the one and only way of making certain of their accuracy, is to think about something else.

Heretics, ch. 10

It is not enough that the unhappy man should desire truth; he must desire health. Nothing can save him but a blind hunger for normality. . . . A man cannot think himself out of mental evil; for it is actually the organ of thought that has become diseased, ungovernable, and, as it were, independent. He can only be saved by will or faith. The moment his mere reason moves, it moves in the old circular rut.

Orthodoxy, ch. 2

1. Mat. 6.31 – 3.

IMPORTANCE OF RELIGION

Nothing but a religion can cast out a religion.
  Letter to Maurice Baring 1919, cited Ward, *Gilbert Keith Chesterton*, p. 376

Men are most moved by their religion.
                                        The Everlasting Man, Part 1, ch. 3

> In a time of sceptic moths and cynic rusts,
> And fatted lives that of their sweetness tire,
> In a world of flying loves and fading lusts,
> It is something to be sure of a desire.
>
> Lo, blessed are our ears for they have heard;
> Yea, blessed are our eyes for they have seen:
> Let thunder break on man and beast and bird
> And the lightning. It is something to have been.

From 'The Great Minimum', in *The Collected Poems of G.K. Chesterton*

The largest idea of all . . . is the idea of the fatherhood that makes the whole world one.
                                        The Everlasting Man, Part 1, ch. 4

Definite opinion must . . . begin with the basic matters of human thought, and these must not be dismissed as irrelevant, as religion, for instance, is too often in our days dismissed as irrelevant. Even if we think religion insoluble, we cannot think it irrelevant. Even if we ourselves have no view of the ultimate verities, we must feel that wherever such a view exists in a man it must be more important than anything else in him. . . . The idea does exist . . . that there is something narrow or irrelevant or even mean about attacking a man's religion, or arguing from it in matters of politics or ethics. . . . Such an accusation of narrowness is itself almost grotesquely narrow. . . . A difference of opinion about the nature of Parliaments matters very much; but a difference of opinion about the nature of sin does not matter at all. A difference of opinion about the object of taxation matters very much; but a difference of opinion about the object of human existence does not matter at all. We have a right to distrust a man who is in a different kind of municipality; but we have no right to mistrust a man who is in a different kind of cosmos. . . . This sort of enlightenment is surely about the most unenlightened that it is possible to imagine. . . . Religion is exactly the thing which cannot be left out – because it includes everything.
                                                        Heretics, ch. 20

Neither reason nor faith will ever die; for men would die if deprived of either.
  'Anti-Religious Thought in the Eighteenth Century', in *The Spice of Life*

NATURE OF RELIGION

[Quotes *Hamlet* Act II, sc. 2, ll. 305-317: 'it goes so heavily with my disposition that this goodly frame . . . ' etc.] It is, perhaps, the most optimistic passage in all human literature. It is the absolute expression of the ultimate fact of the faith of Hamlet; his faith that, although he cannot see the world is good, yet certainly it is good; his faith that, though he cannot see man as the image of God, yet certainly he is the image of God. The modern, like the modern conception of Hamlet, believes only in mood. But the real Hamlet, like the Catholic Church, believes in reason. Many fine optimists have praised man when they felt like praising him. Only Hamlet has praised man when he felt like kicking him as a monkey of the mud. . . . This is the definition of a faith. A faith is that which is able to survive a mood. And Hamlet had this from first to last. Early he protests against a law that he recognises: "O that the Everlasting had not fixed his canon 'gainst self – slaughter." Before the end he declares that our clumsy management will be turned to something, "rough – hew it how we will".

'The Orthodoxy of Hamlet', in *Lunacy and Letters*

We do not really want a religion that is right where we are right. What we want is a religion that is right where we are wrong. . . . [Moderns] take the modern mood, . . . and then require any creed to be cut down to fit that mood. But the mood would exist even without the creed. . . . They say they want it, when they mean that they could do without it. It is a very different matter when a religion, in the real sense of a binding thing, binds men to their morality when it is not identical with their mood.

The Catholic Church and Conversion, ch. 5

The modern habit of saying, 'Every man has a different philosophy; this is my philosophy and it suits me': the habit of saying this is mere weak-mindedness. A cosmic philosophy is not constructed to fit a man; a cosmic philosophy is constructed to fit a cosmos. A man can no more possess a private religion than he can possess a private sun and moon.

'The Book of Job', in *G.K.C. As M.C.*

Strong and genuine religious sentiment has never had any objection to realism; on the contrary, religion was the realistic thing, the brutal thing, the thing that called names. . . . But if it was a chief claim of religion that it spoke plainly about evil, it was the chief claim of all that it spoke plainly about good.

Heretics, ch. 2

Religion is the sense of ultimate reality, of whatever meaning a man finds in his own existence or the existence of anything else.
                          'On Mr. Epstein', in *Come to Think of It*

A religion is not the church a man goes to but the cosmos he lives in.
                          Irish Impressions (1919), p. 235

'There is one mark of all genuine religions: materialism.'
                          'The Honour of Israel Gow', in *The Innocence of Father Brown*

I cannot conceive any religion worth calling a religion without fixed and material observances.
                          'A Cab Ride Across Country', in *Tremendous Trifles*

The first facts are never material facts. The invisible always comes before the visible, the immaterial before the material, even in our everyday experience.
                          Illustrated London News, 14 July 1906

There is one central conception of the book of Job which literally makes it immortal. . . . That is the conception that the universe, if it is to be admired, is to be admired for its strangeness and not for its rationality, for its splendid unreason and not for its reason. Job's friends attempt to comfort him with philosophical optimism, like the intellectuals of the eighteenth century. Job tries to comfort himself with philosophical pessimism, like the intellectuals of the nineteenth century. But God comforts Job with indecipherable mystery, and for the first time Job is comforted. . . . If we are to be reconciled to this great cosmic experience, it must be as something divinely strange and divinely violent, a quest or a conspiracy or some sacred joke.
                          The Speaker, 9 Sept. 1905

A religion is dead when it has ceased to dwell on the positive and happy side of its visions, and thinks only of the stern or punitive side.
                          'On Negative Morality', in *All I Survey*

The whole question in which the existence of religion is involved is whether, while we have feelings about the catastrophic, we are or are not to have feelings about the normal; that, while we curse our luck for a house on fire, we are to thank anything for a house. If we come upon a dead man, we start back in horror. Are we not to start with any generous emotion when we come upon a living man, that far greater mystery?
                          Daily News, 20 June 1903

There has crept into our thoughts, through a thousand small openings, a curious and unnatural idea . . . that unity is itself a good thing; that there is something high and spiritual about things being blended and absorbed into each other. . . . Boys are to be 'at one' with girls; all sects are to be 'at one' in the New Theology; beasts fade into men and men fade into God; union in itself is a noble thing. Now union in itself is not a noble thing. Love is a noble thing; but love is not union. Nay, it is rather a vivid sense of separation and identity. . . . Division and variety are essential to praise; division and variety *are* what is right with the world. There is nothing specially right about mere contact and coalescence.

. . . There is, of course, another kind of unity, . . . unity in the possession of truth and the perception of the need for these varieties. But the varieties themselves; the reflection of man and woman in each other, as in two distinct mirrors; the wonder of man at nature as a strange thing at once above and below him; the quaint and solitary kingdom of childhood; the local affections and the colour of certain landscapes – these actually are the things that are the grace and honour of the earth; these are the things that make life worth living and the whole framework of things well worthy to be sustained. . . . While a few prigs on platforms are talking about 'oneness' and absorption in 'The All', the folk that dwell in all the valleys of this ancient earth are renewing the varieties for ever. With them a woman is loved for being unmanly, and a man loved for being unwomanly. With them the church and the home are both beautiful, because they are both different; with them fields are personal and flags are sacred; they are the virtue of existence, for they are not mankind but men.

'What is Right With the World',
in *G.K. Chesterton: The Apostle and the Wild Ducks*

The man of the true religious tradition understands two things: liberty and obedience. The first means knowing what you really want. The second means knowing what you really trust.

G.K.'s Weekly, 18 Aug. 1928

There never was an age of assurance, . . . an age of faith. Faith is always at a disadvantage; it is a perpetually defeated thing which survives all its conquerors. The desperate modern talk about dark days and reeling altars, and the end of Gods and angels, is the oldest talk in the world: lamentations over the growth of agnosticism can be found in the monkish sermons of the dark ages; horror at youthful impiety can be found in the Iliad. This is the thing that never deserts men and yet always, with daring diplomacy, threatens to desert them. It has indeed dwelt among and controlled all the kings and crowds, but only with the air of a pilgrim passing by. It has indeed warmed and lit men from the beginning of Eden with an unending glow, but it was the glow of an eternal sunset.

G.F. Watts (1920), p. 101

BELIEFS

A religion means something that commits a man to some doctrine about the universe.

'The Angry Author: His Farewell', in *A Miscellany of Men*

All sane men . . . believe firmly . . . in a certain number of things which are unproved and unprovable . . . [e.g.] that the world around him and the people in it are real, and not his own delusion or dream. . . . That anything exists except myself is unproved and unprovable. All sane men believe that this world . . . matters. Every man believes there is a sort of obligation on us to interest ourselves in this vision. . . . That there is any such duty to improve the things we did not make is a thing unproved and unprovable. All sane men believe that there is such a thing as a self or ego, which is continuous. There is no inch of my brain matter the same as it was ten years ago.

Daily News, 22 June 1907

We have a general view of existence, whether we like it or not; it alters, or, to speak more accurately, it creates and involves everything we say or do, whether we like it or not. If we regard the Cosmos as a dream, we regard the Fiscal Question as a dream. If we regard the Cosmos as a joke, we regard St. Paul's Cathedral as a joke. . . . Every man in the street must hold a metaphysical system, and hold it firmly. The utmost possibility is that he may have held it so firmly and so long as to have forgotten all about its existence. . . . The modern world is filled with men who hold dogmas so strongly that they do not even know that they are dogmas. . . .

Let us, then, go upon a long journey and enter on a dreadful search. Let us, at least, dig and seek till we have discovered our own opinions. The dogmas we really hold are far more fantastic, and, perhaps, far more beautiful than we think. . . . We all believe fairy-tales, and live in them. Some, with a sumptuous literary turn, believe in the existence of the lady clothed with the sun.[1] Some, with a more rustic, elvish instinct, . . . believe merely in the impossible sun itself. Some hold the undemonstrable dogma of the existence of God; some the equally undemonstrable dogma of the existence of the man next door.

Heretics, ch. 20

Truths turn into dogmas the instant that they are disputed. Thus every man who utters a doubt defines a religion. And the scepticism of our time does not really destroy the beliefs, rather it creates them; gives them their limits and their plain and defiant shape. . . . We who are Christians

1. Rev. 12.1.

never knew the great philosophic common sense which inheres in that mystery until the anti-Christian writers pointed it out to us. The great march of mental destruction will go on. Everything will be denied. Everything will become a creed. . . . It is a rational thesis that we are all in a dream; it will be a mystical sanity to say that we are all awake. . . . Swords will be drawn to prove that leaves are green in summer. We shall be left defending, not only the incredible virtues and sanities of human life, but something more incredible still, this huge impossible universe which stares us in the face. We shall fight for visible prodigies as if they were invisible. We shall look on the impossible grass and the skies with a strange courage. We shall be of those who have seen and yet have believed.

Heretics, ch. 20

The most practical and important thing about a man is still his view of the universe. . . . Vigorous organisms talk not about their processes, but about their aims. . . . There cannot be any better proof of the practical efficiency of a nation than that it talks constantly of a journey to the end of the world, a journey to the Judgment Day and the New Jerusalem.

Heretics, ch. 1

Man's whole nature and object on the earth is to draw . . . black lines that do not exist in organic nature. He separates things and makes them special. . . . Man is made for revolutions, or rather he makes them; he is formed for abrupt departures and great experiments. He faces the cataclysm called Lunch. It is a thing of black lines; decisive like a religion or a rebellion. It begins at some time and . . . ends at some time. Man makes monogamy, patriotism, oaths before magistrates, monetary obligations, religion, honour, civic obedience, theology, all on the same sacred principle on which he makes lunch. . . . If man were to run about on all fours eating a field full of mutton chops, his meals would not have the meaning they have now, a meaning of hospitality, comradeship, human symbolism. His mutton chops would not be the mystical things that they are at present. Man is the animal that draws black lines. Sometimes they are lines round a land, and they make patriotism. Sometimes they are lines round an animal, and they make humanity. But in all cases this is true, that men learn to love their limitations, that men learn to love not only the picture, but the frame.

Daily News, 9 Sept. 1905

He who believes in the existence of God believes in the equality of man.

The New Jerusalem (1920), p. 28

A man ought to love his gods before he is sure that there are any. The sublime words of St John's Gospel[1] permit of a sympathetic parody; if

1. John 20.29.

a man love not God whom he has not seen, how shall he love God whom he has seen? If we do not delight in Santa Claus even as a fancy, how can we expect to be happy even if we find that he is a fact?

William Blake (1920), p. 102

What is wrong with the world is the devil, and what is right with it is God; the human race will travel for a few more million years in all sorts of muddle and reform, and when it perishes of the last cold or heat it will still be within the limits of that very simple definition. . . .

What is right with the world has nothing to do with future changes, but is rooted in original realities. If groups or peoples show an unexpected independence or creative power; if they do things no one had dreamed of their doing; if they prove more ferocious or more self-sacrificing than the wisdom of the world had ever given them credit for, then such inexplicable outbursts can always be referred back to some elementary and absolute doctrine about the nature of men. No traditions in this world are so ancient as the traditions that lead to modern upheaval and innovation. Nothing nowadays is so conservative as a revolution. . . . And when we ask on what republicanism really rests, we come back to that great undemonstrable dogma of the native dignity of man. And when we come back to the lord of creation, we come back of necessity to creation; and we ask ourselves that ultimate question which St Thomas Aquinas. . . . answered in the affirmative: Are these things ultimately of value at all?

What is right with the world is the world. In fact, nearly everything else is wrong with it. This is that great truth in the tremendous tale of Creation, a truth that our people must remember or perish. It is at the *beginning* that things are good, and not (as the more pallid progressives say) only at the end. The primordial things – existence, energy, fruition – are good so far as they go. You cannot have evil life, though you can have notorious evil livers. Manhood and womanhood are good things, though men and women are often perfectly pestilent. . . . We do praise the Lord that there are birch trees growing amongst the rocks and poppies amongst the corn; we do praise the Lord, even if we do not believe in Him. We do admire and applaud the *project* of a world, just as if we had been called to council in the primal darkness and seen the first starry plan of the skies. We are . . . far more certain that this life of ours is a magnificent and amazing enterprise than we are that it will succeed.

That all this frame of things, this flesh, these stones, are good things, of that I am more brutally certain than I can say. . . . For all I know it may be literally and not figuratively true that the tares are tied into bundles for

1. Mat. 13.31; Ecclesiastes 11.3.

burning, and that as the tree falleth so shall it lie.[1] I am an agnostic, like most people with a positive theology. But I do affirm, with the full weight of sincerity, that trees and flowers are good at the beginning, whatever happens to them at the end; that human lives were good at the beginning, whatever happens to them in the end. The ordinary modern progressive position is that this is a bad universe, but will certainly get better. I say it is certainly a good universe, even if it gets worse. I say that these trees and flowers, stars and sexes, are primarily, not merely ultimately, good. In the Beginning the power beyond words created heaven and earth. In the Beginning He looked on them and saw that they were good.

'What is Right With the World',
in *G.K. Chesterton: The Apostle and the Wild Ducks*

TRUTH

'Go on,' said the priest very gently. 'We are only trying to find the truth. What are you afraid of?'

'I am afraid of finding it,' said Flambeau.

'The Honour of Israel Gow', in *The Innocence of Father Brown*

Truth seems to me to be a condition of the soul; possible in a German professor and also in a Sussex peasant. A man seeking after truth . . . appears to me like a man setting out with a knapsack and an Alpine – stock to discover his own centre of gravity. . . . It is possible to teach truth only in such things as arithmetic . . . or swallowing a sword. But if we wish to teach anything to our children beyond these things, uncontested truth is impossible. If we are content with teaching such things as that the giraffe is a mammal or that three feet make one yard, then of course these things can be taught exactly; and in that case we are independent of all doubt and all controversy, of all philosophy, theology, ethics or aesthetics.

Let the child exist entirely upon these undisputed facts. When the time hangs heavy on his hands, when he yearns for the pulse and dance of some light lyric, let him repeat to himself that three feet make one yard. When the sky of his spirit darkens, when troubles come upon him and tear his soul, let him comfort and reassure himself by remembering that, in spite of all passing storms, the giraffe remains a mammal. If this satisfies him, let him be satisfied. But if we have the least notion of teaching him such things as history and philosophy, religion or ethics, art or literature, let us abandon altogether the notion that we can tell him the truth, in the complete and real sense.

'A Plea for Partial Historians', in *Lunacy and Letters*

The degree to which we can perceive [truths] depends strictly upon how far we have a definite conception inside us of what is truth. It is ludicrous to suppose that the more sceptical we are the more we see good in everything. It is clear that the more we are certain what good is, the more we shall see good in everything.

Heretics, ch. 20

Logic and truth . . . have very little to do with each other. Logic is concerned merely with the fidelity and accuracy with which a certain process is performed, a process which can be performed with any materials, with any assumption. You can be as logical about griffins and basilisks as about sheep and pigs. . . . The relations of logic to truth depend, then, not upon its perfection as logic, but upon certain pre-logical faculties and certain pre-logical discoveries, upon the possession of those faculties, upon the power of making those discoveries. If a man starts with certain assumptions, he may be a good logician and a good citizen, a wise man, a successful figure. If he starts with certain other assumptions, he may be an equally good logician and a bankrupt, a criminal, a raving lunatic. Logic, then, is not necessarily an instrument for finding truth; on the contrary, truth is necessarily an instrument for using logic – for using it, that is, for the discovery of further truth and for the profit of humanity. Briefly, you can only find truth with logic if you have already found truth without it.

Daily News, 25 Feb. 1905

MEANING

Even in our quiet life I think we can feel the great fact that is the core of all religion. However quiet may be the skies, or however cool the meadows, we always feel that if we did know what they meant the meaning would be something mighty and shattering. About the weakest weed there is still a sensational difference between understanding and not understanding. We stare at a tree in an infinite leisure; but we know all the time that the real difference is between a stillness of mystery and an explosion of explanation. We know all the time that the question is whether it will always continue to be a tree or turn suddenly into something else.

'Reading the Riddle', in *The Common Man*

Every human being has forgotten who he is and where he came from. We are all blasted with one great obliteration of memory. We none of us saw ourselves born; and if we had, it would not have cleared up the mystery. Parents are a delight; but they are not an explanation. The one thing that no man, however adventurous, can get behind, is his own existence; the one thing that no man, however learned, can ever know, is his own name. It is easier to comprehend the cosmos than to comprehend the ego; it is easier even to know where you are than to know who you are. We have forgotten our own meaning, and we are all wandering about the streets without keepers. All that we call commonsense and practicality and worldly wisdom only means that we forget that we have forgotten. All that we mean by religion and poetry only means that for one wild moment we remember that we forget.

'A Fairy Tale', in *Lunacy and Letters*

The deepest of all desires for knowledge is the desire to know what the world is for and what we are for.

'The Religious Aim of Education', in *The Spice of Life*

Perhaps one never knows what being a man means until the instant of death. Perhaps . . . all life is a learning to die.

'The Epitaph of Pierpont Morgan', in *The Common Man*

[The despair within the 'modern philosophy' is that] it does not really believe that there is any meaning in the universe; therefore it cannot hope to find any romance; its romances will have no plots. A man cannot expect any adventures in the land of anarchy. But a man can expect any number of adventures if he goes travelling in the land of authority. One can find no meanings in a jungle of scepticism; but the man will find more and more meanings who walks through a forest of doctrine and design.

Orthodoxy, ch. 9

GOD

Woe unto them that keep a God like a silk hat, that believe not in God, but in a God.

'Some Prophecies', cited in Ward, *Gilbert Keith Chesterton*, p. 56

There is one kind of infidelity blacker than all infidelities, worse than any blow of secularist, pessimist, atheist, it is that of those persons who regard God as an old institution.

Notebook, cited in Ward, *Gilbert Keith Chesterton*, p. 61

We have been saved by God out of the sea of nothing and the night that was before the world.

G.K.'s Weekly, 11 Oct. 1930

Voices
The axe falls on the wood in thuds, "God, God."
The cry of the rook, "God," answers it,
The crack of the fire on the hearth, the voice of
    the brook, say the same name;
All things, dog, cat, fiddle, baby,
Wind, breaker, sea, thunderclap
Repeat in a thousand languages – God.
                Notebook, cited in Ward, *Gilbert Keith Chesterton*, p. 61

I had always believed that the world involved magic: now I thought that perhaps it involved a magician. And this pointed a profound emotion always present and sub-conscious; that this world of ours has some purpose; and if there is a purpose, there is a person. I had always felt life first as a story: and if there is a story there is a story-teller.

Orthodoxy, ch. 4

Our existence is . . . a story. . . . A story has behind it, not merely intellect which is partly mechanical, but will, which is in its essence divine.

Heretics, ch. 14

Even in the sense in which man is at one with the universe it is an utterly lonely universality. The very sense that he is united with all things is enough to sunder him from all. Looking around him by this unique light, as lonely as the literal flame that he alone has kindled, this demigod or demon of the visible world makes that world visible. He sees around him a world of a certain style or type. It seems to proceed by certain rules or at least repetitions. He sees a green architecture that builds itself without visible hands. . . . In the very shape of things there is more than green growth; there is the finality of the flower. It is a world of crowns. This impression, whether or no it be an illusion, has so profoundly influenced this race of thinkers and masters of the material world, that the vast majority have been moved to take a certain view of that world. They have concluded, rightly or wrongly, that the world had a plan as the tree seemed to have a plan; and an end and crown like the flower. . . . The admission of this idea of a plan brought with it another thought more thrilling and even terrible. There was some one else, some strange and unseen being, who had designed these things, if indeed they were designed. There was a stranger who was also a friend; a mysterious benefactor who had been before them and built up the woods and hills for their coming, and had kindled the sunrise against their rising, as a servant kindles a fire. Now this idea of a mind that gives a meaning to the universe has received more and more confirmation within the minds of men, by meditations and experiences much more subtle and searching than any such argument about the external plan of the world. . . . Most men, including the wisest men, have come to the conclusion that the world has such a final purpose and therefore such a first cause.

The Everlasting Man, Part 2, Conclusion

It is only in God that we all love each other.

Cited in Maisie Ward, *Return to Chesterton* (1952), p. 207

Part 2

General Approaches to Christianity

PERSPECTIVES

There is no end to the dissolution of ideas, the destruction of all tests of truth, that has become possible since men abandoned the attempt to keep a central and civilized Truth, to contain all truths and trace out and refute all errors. Since then, each group has taken one truth at a time and spent the time in turning it into a falsehood. We have had nothing but movements; or in other words, monomaniacs. But the Church is not a movement but a meeting-place; the trysting-place of all the truths in the world.

'Why I am a Catholic', in *Twelve Modern Apostles and Their Creeds* (1926)

The Faith gives a man back his body and his soul and his reason and his will and his very life. . . . The man who has received it receives all the old human functions which all the other philosophies are already taking away. . . . He alone will have freedom, . . . he alone will have will, because he alone will believe in free will; . . . he alone will have reason, since ultimate doubt denies reason as well as authority; . . . he alone will truly act, because action is performed to an end. . . . All this hardening and hopeless despair of the intellect will leave him at last the only walking and talking citizen in a city of paralytics.

'The Sceptic as Critic', in *The Thing*

All sane men can see that sanity is some kind of equilibrium; that one may be mad and eat too much, or mad and eat too little. . . . Paganism declared that virtue was in a balance; Christianity declared it was in a conflict: the collision of two passions apparently opposite. Of course they were not really inconsistent; but they were such that it was hard to hold simultaneously. . . . This duplex passion was the Christian key to ethics everywhere. Everywhere the creed made a moderation out of the still crash of two impetuous emotions. Take, for instance, the matter of modesty, of the balance between mere pride and mere prostration. . . . [Christianity] separated the two ideas and then exaggerated them both. In one way Man was to be haughtier than he had ever been before; in another way he was to be humbler. . . . In so far as I am Man I am the chief of creatures. In so far as I am *a* man I am the chief of sinners. All humility that had meant pessimism, that had meant man taking a . . . mean view of his whole destiny – all that was to go. . . . Man was a statue of God walking about the garden. . . . Yet at the same time [Christianity] could hold a thought about the abject smallness of man. . . . When one came to think of *one's self*, there was vista and void enough for any amount of bleak abnegation and bitter truth. . . . Christianity got over the difficulty of combining furious opposites, by keeping them both, and keeping them both furious. The Church was positive on both points. One can hardly think too little of one's self. One can hardly think too much of one's soul.

Orthodoxy, ch. 6

If a man saw the world upside down, with all the trees and towers hanging head downwards as in a pool, one effect would be to emphasise the idea of *dependence*. . . . It would make vivid the Scriptural text which says that God has hanged the world upon nothing. If St. Francis [of Assisi] had seen, in one of his strange dreams, the town of Assisi upside down, . . . he would be thankful to God Almighty that it had not been dropped; he would be thankful to God for not dropping the whole cosmos like a vast crystal to be shattered into falling stars. . . . That we all depend in every detail, at every instant, as a Christian would say upon God, as even an agnostic would say upon existence and the nature of things, is not an illusion of imagination; on the contrary, it is the fundamental fact which we cover up, . . . with the illusion of ordinary life. . . . It is much more the ordinary life that is made of imagination than the contemplative life. He who has seen the whole world hanging on a hair of the mercy of God has seen the truth. . . . He who has seen the vision of his city upside-down has seen it the right way up. . . .

In so far as ordinary social relations have in them something that seems solid and self-supporting, some sense of being at once buttressed and cushioned; in so far as they establish sanity in the sense of security and security in the sense of self-sufficiency, the man who has seen the world hanging on a hair does have some difficulty in taking them so seriously as that. . . . The man who has seen the human hierarchy upside down will always have something of a smile for its superiorities. The mystic . . . generally loses something of his status. He can no longer take himself for granted. . . . Such a man may have something of the appearance of the lunatic who has lost his name while preserving his nature; who straightaway forgets what manner of man he was. "Hitherto I have called Pietro Bernardone[1] father; but now I am the servant of God."

St. Francis of Assisi, ch. 5

Christianity emphatically began with the assumptions that God has come on earth because all is wrong with the world; and from those two things the whole Christian theory proceeds.

'On Optimism and Scepticism', in *All is Grist*

The Christian optimism is based on the fact that we do *not* fit in to the world. I had tried to be happy by telling myself that man is an animal, like any other which sought its meat from God. But now I really was happy, for I had learnt that man is a monstrosity. I had been right in feeling all things as odd, for I myself was at once worse and better than all things. . . . The Christian pleasure was poetic, for it dwelt on the unnaturalness of everything in the light of the supernatural. . . . I knew now why grass had always seemed to me as queer as the green beard of a giant, and why I could feel homesick at home.

Orthodoxy, ch. 5

Buddhism is centripetal, but Christianity is centrifugal: it breaks out. For the circle is perfect and infinite in its nature; but it is fixed for ever in its size; it can never be larger or smaller. But the cross, though it has at its heart a collision and a contradiction, can extend its four arms for ever without altering its shape. Because it has a paradox in its centre it can grow without changing. The circle returns upon itself and is bound. The cross opens its arms to the four winds; it is a signpost for free travellers.

Orthodoxy, ch. 2

The great Asiatic symbol of a serpent with its tail in its mouth is really a very perfect image of a certain idea of unity and recurrence that does indeed belong to the Eastern philosophies and religions. It really is a curve that in one sense includes everything, and in another sense comes to nothing. In that sense it does confess . . . that all argument is an argument in a circle. . . . The cross . . . does convey . . . the truth about the real issue; the idea of a conflict stretching outwards into eternity. . . . The cross . . . does really stand for the idea of breaking out of the circle that is everything and nothing. It does escape from the circular argument by which everything begins and ends in the mind. . . . Christianity does appeal to a solid truth outside itself; to something which is in that sense external as well as eternal. It does declare that things are really there; . . .

---

1. Father of St. Francis.

that things are really things. In this Christianity is at one with common sense . . . [which] perishes except where there is Christianity to preserve it. It cannot otherwise . . . endure, because mere thought does not remain sane. . . . The temptation of the philosophers is simplicity rather than subtlety. They are always attracted by insane simplifications.

The Everlasting Man, Part 1, ch. 6

TRANSCENDENCE AND IMMANENCE

[Christianity] divided God from the cosmos. That transcendence and distinctness of the deity which some Christians now want to remove from Christianity, was really the only reason why any one wanted to be a Christian. . . . The root phrase for all Christian theism was this, that God was a creator, as an artist is a creator. A poet is so separate from his poem that he himself speaks of it as a little thing he has "thrown off". . . . This principle that all creation and procreation is a breaking off is at least as consistent through the cosmos as the evolutionary principle that all growth is a branching out. . . . It was the prime philosophic principle of Christianity that this divorce in the divine act of making . . . was the true description of the act whereby the absolute energy made the world. According to most philosophers, God in making the world enslaved it. According to Christianity, in making it, He set it free.

Orthodoxy, ch. 5

The western energy that dethrones tyrants has been directly due to the western theology that says "I am I, thou art thou." . . . That external vigilance which has always been the mark of Christianity (the command that we should *watch* and pray) has expressed itself both in typical western orthodoxy and in typical western politics: but both depend on the idea of a divinity transcendent, different from ourselves, a deity that disappears. Certainly the most sagacious creeds may suggest that we should pursue God into deeper and deeper rings of the labyrinth of our own ego. But only we of Christendom have said that we should hunt God like an eagle upon the mountains: and we have killed all monsters in the chase. . . . By insisting specially on the immanence of God we get introspection, self-isolation, quietism, social indifference. . . . By insisting specially on the transcendence of God we get wonder, curiosity, moral and political adventure, righteous indignation. . . . Insisting that God is inside man, man is always inside himself. By insisting that God transcends man, man has transcended himself.

Orthodoxy, ch. 8

When a man has found something which he prefers to life, he then for the first time begins to live. A promptitude of poetry opens in his soul of which our paltry experiences do not possess the key. When once he has despised this world as a mere instrument, it becomes a musical instrument; it falls into certain artistic harmonies around him.

'The Heroic that Happened', in *Lunacy and Letters*

'Alone on earth, the Church makes reason really supreme. Alone on earth, the Church affirms that God Himself is bound by reason. . . . Reason and justice grip the remotest and the loneliest star. Look at those stars. Don't they look as if they were single diamonds and sapphires? Well, you can imagine any mad botany or geology you please. Think of forests of adamant with leaves of brilliants. Think the moon is a blue moon, a single elephantine sapphire. But don't fancy that all that frantic astronomy would make the smallest difference to the reason and justice of conduct. On plains of opal, under cliffs cut out of pearl, you would still find a noticeboard, "Thou shalt not steal."'

'The Blue Cross', in *The Innocence of Father Brown*

The purely spiritual or mystical side of Catholicism had very much got the upper hand in the first Catholic centuries. . . . Theologians had somewhat stiffened into a sort of Platonic pride, in the possession of intangible and untranslatable truths within: as if no part of their wisdom had any root anywhere in the real world. Now, the first thing that Aquinas did . . . was to say to these pure transcendentalists something substantially like this. . . . 'I find my reason fed by my senses; that I owe a great deal of what I think to what I see and smell and taste and handle; and that so far as my reason is concerned, I feel obliged to treat all this reality as real. . . . I do not believe that God meant Man to exercise only that peculiar, uplifted and abstracted sort of intellect which you are so fortunate as to possess: but I believe that there is a middle field of facts, which are given by the senses to be the subject matter of the reason; and that in that field the reason has a right to rule, as the representative of God in Man. It is true that all this is lower than the angels; but it is higher than the animals, and all the actual material objects Man finds around him.' . . . Thus began what is commonly called the appeal of Aquinas to Aristotle. It might be called the appeal to Reason and the Authority of the Senses. . . . It is a truly and eminently Christian doctrine.

St. Thomas Aquinas, ch. 1

Man . . . is limited. He has not the memory nor the imagination nor the vigilance nor the sheer physical health to realize the Godhead in every atom or object that passes under his hands. . . . The only things which man . . . can do in this matter, are two: first, he can believe (as an absolute thing of faith) that there is this divinity in things, whether he sees it or not; second, he can leave himself reasonably open to those sudden revelations whereby one or two of these things – a cloud, a man's face, a noise in the dark – may for some reason no one has ever been able to offer, capriciously reveal its divinity. . . . I believe that every object is divine in a very definite and thorough sense. I believe . . . there is a great pressure of spiritual reality behind things as they seem. . . . If a man . . . looks steadily and with some special and passionate adoration at some one thing, that thing suddenly speaks to him. Divinity lurks not in the All, but in everything.

Daily News, 24 March 1903

THE PHYSICAL WORLD

'Speller of the stones and weeds,
Skilled in Nature's crafts and creeds,
Tell me what is in the heart
Of the smallest of the seeds.'

'God Almighty, and with Him
Cherubim and Seraphim,
Filling all eternity –
Adonai Elohim.'[1]

From 'The Holy of Holies', in *The Collected Poems of G.K. Chesterton*

[St Thomas Aquinas] did not, like a modern specialist, study the worm as if it were the world; but he was willing to begin to study the reality of the world in the reality of the worm. His Aristotelianism simply meant that the study of the humblest fact will lead to the study of the highest truth.

St. Thomas Aquinas, ch. 3

No human being was ever really so unnatural as to worship Nature. . . . [The reason] is that all human beings are superhuman beings. We have printed our own image upon Nature, as God has printed His image upon us. . . . 'Christ is the Sun of Easter' does not mean that the worshipper is praising the sun under the emblem of Christ. . . . When I look across the sun-struck fields, I know in my inmost bones that my joy is not solely in the spring. . . . My pleasure is in some promise yet possible and in the resurrection of the dead.

"The Priest of Spring', in *A Miscellany of Men*

1. Two Hebrew words alluding to God.

Granted . . . that certain transformations do happen, it is essential that
we should regard them in the philosophic manner of fairy tales, not in
the unphilosophic manner of science and the "Laws of Nature." When
we are asked why eggs turn to birds or fruits fall in autumn, we must
answer exactly as the fairy godmother would answer if Cinderella asked
her why mice turned to horses or her clothes fell from her at twelve
o'clock. We must answer that it is *magic*. It is not a "law," for we do not
understand its general formula. It is not a necessity, for though we can
count on it happening practically, we have no right to say that it must
always happen. . . . All the terms used in the science books, "law,"
"necessity," "order," "tendency," and so on, are really unintellectual,
because they assume an inner synthesis which we do not possess. The
only words that ever satisfied me as describing Nature are the terms
used in the fairy books, "charm," "spell," "enchantment." They express
the arbitrariness of the fact and its mystery.

. . . All the towering materialism which dominates the modern mind
rests ultimately upon one . . . false assumption . . . that if a thing goes
on repeating itself it is probably dead; a piece of clockwork. People
feel that if the universe was personal it would vary; if the sun were alive
it would dance. . . . But perhaps God is strong enough to exult in
monotony. . . . It may not be automatic necessity that makes all daisies
alike; it may be that God makes every daisy separately, but has never
got tired of making them. . . . Repetition may go on for millions of
years, by mere choice, and at any instant it may stop.

Orthodoxy, ch. 4

In a book from America which I have read recently the author points
out, truly, as it seems to me, that science has not explained and is in its
nature incapable of explaining what actually is the original impulse or
motive, the original élan or prompting in spirit or matter, which has
given it the strength and consistency necessary to pursue life through
so strange an evolution, culminating in so sensational a product. He
says that as a matter of fact the birds and brutes and insects have
persisted continuously because they have faith; in other and inferior
words, because they never for a moment doubt the essential goodness
of the ideal of existence. . . . All these creatures truly have a religion,
the dark, blind and triumphant religion of the goodness of God, of
the supreme value of his terrible trumpet calling them together to life.

'A Wild Reconstruction', in *Lunacy and Letters*

All good things are one thing. Sunsets, schools of philosophy, babies,
constellations, cathedrals, operas, mountains, horses, poems – all these
are merely disguises. One thing is always walking among us in fancy-

dress, in the grey cloak of a church or the green cloak of a meadow. He is always behind, His form makes the folds fall so superbly. And that is what the savage old Hebrews, alone among the nations, guessed, and why their rude tribal god has been erected on the ruins of all polytheistic civilisations. For the Greeks and Norsemen and Romans saw the superficial wars of nature and made the sun one god, the sea another, the wind a third. They were not thrilled, as some rude Israelite was, one night in the wastes, alone, by the sudden blazing idea of all being the same God: an idea worthy of a detective story.

> Letter of 1899, cited Ward, *Gilbert Keith Chesterton*, pp. 99-100

. . . that great and central sacramental idea which is the one thing which marks religion from all imitations of religion or false definitions of it. . . . This element can only be called the materialism of the true mystic. . . . It is the idea that to enter upon abstractions and infinities is to get further and further from the mystery; to come near some particular stone or flame or boundary is to get nearer and nearer to the mystery. All unsophisticated human beings instinctively accept the sacramental principle that the particular thing is closest to the general, the tangible thing closest to the spiritual; the child with a doll, the priest with a relic, the girl with an engagement ring, the soldier with a medal, the modern agnostic with his little scarab for luck. One can recall the soul of boyhood better by smelling peppermint than by reading about adolescence; one could talk for hours about a person's identity and still jump on hearing his voice; and it is possible for Putney to be a much more pathetic word than Memory. . . . Every genuine mystic . . . adores something material. In short, both the mystic and the mere philosopher agree that the spiritual is more important than the material considered in itself. The philosopher thinks that the spiritual lies very far beyond the material, like a remote landmark behind a plain. The mystic thinks that the spiritual is very close behind the material, like a brigand hiding behind a bush. Science is always saying that the other world, if it exists, is too distant to be seen. Religion is always saying that it is too close to be seen. The kingdom of heaven is at hand.[1]

> 'The Moral Philosophy of Meredith', in *A Handful of Authors*

The essence of all pantheism, evolutionism, and modern cosmic religion is really in this proposition: that Nature is our mother. . . . The main point of Christianity was . . . that Nature is not our mother: Nature is our sister. We can be proud of her beauty, since we have the same father; but she has no authority over us; we have to admire, but not to

---

1. Mat. 3.2.

imitate. . . . Nature is not solemn to Francis of Assisi. . . . To St. Francis, Nature is . . . a little, dancing sister, to be laughed at as well as loved. . . . We must have in us enough reverence for all things outside us to make us tread fearfully on the grass. We must also have enough disdain for all things outside us, to make us, on due occasion, spit at the stars. Yet these two things (if we are to be good or happy) must be combined, not in any combination, but in one particular combination. The perfect happiness of men on the earth (if it ever comes) will not be a flat and solid thing, like the satisfaction of animals. It will be an exact and perilous balance; like that of a desperate romance. Man must have just enough faith in himself to have adventures, and just enough doubt of himself to enjoy them.

Orthodoxy, ch. 7

[St Thomas Aquinas] lays down the almost startlingly modern or materialist statement; "Everything that is in the intellect has been in the senses." This is where he began . . . at the very opposite end of inquiry from that of the mere mystic. The Platonists, or at least the Neo-Platonists, all tended to the view that the mind was lit entirely from within; St. Thomas insisted that it was lit by five windows, that we call the windows of the senses. . . . For him the point is always that Man is not a balloon going up into the sky, nor a mole burrowing merely in the earth; but rather a thing like a tree, whose roots are fed from the earth, while its highest branches seem to rise almost to the stars.

St. Thomas Aquinas, ch. 7

Sunlight in a child's hair.
It is like the kiss of Christ upon all children.
Chesterton's Notebook, cited Ward, *Gilbert Keith Chesterton*, p. 210

Substances have . . . a real intrinsic spirituality.
The Coloured Lands (1938), p. 119

That "God looked on all things and saw that they were good" contains a subtlety which the popular pessimist cannot follow. . . . It is the thesis that there are no bad things; but only bad uses of things. If you will, there are no bad things but only bad thoughts; and especially bad intentions. . . . It is possible to have bad intentions about good things; and good things, like the world and the flesh, have been twisted by a bad intention called the devil. But he cannot make *things* bad; they remain as on the first day of creation. The work of heaven alone was material; the making of a material world. The work of hell is entirely spiritual.

St. Thomas Aquinas, ch. 4

Sane peasants, healthy hunters, are all superstitious; they are superstitious because they are healthy and sane. They have a reasonable fear of the unknown; for superstition is only the creative side of agnosticism. The superstitious man sees quite plainly that the universe is a thing to be feared. The religious man maintains paradoxically that the universe is a thing to be trusted.

'Ibsen', in *A Handful of Authors*

BELIEFS

[Chesterton is asked by the socialist anti-Christian Robert Blatchford:]
1. *Are you a Christian?* Certainly.
2. *What do you mean by the word Christianity?* A belief that a certain human being whom we call Christ stood to a certain superhuman being whom we call God in a certain unique transcendental relationship which we call sonship.
3. *What do you believe?* A considerable number of things. That Mr Blatchford is an honest man, for instance. And (but less firmly) that there is a place called Japan. If he means what do I believe in religious matters, I believe the above statement (answer 2) and a large number of other mystical dogmas, ranging from the mystical dogma that man is the image of God to the mystical dogma that all men are equal and that babies should not be strangled.
4. *Why do you believe it?* Because I perceive life to be logical and workable with these beliefs and illogical and unworkable without them.

Daily News, 1903, cited
in Dudley Barker, *G.K. Chesterton A Biography* (1973), p. 169

[St. Thomas Aquinas] did, with a most solid and colossal conviction, believe in Life; and in something like what [Robert Louis] Stevenson called the great theorem of the livableness of life. . . . If the morbid Renaissance intellectual is supposed to say, "To be or not to be – that is the question," then the massive medieval doctor does most certainly reply in a voice of thunder, "To be – that is the answer."

St. Thomas Aquinas, ch. 4

St. Thomas Aquinas . . . says emphatically that the child is aware of *Ens* ['Being']. Long before he knows that grass is grass, or self is self, he knows that something is something. . . . "There *is* an Is." . . . There is no doubt about the being of being, even if it does sometimes look

like becoming; that is because what we see is not the fullness of being;
. . . we never see being being as much as it can. Ice is melted into cold
water and cold water is heated into hot water; it cannot be all three at
once. But this does not make water unreal or even relative; it only means
that its being is limited to being one thing at a time. But the fullness of
being is everything that it can be; and without it the lesser or approximate
forms of being cannot be explained as anything. . . .

St. Thomas maintains that the ordinary thing at any moment is
something; but it is not everything that it could be. There is a fullness
of being, in which it could be everything that it can be. Thus, while
most sages come at last to nothing but naked change, he comes to the
ultimate thing that is unchangeable, because it is all the other things at
once. While they describe a change which is really a change in nothing,
he describes a changelessness which includes the changes of everything.
Things change because they are not complete; but their reality can only
be explained as part of something that is complete. It is God. . . . The
defect we see, in what is, is simply that it is not all that is. God is more
actual even than Man; more actual even than Matter; for God with all
His powers at every instant is immortally in action. . . .

Looking at Being as it is now, . . . we see a second thing about it; . . . it
looks secondary and dependent. Existence exists; but it is not sufficiently
self-existent; and would never become so merely by going on existing.
The same primary sense which tells us it is Being, tells us that it is not
perfect Being; not merely imperfect in the popular controversial sense of
containing sin or sorrow; but imperfect as Being; less actual than the
actuality it implies. For instance, its Being is often only Becoming;
beginning to Be or ceasing to Be; it implies a more constant or complete
thing of which it gives in itself no example. That is the meaning of that
basic medieval phrase, "Everything that is moving is moved by another";
which, in the clear subtlety of St. Thomas, means inexpressibly more
than the mere Deistic "somebody wound up the clock" with which it is
probably often confounded. . . . There is always something really
unthinkable about the whole evolutionary cosmos . . . because it is
something coming out of nothing; an ever-increasing flood of water
pouring out of an empty jug. . . . The world does not explain itself, and
cannot do so merely by continuing to expand itself. . . . It is absurd for
the Evolutionist to complain that it is unthinkable for an admittedly
unthinkable God to make everything out of nothing; and then pretend
that it is *more* thinkable that nothing should turn itself into everything.

What [the Evolutionists] really mean is that change is not mere change,
but is the unfolding of something; and if it is thus unfolded, though the
unfolding takes twelve million years, it must be there already. In other

words, they agree with Aquinas that there is everywhere potentiality that has not reached its end in act. But if it is a definite potentiality, and if it can only end in a definite act, why then there is a Great Being, in whom all potentialities already exist as a plan of action. In other words, it is impossible even to say that the change is for the better, unless the best exists somewhere, both before and after the change.

St. Thomas Aquinas, ch. 7

The Faith itself enlarges the world; which would be a small thing without it.

'The Church and Agoraphobia', in *The Well and the Shallows*

You cannot evade the issue of God. . . . If Christianity should happen to be true – that is to say, if its God is the real God of the universe – then defending it may mean talking about anything or everything. Things can be irrelevant to the proposition that Christianity is false, but nothing can be irrelevant to the proposition that Christianity is true. . . . All . . . things not only may have something to do with the Christian God, but must have something to do with Him if He really lives and reigns.

Daily News, 12 Dec. 1903

> There is one creed: 'neath no world-terror's wing
>   Apples forget to grow on apple-trees.
> There is one thing is needful – everything –
>   The rest is vanity of vanities.

From 'Ecclesiastes', in *The Collected Poems of G.K. Chesterton*

Thinkers of [a particular] school have a tendency to believe that the concrete is the symbol of the abstract. The truth, the truth at the root of all mysticism, is quite the other way. The abstract is the symbol of the concrete. . . . Just in so far as we get into the abstract, we get away from the reality, we get away from the mystery. . . . God made the concrete, but man made the abstract.

The Speaker, 31 May 1902

It is a mark of false religion that it is always trying to express concrete facts as abstract. . . . The test of true religion is that its energy drives exactly the other way; it is always trying to make men feel truths as facts; always trying to make abstract things as plain and solid as concrete things.

'The Appetite of Earth', in *Alarms and Discursions*

There is . . . a particular sort of prig who is always lecturing us about having the spirit of true Christianity, apart from all names and forms. As far as I can make out, he means the very opposite of what he says.

He means that we are to go on using the names "Christian" and
"Christianity," . . . for something in which it is quite specially the spirit
that is not Christian; something that is a sort of combination of the
baseless optimism of an American atheist with the pacifism of a mild
Hindoo.

'The Spirit of Christmas', in *The Thing*

Religion is revelation. In other words, it is a vision, and a vision received
by faith; but it is a vision of reality. The faith consists in a conviction
of its reality. That . . . is the difference between a vision and a day-
dream. And that is the difference between religion and mythology. . . .
But if it is not a mythology neither is it a philosophy. It is not a
philosophy because, being a vision, it is not a pattern but a picture. It is
not one of those simplifications which resolve everything into an
abstract explanation. . . . It is not a process but a story. It has
proportions, of the sort seen in a picture or a story; it has not the
regular repetitions of a pattern or a process; but it replaces them by
being convincing as a picture or a story is convincing. In other words, it
is exactly . . . like life. For indeed it is life. . . .

The Catholic faith is the reconciliation because it is the realisation
both of mythology and philosophy. It is a story. . . . It is a philosophy
. . . it is a reconciliation because it is something that can only be called
the philosophy of stories. That normal narrative instinct which produced
all the fairy-tales is something that is neglected by all the philosophies
– except one. The Faith is the justification of that popular instinct; the
finding of a philosophy for it or the analysis of the philosophy in it.
Exactly as a man in an adventure story has to pass various tests to save
his life, so the man in this philosophy has to pass several tests and save
his soul. . . . It met the mythological search for romance by being a
story and the philosophical search for truth by being a true story. That
is why the ideal figure had to be a historical character. . . . But that is
also why the historical character had to be the ideal figure. . . . If there
be indeed a God, his creation could hardly have reached any other
culmination than this granting of a real romance to the world. Otherwise
the two sides of the human mind could never have touched at all; and
the brain of man would have remained cloven and double; one lobe of
it dreaming impossible dreams and the other repeating invariable
calculations. The picture-makers would have remained for ever painting
the portrait of nobody. The sages would have remained for ever adding
up the numerals that come to nothing. It was the abyss that nothing but
an incarnation could cover; a divine embodiment of our dreams. . . .

The Everlasting Man, Part 2, ch. 5

All Christianity concentrates on the man at the cross-roads. The vast and shallow philosophies . . . all talk about ages and evolution. . . . The true philosophy is concerned with the instant. Will a man take this road or that? The aeons are easy enough to think about, any one can think about them. The instant is really awful: and it is because our religion has intensely felt the instant, that it has in literature dealt much with battle and in theology dealt much with hell.

Orthodoxy, ch. 8

Christianity (which is still the only coherent ethic of Europe) rests on two or three paradoxes or mysteries which can easily be impugned in argument and as easily justified in life. One . . . is the paradox of hope or faith – that the more hopeless is the situation the more hopeful must be the man. . . . Another is the paradox of charity or chivalry that the weaker a thing is the more it should be respected, that the more indefensible a thing is the more it should appeal to us for a certain kind of defence. . . . One of the very practical and working mysteries in the Christian tradition . . . is the conception of the sinfulness of pride. Pride is a weakness in the character; it dries up laughter, it dries up wonder, it dries up chivalry and energy.

Heretics, ch. 9

MISCELLANY

The object of philanthropy is to do good; the object of religion is to be good.

Heretics, ch. 6

'The Grace of Our Lord Jesus Christ'

'I live in an age of varied powers and knowledge,
Of steam, science, democracy, journalism, art;
But when my love rises like a sea,
I have to go back to an obscure tribe and a slain man
To formulate a blessing.'

Notebook, cited Ward, *Gilbert Keith Chesterton*, p. 62

To the orthodox there must always be a case for revolution; for in the hearts of men God has been put under the feet of Satan. In the upper world hell once rebelled against heaven. But in this world heaven is rebelling against hell.

Orthodoxy, ch. 7

If clean homes and clean air make clean souls, why not give the power
. . . to those who undoubtedly have the clean air? If better conditions
will make the poor more fit to govern themselves, why should not better
conditions already make the rich more fit to govern them? . . . Only the
Christian Church can offer any rational objection to a complete
confidence in the rich. For she has maintained from the beginning that
the danger was not in man's environment, but in man. Further, she has
maintained that if we come to talk of a dangerous environment, the
most dangerous environment of all is the commodious environment.

Orthodoxy, ch. 7

The extraordinary position of man in the physical universe makes it
practically impossible to treat him in either one direction or the other
in a purely physical way. Man is an exception . . . . If he is not the image
of God, then he is a disease of the dust. If it is not true that a divine
being fell, then we can only say that one of the animals went entirely
off its head. In neither case can we really argue very much from the
body of man simply considered as the body of an innocent and healthy
animal. His body has got too much mixed up with his soul, as we see in
the supreme instance of sex . . . . All the human things are more
dangerous than anything that affects the beasts – sex, poetry, property,
religion. The real case against drunkenness is not that it calls up the
beast, but that it calls up the Devil . . . . Man is always something worse
or something better than an animal; and a mere argument from animal
perfection never touches him at all. Thus, in sex no animal is either
chivalrous or obscene. And thus no animal ever invented anything so
bad as drunkenness – or so good as drink.

'Wine when it is Red', in *All Things Considered*

Christianity [rests wholly] on the recognition of pain.

'Unknown America', in *Sidelights on New London and Newer York*

I have doubted if I believed anything: but I have found the trick of
saying: "If I did not *really* believe I should not have done this work, or
resisted that temptation . . . . My Will knows me better than my Mind
does." Think about solid things outside you; especially about the most
solid thing in the world – affection . . . . I doubt if there is a doubt
anywhere I have not entertained, examined and dismissed. I believe in
God the Father Almighty, Maker of Heaven and Earth and in the other
extraordinary things in the same statement. I believe them more, the
more I see of human experience.

Letter, cited Maisie Ward, *Return to Chesterton* (1952), p. 202

Part 3

Anti-Religion

'Ten false philosophies will fit the universe.'
                'The Honour of Israel Gow', in *The Innocence of Father Brown*

ATTACK ON CHRISTIANITY

[Christianity] was attacked on all sides and for all contradictory reasons. . . . One accusation against Christianity was that it prevented men, by morbid tears and terrors, from seeking joy and liberty in the bosom of Nature. But another accusation was that it comforted men with a fictitious providence. . . . One rationalist had hardly done calling Christianity a nightmare before another began to call it a fool's paradise. . . . The very people who reproached Christianity with the meekness and non-resistance of the monasteries were the very people who reproached it also with the violence and valour of the Crusades.

Orthodoxy, ch. 6

When Christianity was heavily bombarded in the last century, upon no point was it more persistently and brilliantly attacked than upon that of its alleged enmity to human joy. Shelley and Swinburne and all their armies have passed again and again over the ground, but they have not altered it. They have not set up a single new trophy or ensign for the world's merriment to rally to. . . . Mr. Swinburne does not hang up his stocking on the eve of the birthday of Victor Hugo. Mr. William Archer does not sing carols descriptive of the infancy of Ibsen outside people's doors in the snow.[1] In the round of our rational and mournful year one festival remains out of all those ancient gaieties that once covered the whole earth. Christmas remains to remind us of those ages, whether Pagan or Christian, when the many acted poetry instead of the few writing it. In all the winter in our woods there is no tree in glow but the holly.

Heretics, ch. 6

1. The poet Swinburne was strongly influenced by Hugo, and the theatre figure Archer (1856-1924) was a chief advocate of Ibsen.

The great Victorian rationalism has succeeded in doing damage to religion. It has done what is perhaps the worst of all damages to religion. It has driven it entirely into the power of the religious people. . . . Men who would have been mystics in any case, were driven back upon being much more extravagantly religious than they would have been in a religious country. Men like [T.H.] Huxley . . . were equally driven back on being irreligious; that is, on doubting things which men's normal imagination does not necessarily doubt. . . . They have left to their descendants a treaty that has become a dull torture. Men may believe in immortality, and none of the men know why. Men may not believe in miracles, and none of the men know why.

. . . Darwin, especially through the strong journalistic genius of Huxley, had won a very wide spread though an exceedingly vague victory. . . . It was and is hazily associated with the negation of religion. But . . . it was also associated with the negation of democracy. The same Mid-Victorian muddle-headedness that made people think that "evolution" meant that we need not admit the supremacy of God, also made them think that "survival" meant that we must admit the supremacy of men. . . . As so often happens when a rather unhealthy doubt is in the atmosphere, the strongest words of their great captain [Huxley] could not keep the growing crowds of agnostics back from the most hopeless and inhuman extremes of destructive thought. Nonsense not yet quite dead about the folly of allowing the unfit to survive began to be more and more wildly whispered . . . The harshness of Utilitarianism began to turn into downright tyranny. That beautiful faith in human nature and in freedom which had made delicate the dry air of John Stuart Mill; that robust, romantic sense of justice which had redeemed even the injustices of Macaulay – all that seemed slowly and sadly to be drying up. Under the shock of Darwinism all that was good in the Victorian rationalism shook and dissolved like dust. All that was bad in it abode and clung like clay. The magnificent emancipation evaporated; the mean calculation remained. One could still calculate in clear statistical tables, how many men lived, how many men died. One must not ask how they lived; for that is politics. One must not ask how they died; for that is religion. And religion and politics were ruled out of all the Later Victorian debating clubs; even including the debating club at Westminster.

. . . There had begun that easy automatic habit, of science as an oiled and smooth-running machine, that habit of treating things as obviously unquestionable, when, indeed, they are obviously questionable. . . . The point was not so much that the [scientific] pioneers had not proved their case; it was rather that, by an unexpressed rule of respectability, they were not required to prove it. This rather abrupt twist of the rationalistic mind in the direction of arbitrary power, certainly weakened the Liberal movement from within.

The Victorian Age in Literature, ch. 4

The thing which the evolutionary attitude of mind in our day does deny is that there is any particular sanctity about this particular two-legged being who has come from the ape by imperceptible gradations, and who may be going back again to the ape, with equally imperceptible gradations! In other words, Science attacks that thing which I have called the "corner stone of Christianity" – the sacredness of the ordinary man, that the ordinary man is a person to be reverenced. . . . The sense of the sacredness of every human being, the sense that he is different from nature, that he is above nature, is the whole essence and power and force of Christianity, and indeed not only of Christianity, but of every other religion – or (as is so finely expressed in that well-known paraphrase of Sir Thomas Browne's) "There is that in man which is older than the elements, and which owes no homage unto the sun."[1]

'Vox Populi, Vox Dei',
in *Preachers from the Pew*, ed. Rev. W. Henry Hunt (1906)

THE MIND-SET OF ANTI-RELIGION

We accept in a blind and literal spirit, not only images of speculation, but even figures of speech. The nineteenth century prided itself on having lost its faith in myths, and proceeded to put all its faith in metaphors. It dismissed the old doctrines about the way of life and the light of the world; and then it proceeded to talk as if the light of truth were really and literally a light, that could be absorbed by merely opening our eyes; or as if the path of progress were really and truly a path, to be found by merely following our noses. Thus the purpose of God is an idea, true or false; but the purpose of Nature is merely a metaphor; for obviously if there is no God there is no purpose. Yet while men, by an imaginative instinct, spoke of the purpose of God with a grand agnosticism, as something too large to be seen, something reaching out to worlds and to eternities, they speak of the purpose of Nature in particular and practical problems of curing babies or cutting up rabbits.
. . . We must free ourselves from the talismanic tyranny of a metaphor

---

1. 'There is surely a piece of Divinity in us, something that was before the Elements, and owes no homage unto the Sun': Sir Thomas Browne *Religio Medici* (1643), part 2, sec. 11.

which we do not recognize as a metaphor. Men realized that the old mystical doctrines were mystical; they do not realize that the new metaphors are metaphorical.

What I Saw in America, ch. 12, 'The Republican in the Ruins'

Just before the French Revolution, among the first eighteenth-century philosophers, it was generally assumed that Liberty was not merely a good thing, but the one and only origin of all good things. The man living according to Nature, the Natural Man or the Noble Savage, would find himself immediately free and happy so long as he never went to church, and was careful to cut the parish priest in the street. . . . The philosophers who did not believe in God, whom they regarded as a myth, managed to believe in Nature without realising that she is a metaphor.

Then . . . came the industrial revolution; and with it the enormous new importance attached to science. . . . The second atheist philosophy was founded, not on the fact that Nature is kind, but on the fact that Nature is cruel; not that fields are free and beautiful, but that scientific men and industrialists are so energetic, that they will soon cover all the fields with factories and warehouses. . . . It was now positively stated that economic liberty, the freedom to buy and sell and hire and exploit, would make people so blissfully happy that they would forget all their dreams of the fields of heaven; or for that matter of the fields of earth.

'God and Goods', in *The Common Man*

Every one of the popular modern phrases and ideals is a dodge in order to shirk the problem of what is good. We are fond of talking about "liberty;" that, as we talk of it, is a dodge to avoid discussing what is good. We are fond of talking about "progress;" that is a dodge to avoid discussing what is good. . . . The modern man says, "Let us leave all these arbitrary [religious] standards and embrace liberty." This is, logically rendered, "Let us not decide what is good, but let it be considered good not to decide it." He says, "Away with your old moral formulae; I am for progress." This, logically stated, means, "Let us not settle what is good; but let us settle whether we are getting more of it." He says, "Neither in religion nor morality . . . lie the hopes of the race, but in education." This, clearly expressed, means, "We cannot decide what is good, but let us give it to our children."

As enunciated today "progress" is simply a comparative of which we have not settled the superlative. We meet every ideal of religion, patriotism, beauty, or brute pleasure with the alternative ideal of progress – that is to say, we meet every proposal of getting something that we know about, with an alternative proposal of getting a great deal more of nobody knows what . . . Nobody has any business to use the word "progress" unless he has a definite creed and a cast-iron code of morals. Nobody can be progressive without being doctrinal; I might almost say that nobody can be progressive without being infallible – at any rate, without believing in some infallibility. For progress by its very name indicates a direction; and the moment we are in the least doubtful about the direction, we become in the same degree doubtful about the progress.

Heretics, ch. 2

"Progress" is a useless word; for progress takes for granted an already defined direction; and it is exactly about the direction that we disagree.

'American Notes',
in *Appreciations and Criticisms of the Works of Charles Dickens*

While there is a perfectly genuine danger of fanaticism from the men who have unworldly ideals, the permanent and urgent danger of fanaticism is from the men who have worldly ideals. People who say that an ideal is a dangerous thing, that it deludes and intoxicates, are perfectly right. But the ideal which intoxicates most is the least idealistic kind of ideal. The ideal which intoxicates least is the very ideal ideal; that sobers us suddenly, as all heights and precipices and great distances do.

Heretics, ch. 18

A common hesitation in our day touching the use of extreme convictions is a. . . . notion that extreme convictions, specially upon cosmic matters, have been responsible in the past for the thing which is called bigotry . . . The people who are most bigoted are the people who have no convictions at all. . . . It is the vague modern who is not at all certain what is right who is most certain that Dante was wrong. The serious opponent of the Latin Church in history, even in the act of showing that it produced great infamies, must know that it produced great saints. It is the hard-headed stockbroker, who knows no history and believes in no religion, who is, nevertheless, perfectly convinced that all these priests are knaves. . . . Bigotry . . . [is] the anger of men who have no opinions. It is the resistance offered to definite ideas by that vague bulk of people whose ideas are indefinite to excess. Bigotry . . . [is] the appalling frenzy of the indifferent. . . . It was not the people who cared who ever persecuted; the people who cared were not sufficiently numerous. It was the people who did not care who filled the world with fire and oppression.

Heretics, ch. 20

The new Freethinker does not *read* a book. He looks through it feverishly for texts to be twisted in favour of a prejudice, like the religious maniac with the Bible.

'Frozen Free Thought', in *The Well and the Shallows*

At a very early age I had thought my way back to thought itself. It is a very dreadful thing to do; for it may lead to thinking that there is nothing but thought. . . . It was as if I had myself projected the universe from within, with all its trees and stars; and that is so near to the notion of being God that it is manifestly even nearer to going mad. Yet I was not mad, in any medical or physical sense; I was simply carrying the scepticism of my time as far as it would go. . . . While dull atheists came and explained to me that there was nothing but matter, I listened with a sort of calm horror of detachment, suspecting that there was nothing but mind. . . . The atheist told me so pompously that he did not believe there was any God; and there were moments when I did not even believe there was any atheist.

Autobiography, ch. 4

The men who really believe in themselves are all in lunatic asylums. . . . Complete self-confidence is not merely a sin; complete self-confidence is a weakness. Believing utterly in one's self is a hysterical and superstitious belief. . . . It is possible to meet the sceptic who believes that everything began in himself. He doubts not the existence of angels or devils, but the existence of men and cows. For him his own friends are a mythology made up of himself. He created his own father and his own mother. This horrible fancy has in it something decidedly attractive to the somewhat mystical egoism of our day. . . . When the man, believing in nothing and in no man, is alone in his own nightmare, then the great individualistic motto shall be written over him in avenging irony. The stars will be only dots in the blackness of his own brain; his mother's face will be only a sketch from his own insane pencil on the walls of his cell. But over his cell shall be written, with dreadful truth, "He believes in himself."

Orthodoxy, ch. 2

Some people, especially young people, abandon practising Catholicism. But none of them abandon it for Protestantism. All of them practically abandon it for paganism. Most of them abandon it for something that is really rather too simple to be called an *ism* of any kind. They abandon it for things and . . . practically never the theological theories of Protestantism. . . . They leave it to have a high old time; and considering what a muddle we have made of modern morality, they can hardly be blamed. . . . It is the cant phrase of the old rationalists that their reason prevents a return to the Faith, but it is false: it is no longer reason but rather passion.

The Catholic Church and Conversion, ch. 6

THE POVERTY OF SECULARISM

[W.E. Henley] was what every poet must be who shares the unbelief of his age; a man melancholy though not without happiness; a man reconciled to a second best. A poet who has lost his gods must always be like a lover who has lost his love and has married a sensible woman. For the earth which Henley enjoyed has never been the original starting point of men's thoughts or labours. Heaven was man's first love; and the earth is only a substitute; even when it is not only a marriage of convenience.

'W.E. Henley: Poet', in *A Handful of Authors*

The rationalists and realists who were praising the adult pursuit of happiness . . . were (and still are) mainly occupied with describing unhappiness. They only prove that free life and free love are really worse than any ascetic had ever represented them. The naturalistic philosophies did not only contradict Christianity. The naturalistic philosophies also contradicted the naturalistic novels. Their own exercise of their own right of expression was quite enough to show that the mere combination of the maturity of reason with the pleasures of passion does not in fact produce a Utopia. We need not debate here whether the Zolaists were justified in so laboriously describing horrors. If mere liberty had really led to happiness, they would have been describing happiness.

Robert Louis Stevenson, ch. 10

At present [people] are suffering from an utterly abnormal unhappiness. They have got all the tragic elements essential to the human lot to contend with; time and death and bereavement and unrequited affection and dissatisfaction with themselves. But they have not got the elements of consolation and encouragement that ought normally to renew their hopes or restore their self-respect. They have not got vision or conviction, or the mastery of their work, or the loyalty of their household, or any form of human dignity. Even the latest Utopians, the last lingering representatives of that fated and unfortunate race, do not really promise the modern man that he shall do anything, or own anything, or in any effectual fashion be anything. They only promise that, if he keeps his eyes open, he will see something; he will see the Universal Trust or the World State or Lord Melchett[1] coming in the clouds in glory. But the modern man cannot even keep his eyes open. He is too weary with toil and a long succession of unsuccessful Utopias. He has fallen asleep.

G.K.'s Weekly, 20 Oct. 1928

1. Alfred Mond, an industrialist M.P., recently created 'Baron Melchett', was promoting union-business cooperation, though he strongly opposed socialism.

The world cannot keep its own ideals. The secular order cannot make secure any one of its own noble and natural conceptions of secular perfection. That will be found, as time goes on, the ultimate argument for a Church independent of the world and the secular order. What has become of all those ideal figures from the Wise Man of the Stoics to the democratic Deist of the eighteenth century? What has become of all that purely human hierarchy of chivalry . . . ? The very name of 'knight' has come to represent the petty triumph of a profiteer, and the very word squire the petty tyranny of a landlord. What has become of all that golden liberality of the Humanists . . . ? The very Greek language that they loved has become a mere label for snuffy and snobbish dons, and a mere cock-shy for cheap and half-educated Utilitarians, who make it a symbol of superstition and reaction. We have lived to see a time when the heroic legend of the Republic and the Citizen, which seemed to Jefferson the eternal youth of the world, has begun to grow old in its turn. . . . These old experiences are now only alive where they have found a lodgment in the Catholic tradition of Christendom, and made themselves friends for ever. St. Francis [of Assisi] is the only surviving troubadour. St. Thomas More is the only surviving Humanist. St. Louis is the only surviving knight.

What I Saw in America, ch. 19, 'The Future of Democracy'

Mr. Bernard Shaw has put the view . . . : "The golden rule is that there is no golden rule." . . . A man's opinion on tramcars matters; his opinion on Botticelli matters; his opinion on all things does not matter. He may turn over and explore a million objects, but he must not find that strange object, the universe; for if he does he will have a religion, and be lost. Everything matters – except everything.

Heretics, ch. 1

As an explanation of the world, materialism has a sort of insane simplicity. . . . We have at once the sense of it covering everything and the sense of it leaving everything out. . . . [The materialist] understands everything, and everything does not seem worth understanding. His cosmos may be complete in every rivet and cog-wheel, but still his cosmos is smaller than our world. Somehow his scheme . . . seems unconscious of the alien energies and the large indifference of the earth; it is not thinking of the real things of the earth, of fighting peoples or proud mothers, or first love or fear upon the sea.

. . . The materialist philosophy . . . is certainly much more limiting than any religion. . . . The Christian is quite free to believe that there is a considerable amount of settled order and inevitable development in the universe. But the materialist is not allowed to admit into his spotless machine the slightest speck of spiritualism or miracle. . . . The Christian admits that the universe is manifold. . . . The sane man knows that he has a touch of the beast, a touch of the devil, a touch of the saint, a touch of the citizen. . . . But the materialist's world is quite simple and solid, just as the madman is quite sure he is sane. The materialist is sure that history has been simply and solely a chain of causation. . . . Spiritual doctrines do not actually limit the mind as do materialistic denials. Even if I believe in immortality I need not think about it. But if I disbelieve in immortality I must not think about it. In the first case the road is open and I can go as far as I like; in the second the road is shut. . . . The main deductions of the materialist . . . gradually destroy his humanity; I do not mean only kindness, I mean hope, courage, poetry, initiative, all that is human. For instance, when materialism leads men to complete fatalism, . . . it is quite idle to pretend that it is in any sense a liberating force. It is absurd to say that you are especially advancing freedom when you only use free thought to destroy free will.

Orthodoxy, ch. 2

The danger which I anticipate from the disappearance of religion is . . . a decrease in life. I do not think that under modern Western materialism we should have anarchy. I doubt whether we should have enough individual valour and spirit even to have liberty. It is quite an old-fashioned fallacy to suppose that our objection to scepticism is that it removes the discipline from life. Our objection to scepticism is that it removes the motive power. Materialism is not a thing which destroys mere restraint. Materialism itself is the great restraint.

Heretics, ch. 16

A world in which men know that most of what they know is probably untrue cannot be dignified with the name of a sceptical world; it is simply an impotent and abject world, not attacking anything, but accepting everything while trusting nothing; accepting even its own incapacity to attack; accepting its own lack of authority to accept; doubting its very right to doubt. . . . We did not ourselves think that the mere denial of our dogmas could end in such dehumanised and demented anarchy. . . . The organic thing called religion has in fact the organs that take hold on life. It can feed where the fastidious doubter finds no food; it can reproduce where the solitary sceptic boasts of being barren. It may be accepting a miracle to believe in free will; but it is accepting madness, sooner or later, to disbelieve in it. It may be a wild risk to make a vow; but it is a quiet, crawling and inevitable ruin to refuse to make a vow.

'The Return to Religion', in *The Well and the Shallows*

Sceptics do not succeed in pulling up the roots of Christianity; but they do succeed in pulling up the roots of every man's ordinary vine and fig tree, of every man's garden. . . . Secularists have not succeeded in wrecking divine things; but Secularists have succeeded in wrecking secular things.

A religion cannot be shown to be monstrous at the last; a religion is monstrous from the beginning. It announces itself as extraordinary. It offers itself as extravagant. The sceptics at the most can only ask us to reject our creed as something wild. And we have accepted it as something wild. . . . With your queries and dilemmas you have made no havoc in faith; from the first it was a transcendental conviction; it cannot be made any more transcendental than it was. But you have . . . made a certain havoc in common morals and commonsense. . . . Evolutionists cannot drive us, because of the nameless gradation in Nature, to deny the personality of God, for a personal God might as well work by gradations as in any other way; but they do drive themselves, through those gradations, to deny the existence of a personal Mr. Jones, because he is within the scope of evolution and his edges are rubbed away. The evolutionists uproot the world, but not the flowers. The Titans never scaled heaven, but they laid waste the earth.

'The Roots of the World', in *Lunacy and Letters*

RATIONALISMS

It is idle to talk always of the alternative of reason and faith. Reason is itself a matter of faith. It is an act of faith to assert that our thoughts have any relation to reality at all. . . . A sceptic . . . must sooner or later ask . . . the question, "Why should *anything* go right; even observation and deduction? Why should not good logic be as misleading as bad logic? They are both movements in the brain of a bewildered ape?"

Orthodoxy, ch. 3

Everybody knows by this time that science has had its revenge on scepticism. The border between the credible and the incredible has not only become once more as vague as in any barbaric twilight; but the credible is obviously increasing and the incredible shrinking. A man in Voltaire's time did not know what miracle he would next have to throw up. A man in our time does not know what miracle he will next have to swallow.

St. Francis of Assisi, ch. 9

As soon as the men of science began to doubt the rules of the game, the game was up. They could no longer rule out all the old marvels as impossible, in face of the new marvels which they had to admit as possible. They were themselves dealing now with a number of unknown quantities. . . . They knew by a hundred hints that their non-miraculous world was no longer water-tight.

The New Jerusalem (1920), pp. 161-2

'What is it gets hold of a man on these cursed cold mountains? I think it's the black, brainless repetition; all these forests, and over all an ancient horror of unconsciousness. It's like the dream of an atheist. Pine-trees and more pine-trees and millions more pine-trees.'

'The Honour of Israel Gow', in *The Innocence of Father Brown*

Atheism is abnormality. It is not merely the denial of a dogma. It is the reversal of a subconscious assumption in the soul; the sense that there is a meaning and a direction in the world it sees.

The Everlasting Man, Part 1, ch. 8

Heavens! to think of the dull rut of the sceptics who go on asking whether we possess a future life. The exciting question for real scepticism is whether we possess a past life. What is a minute ago, rationalistically considered, except a tradition and a picture?

'The Extraordinary Cabman', in *Tremendous Trifles*

If a man feels that all the movements of his own mind are meaningless, then his mind is meaningless, and he is meaningless; and it does not mean anything to attempt to discover his meaning. Most fundamental sceptics appear to survive, because they are not consistently sceptical and not at all fundamental. They will first deny everything and then admit something, if for the sake of argument.

St. Thomas Aquinas, ch. 6

The essence of the Thomist common sense is that two agencies are at work; reality and the recognition of reality; and their meeting is a sort of marriage. . . . God made Man so that he was capable of coming in contact with reality; and those whom God hath joined, let no man put asunder.

. . . No sceptics work sceptically; no fatalists work fatalistically; all without exception work on the principle that it is possible to assume what it is not possible to believe. No materialist who thinks his mind was made up for him, by mud and blood and heredity, has any hesitation in making up his mind. No sceptic who believes that truth is subjective has any hesitation about treating it as objective.

St. Thomas Aquinas, ch. 8

Atheism is indeed the most daring of all dogmas, more daring than the vision of a palpable day of judgment. For it is the assertion of a universal negative; for a man to say that there is no God in the universe is like saying that there are no insects in any of the stars.

'Charles II', in *Twelve Types*

[The eighteenth century] had no great understanding of children. The men of that time had forgotten the Holy Child of medieval times and had not yet heard of the Happy Child of modern literature. They could not imagine a Peter Pan, for they had lost the religious traditions both of Pan and Peter. They had silenced all those subconscious voices which speak to simple people of the wonders hidden in this world. In short, they were ignorant of all the thousand things that only the ignorant ever know.

. . . The religion of the eighteenth century was finely expressed in the motto of a group of Scottish debating societies famous as the Associated Societies of Edinburgh University. It was *Gloria hominis ratio et oratio*: the glory of man is reason and speech.

'The Age of Reason', in *The Glass Walking-Stick*

That great wave of barbarism that swept over Western Europe in the nineteenth century, and which has been called the Rise of Rationalism,[1] has this note in it even more savage than its other notes of savagery: that it sought to make a man's soul the slave of his body. It did not say that the spirit was willing but the flesh was weak[2] – the free and generous doctrine of religion. It said that the spirit was unwilling because the flesh was strong. The body was not a timid slave, but an insulting tyrant. The most abstruse pleasure, the most ethereal agony, was to be explained by physiological causes that nobody could possibly test. Every happy morning was due to a good breakfast; every unhappy morning was due to a bad night.

. . . I have always . . . had a notion that the truth was exactly the other way about. So far from thinking that most moral pleasures are really material, I fancy that a great many apparently material pleasures are chiefly moral. So far from admitting that the bacon makes you enjoy the beautiful morning, I think it highly probable that only the beautiful morning makes you tolerate the bacon. . . . I fancy that if every one of those queer indestructible dreads [i.e. people's phobias] were sympathetically

1. Probably referring to William Lecky's *History of the Rise and Influence of the Spirit of Rationalism in Europe* (1865), which celebrated the damage done to Catholicism by rationalism.
2. Mat. 26.50.

examined it would be found that in each case the core of the terror was spiritual. . . . A man is afraid of animals, not because they are dangerous, but because they are animal; they represent that rude, unquenchable life in the universe that is the rival of man and his rebuke. Fear is of the body, perhaps; but terror is only of the soul. The body runs with fear: it is only the soul that stands still with it.

'Fear', in *Lunacy and Letters*

The general notion that science establishes agnosticism is a sort of mystification produced by talking Latin and Greek instead of plain English. Science is the Latin for knowledge. Agnosticism is the Greek for ignorance. It is not self-evident that ignorance is the goal of knowledge. It is the ignorance and not the knowledge that produces the current notion that free thought weakens theism.

'Obstinate Orthodoxy', in *The Thing*

The modern Anthropologists, who called themselves Agnostics, completely failed to be Anthropologists at all. Under their limitations, they could not get a complete theory of Man, let alone a complete theory of Nature. They began by ruling out something which they called the Unknowable. The incomprehensibility was almost comprehensible, if we could really understand the Unknowable in the sense of the Ultimate. But it rapidly became apparent that all sorts of things were Unknowable, which were exactly the things that a man has got to know. It is necessary to know whether he is responsible or irresponsible, perfect or imperfect, perfectible or unperfectible, mortal or immortal, doomed or free: not in order to understand God, but in order to understand Man. . . . Has a man free will; or is his sense of choice an illusion? Has he a conscience, or has his conscience any authority; or is it only the prejudice of the tribal past? Is there any real hope of settling these things by human reason; and has *that* any authority? Is he to regard death as final; and is he to regard miraculous help as possible?

St. Thomas Aquinas, ch. 7

Science [cannot] forbid men to believe in something which science does not profess to investigate. Science is the study of the admitted laws of existence; it cannot prove a universal negative about whether those laws could ever be suspended by something admittedly above them. . . . The visible order of nature follows a certain course if there is nothing behind it to stop it. But that fact throws no sort of light on whether there *is* anything behind it to stop it. That is a question of philosophy or metaphysics and not of material science.

'Inge versus Barnes', in *The Thing*

Science is claiming much less than it did to show us a solid and objective reality. . . . The Atom has entirely lost the objective solidity it had for the nineteenth-century materialists. . . . The science of physics has almost become a science of metaphysics. . . . [Sir Arthur] Eddington is more agnostic about the material world than Huxley ever was about the spiritual world. A very unfortunate moment at which to say that science deals directly with reality and objective truth. . . . The . . . importance for Catholics of this collapse of materialism is simply the fact that the most confident cosmic statements of science can collapse. If fifty years hence the electron is as entirely exploded as the atom, it will not affect us; for we have never founded our philosophy on the electron any more than on the atom. But the materialists did found *their* philosophy on the atom. . . . The importance of the change . . . does consist in its destroying the accepted, universal and proclaimed and popularised dogma: "You must accept the conclusions of science."

'The Collapse of Materialism', in *The Well and the Shallows*

[Catholicism] does not, in the conventional phrase, accept the conclusions of science, for the simple reason that science has not concluded. To conclude is to shut up, and the man of science is not at all likely to shut up.

'Why I am a Catholic', in *Twelve Modern Apostles and Their Creeds* (1926)

THE SOCIAL DIMENSION

Humanitarianism is . . . the dregs of Christianity.

William Blake (1920), p. 117

Now Progress is Providence without God. That is, it is a theory that everything has always perpetually gone right by accident. It is a sort of atheistic optimism, based on an everlasting coincidence far more miraculous than a miracle. If there be no purpose, or if the purpose permits of human free will, then in either case it is almost insanely unlikely that there should be in history a period of steady and uninterrupted progress; or in other words a period in which poor bewildered humanity moves amid a chaos of complications, without making a single mistake. What has to be hammered into the heads of most normal newspaper-readers to-day is that Man has made a great many mistakes. Modern Man has made a great many mistakes.

What I Saw in America, ch. 15, 'Wells and the World State'

Progress has been merely the persecution of the Common Man. Progress has a hagiology, a martyrology, a mass of miraculous legends of its own, like any other religion; and they are mostly false and belong to a false religion.
'The Common Man', in *The Common Man*

The brotherhood of man is a fact which in the long run wears down all other facts. Therefore, a privileged class, if it would avoid sliding naturally back into the body of mankind must keep up an incessant excitement about new projects, new cultures and new prejudices, new skirts and stockings. It must tell a new tale every day or perish, like the lady of the *Arabian Nights*. . . . And so, out of luxury and waste and weariness, the fever they call Progress came into the world.
'Asparagus', in *G.K. Chesterton: The Apostle and the Wild Ducks*

It is this modern suggestion, that Man was right to be bored with Eden and to demand evolution (otherwise mere change), that is very relevant. . . . For upon this modern theory the Fall really was the Fall; for it was the first action that had only tedium as a motive. Progress began in boredom; and, heaven knows, it sometimes seems likely to end in it. And no wonder; for of all utter falsehoods the most false . . . is this notion that men can be happy in movement, when nothing but dullness drives them on from behind. . . . If ever there was a whisper that might truly come from the devil, it is the suggestion that men can despise the beautiful things they have got, and only delight in getting new things because they have not got them. It is obvious that, on that principle, Adam will tire of the tree just as he has tired of the garden. "It is enough that there is always a beyond"; that is, there is always something else to get tired of. All progress based on that mood is truly a Fall; man did fall, does fall, and we can today see him falling. It is the great progressive proposition; that he must seek only for enjoyment because he has lost the power to enjoy.
'If Don John of Austria had Married Mary Queen of Scots',
in *The Common Man*

These evolutionary optimists who call themselves Meliorists[1] (a patient and poor-spirited lot they are) always talk as if we were certain of the end, though not of the beginning. In other words, they don't know what life is aiming at, but they are quite sure it will get there. Why anybody who has avowedly forgotten where he came from should be quite so certain of

---

1. Meliorists suppose that Man is subject to determinist forces, which can, however, be modified through the application of human effort and intelligence, leading to the progressive improvement of humanity: as a form of Humanism, it rejected the Christian scheme of salvation.

where he is going to I have never been able to make out; but Meliorists are like that. They are ready to talk of existence itself as the product of purely evil forces. . . . Life itself, crude, uncultivated life, is horrible to them. They belong very largely to the same social class and creed as the lady who objected that the milk came to her from a dirty cow, and not from a nice clean shop. But they are sure how everything will end.

'What is Right With the World',
in *G.K. Chesterton: The Apostle and the Wild Ducks*

The appearance of [Darwin's] 'The Descent of Man' was that it was really a descent of man – that man had been kicked off his pedestal on to the floor.

Daily News, 26 June 1909

Ancient Calvinism and modern Evolutionism are essentially the same things. They are both ingenious logical blasphemies against the dignity and liberty of the human soul.

'Little Dorrit',
in *Appreciations and Criticisms of the Works of Charles Dickens*

Darwinism can be used to back up two mad moralities, but it cannot be used to back up a single sane one. The kinship and competition of all living creatures can be used as a reason for being insanely cruel or insanely sentimental; but not for a healthy love of animals. On the evolutionary basis you may be inhumane, or you may be absurdly humane; but you cannot be human.

Orthodoxy, ch. 7

The great number of abuses peculiar to our present social state work back to that one great heresy which is the perversion of Darwin; I mean the heresy that man is an animal first and a spirit afterwards. The truth is that man is an animal and a spirit simultaneously, and his spiritual life is no more a luxury than his physical; except in the sense that he cannot rationally explain why he denies either of them.

The Open Review, July 1906

The thing once called free thought has come finally to threaten everything that is free. It denies personal freedom in denying free will and the human power of choice. . . . The whole trend of it . . . is towards some . . . theory that a man cannot help himself; that a man cannot mend himself; above all, that a man cannot free himself. . . . We are practically told that we might as well ask a fossil to reform itself. . . . We are all dead, and the only comfort is that we are all classified. . . . As it is Kismet without Allah, so also it is Calvinism without God.

'The Return to Religion', in *The Well and the Shallows*

Determinism is not inconsistent with the cruel treatment of criminals. What it is (perhaps) inconsistent with is the generous treatment of criminals; with any appeal to their better feelings or encouragement in their moral struggle. The determinist does not believe in appealing to the will, but he does believe in changing the environment. He must not say to the sinner, "Go and sin no more," because the sinner cannot help it. But he can put him in boiling oil; for boiling oil is an environment.

Orthodoxy, ch. 2

There is no faith in freedom without faith in free will. A servile fatalism dogs the creed of materialism; because nothing, as Dante said, less than the generosity of God could give to Man, after all ordinary orderly gifts, the noblest of all things, which is Liberty.

Broadcast talk, 1934, cited Ward, *Gilbert Keith Chesterton*, p. 545

A philosophy begins with Being; with the end and value of a living thing; and it is manifest that a materialism that only considers economic ethics, cannot cover the question at all. If the problem of happiness were so solved by economic comfort, the classes who are now comfortable would be happy, which is absurd.

'The Backward Bolshie', in *The Well and the Shallows*

The materialist theory of history, that all politics and ethics are the expression of economics, is a very simple fallacy indeed. It consists simply of confusing the necessary conditions of life with the normal preoccupations of life, that are quite a different thing. It is like saying that because a man can only walk about on two legs, therefore he never walks about except to buy shoes and stockings. . . . Cows may be purely economic, in the sense that we cannot see that they do much beyond grazing . . . and that is why a history of cows in twelve volumes would not be very lively reading . . . But so far from the movements that make up the story of man being economic, we may say that the story only begins where the motive of the cows . . . leaves off. . . . If you leave things like all the religious wars and all the merely adventurous explorations out of the human story, it will not only cease to be human at all but cease to be a story at all. The outline of history is made of these decisive curves and angles determined by the will of man. Economic history would not even be history. . . . The thing most present to the mind of man is not the economic machinery necessary to his existence, but rather that existence itself. . . . There is something that is nearer to him than livelihood, and that is life.

The Everlasting Man, Part 1, ch. 7

Trade has been put in the place of Truth. Trade, which is in its nature a secondary or dependent thing, has been treated as a primary and independent thing; as an absolute. The moderns . . . have taken what all ancient philosophers called the Good, and translated it as the Goods. . . . When God looked on created things and saw that they were good, it meant that they were good in themselves and as they stood. . . . The idea of a man enjoying a thing in itself, for himself, is inconceivable to them. . . . The fall from that first creation that was called good has very largely come from the restless impotence for valuing things in themselves; the madness of the trader who cannot see any good in a good, except as something to get rid of. . . . Nothing solid can be built on any other philosophy [than one based on values]; certainly not upon the utterly unphilosophical philosophy of blind buying and selling; of bullying people into purchasing what they do not want; of making it badly so that they may break it and imagine they want it again; of keeping rubbish in rapid circulation like a dust-storm in a desert; and pretending that you are teaching men to hope, because you do not leave them one intelligent instant in which to despair.

'Reflections on a Rotten Apple', in *The Well and the Shallows*

The materialistic state, cemented only with money as with mud, will fall apart under the blow of any people who have love or loyalty to their leaders or their cause; for the simple reason that those who care most for money care more for life.

'Trade Terms', in *The Well and the Shallows*

I have ended by doubting the existence of Materialism. I do not believe there is any person who is not primarily dominated by his religion, by his views of the universe. . . . I do not say that every man has a religion but I do say that there is a subconscious part of his mind of which probably he is entirely unaware, and that almost every act he performs is dictated by his conception of the universe. . . . The Sceptic is a man who does not believe in other people's religion. . . . Men's pockets are almost always dependent upon their theories about man's existence. In that sense, there is no Materialist, that is, there are no people who act on practical and economic principles only. . . . The people who do not follow any vision at all do not exist or cannot exist for long.

'The Citizen, the Gentleman, and the Savage',
in *Preachers from the Pew*, ed. Rev. W. Henry Hunt (1906)

Two Earthly Paradises had collapsed. The first was the natural paradise of Rousseau; the second the economic paradise of Ricardo. Men did not become perfect through being free to live and love; men did not become perfect through being free to buy and sell. It was obviously time for the atheists to find a third inevitable and immediate ideal. They have found it in Communism. And it does not trouble them that it is quite different from their first ideal and quite contrary to their second. All they want is some supposed betterment of humanity which will be a bribe for depriving humanity of divinity.

'God and Goods', in *The Common Man*

Bolshevism and every shade of any such theory of brotherhood is based upon one unfathomably mystical Catholic dogma; the equality of men. The Communists stake everything on the equality of men. . . . They ride it to death, . . . turning their horse into a nightmare.

The Catholic Church and Conversion, ch. 4

It is only by believing in God that we can ever criticise the Government. Once abolish the God, and the Government becomes the God. That fact . . . is written most plainly across that recent history of Russia. . . . There the Government is the God.

Christendom in Dublin, Part 3

Supermen, if not good men, are vermin. . . . The modern world, when it praises its little Caesars, talks of being strong and brave: but it does not seem to see the eternal paradox involved in the conjunction of these ideas. The strong cannot be brave. Only the weak can be brave; and yet again, in practice, only those who can be brave can be trusted, in time of doubt, to be strong. . . . The meaning of all modern hero-worship and celebration of the Strong Man, the Caesar, the Superman [is] that he may be something more than man; we must be something less. . . . A great man is not a man so strong that he feels less than other men; he is a man so strong that he feels more. And when Nietzsche[1] says, "A new commandment I give to you, 'be hard,'" he is really saying, "A new commandment I give to you, 'be dead.'" Sensibility is the definition of life.

Heretics, ch. 5

---

1. Friedrich Nietzsche despised Christianity as a 'slave morality', his ideal the *Übermensch*, or 'Superman', who would impose his own will and morality on the weak.

Part 4

Religions other than Christianity

BUDDHISM

Buddha . . . belongs to that class of philosophical mystics for whom what we commonly call religion was really only symbolical, and the main matter was a metaphysical unification. He may have had some of the virtues of a saint, but he was in reality a sage. He may have been what we call an idealist; he was also something very like a pessimist. But anyhow he was not a Church and did not found a Church. . . . Buddhism is certainly the very opposite of nature-worship. It would be true to call it an iconoclasm directed to destroy the idol called nature.

Blackfriars, March 1923

Buddha . . . proposed a way of escaping from all this recurrent sorrow; and that was simply by getting rid of the delusion that is called desire. . . . If once a man realised that there is really no reality, that everything, including his soul, is in dissolution at every instant, he would anticipate disappointment and be intangible to change, existing . . . in a sort of ecstasy of indifference. The Buddhists call this beatitude; . . . to us it is indistinguishable from despair. I do not see, for instance, why the disappointment of desire should not apply as much to the most benevolent desires as to the most selfish ones. Indeed the Lord of Compassion seems to pity people for living rather than for dying.

The Everlasting Man, Part 1, ch. 6

The Christian pities men because they are dying, and the Buddhist pities them because they are living. The Christian is sorry for what damages the life of a man; but the Buddhist is sorry for him because he is himself. . . . When a Christian hospital cures a sick man, it assumes that life is a potential pleasure. I cannot see . . . why a Buddhist saint or hospital should help a man to anything – except perhaps to Buddhism.

'On Buddhism', in *Generally Speaking*

To the Buddhists was given a conception of God of extraordinary intellectual purity; but in growing familiar with the featureless splendour, they have lost their heads; . . . they say that everything is nothing and nothing is everything, that black is white because white is black. We fancy that the frightful universal negatives at which they have at last arrived, are really little more than the final mental collapse of men trying always to find an abstraction big enough for all things. . . . Buddhism stands for a simplification of the mind and a reliance on the most indestructible ideas; Christianity stands for a simplification of the heart and a reliance on the most indestructible sentiments. The greater Christian insistence upon personal deity and immortality is not, we fancy, the cause so much as the effect of this essential trend towards an ancient passion and pathos as the power that most nearly rends the veil from the nature of things. Both creeds grope after the same secret sun, but Buddhism dreams of its light and Christianity of its heat. Buddhism seeks after God with the largest conception it can find, the all-producing and all-absorbing One; Christianity seeks after God with the most elementary passion it can find – the craving for a Father, the hunger that is as old as the hills. It turns the whole cry of a lost universe into the cry of a lost child.

The Speaker, 17 Nov. 1900

The more we really appreciate the noble revulsion and renunciation of Buddha, the more we see that intellectually it was the converse and almost the contrary of the salvation of the world by Christ. The Christian would escape from the world into the universe; the Buddhist wishes to escape from the universe even more than from the world. One would uncreate himself; the other would return to his Creation: to his Creator. . . . And he who will not climb the mountain of Christ does indeed fall into the abyss of Buddha.

St. Thomas Aquinas, ch. 4

Christ said 'Seek first the kingdom, and all these things shall be added unto you.' Buddha said 'Seek first the kingdom, and then you will need none of these things.'

The Everlasting Man, Part 2, ch. 3

No two ideals could be more opposite than a Christian saint in a Gothic cathedral and a Buddhist saint in a Chinese temple. . . . The Buddhist saint always has his eyes shut, while the Christian saint always has them very wide open. The Buddhist saint has a sleek and harmonious body, but his eyes are heavy and sealed with sleep. The mediaeval saint's body is wasted, . . . but his eyes are frightfully alive. . . . The Buddhist is looking with a peculiar intentness inwards. The Christian is staring with a frantic intentness outwards. . . . For the Buddhist or Theosophist personality is the fall of man, for the Christian it is the purpose of God, the whole point of his cosmic idea. The world-soul of the Theosophists asks man to love it only in order that man may throw himself into it. But the divine centre of Christianity actually threw man out of it in order that he might love it. . . . The Christian saint is happy because he has verily been cut off from the world; he is separate from things and is staring at them in astonishment. But why should the Buddhist saint be astonished at things? since there is really only one thing, and that being impersonal can hardly be astonished at itself.

Orthodoxy, ch. 8

JUDAISM

With all their fine apprehensions, the Jews suffer from one heavy calamity; that of being a Chosen Race. It is the vice of any patriotism or religion depending on race that the individual is himself the thing to be worshipped; the individual is his own ideal, and even his own idol.

The New Jerusalem (1920), p.29

Humanly speaking, . . . the world owes God to the Jews. It owes that truth to much that is blamed in the Jews. . . . Through all their wanderings, . . . they did indeed carry the fate of the world in that wooden tabernacle. . . . Much as we may prefer that creative liberty which the Christian culture has declared . . . we must not underrate the determining importance at the time of the Hebrew inhibition of images. It is a typical example of one of those limitations that did in fact preserve and perpetuate enlargement, like a wall built round a wide open space. The God who could not have a statue remained a spirit. . . . It is often said with a sneer that the God of Israel was only a God of Battles, . . . pitted in rivalry against the other gods only as their envious foe. Well it is for the world that he was a God of Battles . . . [that] he was to all the rest only a rival and a foe. . . . It would have been easy enough for his worshippers to follow the enlightened course of Syncretism and the pooling of all the pagan traditions. . . . It required the almost demoniac energy of certain inspired demagogues [to testify] to the divine unity in words that are still like winds of inspiration and ruin. . . . The world's destiny would have been distorted still more fatally if monotheism had failed in the Mosaic tradition. . . . That we do preserve something of that primary simplicity, that poets and philosophers can still indeed in some sense say an Universal Prayer, . . . that philosophy and philanthropy are truisms in a religion of reasonable men, all that we do most truly owe, under heaven, to a . . . nomadic people; who bestowed on men the supreme and serene blessing of a jealous God.

The Everlasting Man, Part 1, ch. 4

ISLAM

Some six hundred years after Christianity sprang up in the East and swept westwards, another great faith arose in almost the same eastern lands and followed it like its gigantic shadow. Like a shadow, it was at once a copy and a contrary . . . [Islam] . . . was the final flaming up of the accumulated Orientalisms, perhaps of the accumulated Hebraisms, gradually rejected as the Church grew more European, or as Christianity turned into Christendom. Its highest motive was a hatred of idols, and in its view Incarnation was itself an idolatry. The two things it persecuted were the idea of God being made flesh and of His being afterwards made wood or stone. . . . This fanaticism against art or mythology was at once a development and a reaction from that [Christian] conversion, a sort of minority report of the Hebraists. In this sense Islam was something like a Christian heresy. The early heresies had been full of mad reversals and evasions of the Incarnation, rescuing their Jesus from the reality of his body even at the expense of the sincerity of his soul. And the Greek Iconoclasts had poured into Italy, breaking the popular statues and denouncing the idolatry of the Pope. . . . It was all these disappointed negations that took fire from the genius of Mahomet, and launched out of the burning lands a cavalry charge that nearly conquered the world. . . . This Semite god haunted Christianity like a ghost.

A Short History of England, ch. 6

Islam was the ultimate fulfilment of the Iconoclasts.

St. Thomas Aquinas, ch. 3

The Moslem is the nearest approach to a militant Christian; . . . he is . . . an envoy from western civilisation. . . . Islam . . . owed something to the quite isolated and unique individuality of Israel; but it owed more to Byzantium and the theological enthusiasm of Christendom.

The Everlasting Man, Part 2, ch. 5

The more we know of the great Moslem movement, the more we see that it was really a post-Christian revision, or subsequent simplification rather like the Arian movement. . . . Islam would never have existed without Christianity. . . . Nor was the Muslim movement in the modern sense anti-Christian. It gave to Christ as high a moral position as is given Him by most Unitarians, and indeed a more supernatural status than is given by some Broad Churchmen.

Blackfriars, Mar. 1923

Islam . . . was a . . . reaction against that very humane complexity that is really a Christian character; that idea of balance in the deity, as of balance in the family, that makes that creed a sort of sanity, and that sanity the soul of civilisation.

The Everlasting Man, Part 2, ch. 4

The Moslem had one thought, and that a most vital one; the greatness of God which levels all men. But the Moslem had not one thought to rub against another, because he really had not another. It is the friction of two spiritual things, of tradition and invention, or of substance and symbol, from which the mind takes fire. The creeds condemned as complex have something like the secret of sex; they can breed thoughts.

The New Jerusalem (1920), pp. 34-5

PAGANISM AND PANTHEISM

Nature-worship is more morally dangerous than the most vulgar man-worship of the cities; since it can easily be perverted into the worship of an impersonal mystery, carelessness or cruelty.

'The Surrender of a Cockney', in *Alarms and Discursions*

The direct appeal to Nature is utterly unnatural. . . . We must descend from God down to God's Nature. Nature is only right when seen in the light of the highest right; whether it be, as some Humanists would say, in the mind of Man, or as Christians would say, in the mind of God.

'The End of the Moderns', in *The Common Man*

The only objection to Natural Religion is that somehow it always becomes unnatural. A man loves Nature in the morning for her innocence and amiability, and at nightfall, if he is loving her still, it is for her darkness and cruelty. . . . The mere pursuit of health always leads to something unhealthy. Physical nature must not be made the direct object of obedience; it must be enjoyed, not worshipped. Stars and mountains must not be taken seriously. If they are, we end where the pagan nature worship ended. Because the earth is kind, we can imitate all her cruelties. Because sexuality is sane, we can all go mad about sexuality.

Orthodoxy, ch. 5

The Church will be facing once more her first and most formidable enemy; a thing more attractive because more human than any of the heresies. . . . [Paganism] may be called practical materialism. . . . The Pagan looks for his pleasures to the natural forces of this world. . . . The natural forces, when they are turned into gods, betray mankind by something that is in the very nature of nature-worship. We can already see men becoming unhealthy by the worship of health; becoming hateful by the worship of love; becoming paradoxically solemn and overstrained even by the idolatry of sport. . . . Unless all these things are subject to a more centralised and well-balanced conception of the universe, the local god becomes too vivid, we might say too visible, and strikes his worshippers with madness. The pantheist is always too near to the polytheist and the polytheist to the idolater; the idolater to the man offering human sacrifice. There is nothing in Paganism to check its own exaggerations.

'A Century of Emancipation', in *The Well and the Shallows*

Since Christianity broke the heart of the world and mended it, one cannot really be a Pagan; one can only be an anti-Christian. . . . The Pagan felt that there was a sort of easy and equable force pressing upon us from Nature; that this force was breezy and beneficent, though not specially just or loving; in other words, that there was, as the strength in wine or trees or the ocean, the energy of kindly but careless gods. This Paganism is now impossible, either to the Christian or the sceptic. We believe so much less than that – and we desire so much more.

'The Moral Philosophy of Meredith', in *A Handful of Authors*

The pantheist cannot wonder, for he cannot praise God or praise anything as really distinct from himself. . . . There is no real possibility of getting out of pantheism any special impulse to moral action. For pantheism implies in its nature that one thing is as good as another; whereas action implies in its nature that one thing is greatly preferable to another.

Orthodoxy, ch. 8

Paganism is better than pantheism, for paganism is free to imagine divinities, while pantheism is forced to pretend, in a priggish way, that all things are equally divine.

The Catholic Church and Conversion, ch. 4

It is . . . the greatest glory of the Christian tradition that it has incorporated so many Pagan traditions. . . . And the best and most obvious example is the way in which Christianity did incorporate . . . the old human and heathen conception of the Winter Feast. . . . What was then heathen was still human; that is, it was both mystical and material; it expressed itself in sacred substances and sacramental acts; it understood the mystery of trees and waters and the holy flame. . . . The Pagan element in Christmas came quite natural to Christians, because it was not in fact very far from Christianity. Take, for example, the whole fundamental idea of the Winter Feast. There is a perfectly natural parallel between a religion that defies the world and a ritual that defies the weather. . . . In winter even a rich man receives some faint hint of the problem of a poor man; he may avoid being hungry, but he cannot always avoid being cold. To choose that moment of common freezing for the assertion of common fraternity is, in its own intrinsic nature, a foreshadowing of what we call the Christian idea. It involves the suggestion that joy comes from within and not from without. It involves the suggestion that peril and the potentiality of pain are themselves a ground of gratitude and rejoicing. It involves the suggestion that even when we are merely Pagans we are not merely Pantheists.

'The Winter Feast', in *G.K. Chesterton: The Apostle and the Wild Ducks*

OTHERS

The modern European seeking his religion in Asia is reading his religion into Asia. Religion there is something different.

The Everlasting Man, Part 2, ch. 5

The Caste System of ancient India ... contrasts ... with ... Christian democracy ... in the fact that it does really conceive the social superiority as a spiritual superiority. This ... divides it fundamentally from the fraternity of Christendom.

The Everlasting Man, Part 1, ch. 6

Reincarnation is not really a mystical idea. It is not really a transcendental idea, or in that sense a religious idea. Mysticism conceives something transcending experience; religion seeks glimpses of a better good or a worse evil than experience can give. Reincarnation need only extend experiences in the sense of repeating them. It is no more transcendental for a man to remember what he did in Babylon before he was born than to remember what he did in Brixton before he had a knock on the head. ... It has nothing to do with seeing God or even conjuring up the devil.

The Everlasting Man, Part 1, ch. 6

The difference between having a real religion and having a mere curiosity about psychic marvels is really very like the difference between drinking beer and drinking brandy, between drinking wine and drinking gin. Beer is a food as well as a stimulant; so a positive religion is a comfort as well as an adventure. A man drinks his wine because it is his favourite wine, the pleasure of his palate or the vintage of his valley. A man drinks alcohol merely because it is alcoholic. So a man calls upon his gods because they are good or at any rate good to him, because they are the idols that protect his tribe or the saints that have blessed his birthday. But spiritualists call upon spirits merely because they are spirits; they ask for ghosts merely because they are ghosts.

William Blake (1920), p. 98

... the religion of Comte,[1] generally known as Positivism, or the worship of humanity. ... It is surely unreasonable to attack the doctrine of the Trinity as a piece of bewildering mysticism, and then to ask men to worship a being who is ninety million persons in one God, neither confounding the persons nor dividing the substance.

Heretics, ch. 6

The question really is whether Humanism can perform all the functions of religion. ... I do not believe that Humanism can be a complete substitute for Superhumanism. ... The [Humanist] discovery of brotherhood seemed like the discovery of broad daylight; of something that men could never grow tired of. Yet even in my own short lifetime, men have already grown tired of it. We cannot now appeal to the love of equality as an *emotion*. ... In most men it has died, because it was a mood and not a doctrine. ...

I do not therefore believe that Humanism and Religion are rivals on equal terms. I believe it is a rivalry between the pools and the fountain; or between the firebrands and the fire. [The Humanists] snatched one firebrand out of the undying fire; but ... the torch went out very soon. ... In short, I distrust spiritual experiments outside the central spiritual tradition; for the simple reason that I think they do not last. ... Humanism may try to pick up the pieces; but can it stick them together? Where is the *cement* which made religion corporate and popular, which can prevent it falling to pieces in a débris of individualistic tastes and degrees. What is to prevent one Humanist wanting chastity without humility, and another humility without chastity, and another truth or beauty without either? The problem of an enduring ethic and culture consists in finding an arrangement of the pieces by which they remain related, as do the stones in an arch.

'Is Humanism a Religion?', in *The Thing*

1. Auguste Comte was a humanist who believed that society was progressing towards the domination of science ('positivism' being his word for the scientific approach), but in need of the good qualities of the Middle Ages, so that his pseudo-religion was called 'Catholicism plus Science'.

Part 5

The Christian Denominations

ROMAN CATHOLICISM

The Catholic Church remains in the best sense a mystery even to believers.

'What do they think?', in The Thing

The Church really is like Antichrist in the sense that it is as unique as Christ. Indeed, if it be not Christ it probably is Antichrist.

The Catholic Church and Conversion, ch. 3

The Catholic Church is the only thing which saves a man from the degrading slavery of being a child of his age. . . . The New Religions are in many ways suited to the new conditions; but they are only suited to the new conditions. When those conditions shall have changed in only a century or so, the points upon which alone they insist at present will have become almost pointless. If the Faith has all the freshness of a new religion, it has all the richness of an old religion; it has especially all the reserves of an old religion. . . . In an intellectual sense old things are flexible. Above all, they are various and have many alternatives to offer. There is a sort of rotation of crops in religious history; and old fields can lie fallow for a while and then be worked again. But when the new religion or any such notion has sown its one crop of wild oats, which the wind generally blows away, it is barren. A thing as old as the Catholic Church has an accumulated armoury and treasury to choose from; it can pick and choose among the centuries and brings one age to the rescue of another. It can call in the old world to redress the balance of the new. . . .

The world deceived me and the Church would at any time have undeceived me. The thing that a man may really shed at last like a superstition is the fashion of this world that passes away.

The Catholic Church and Conversion, ch. 5

I began to make for myself a sort of rudimentary philosophy . . . which was founded on the first principle that it is . . . a precious and wonderful privilege to exist at all. . . . The half-truth must be linked up with the whole truth; and who is to link it up? . . . In a word, wonder and humility and gratitude are good things, but they are not the only good things; and there must be something to make the poet who praises them admit that justice and mercy and human dignity are good things too. . . . The young man specialising in the half-truth . . . should take his half-truth into the culture of the Catholic Church, which really is a culture and where it really will be cultivated. For that place is really a garden; and the noisy world outside nowadays is none the less a wilderness because it is a howling wilderness. That is, he can take his idea where it will be valued for what is true in it, where it will be balanced by other truths and often supported by better arguments. . . . [The Church] does not condemn a love of poetry or fantasy; she does not condemn, but rather commends, a sentiment of gratitude for the breath of life. Indeed, it is a spirit in which many Catholic poets have rather specialised, and its first and finest appearance, perhaps, is in the great Canticle of St. Francis. But in that sane spiritual society, I know that optimism will never be turned into an orgy of anarchy or a stagnation of slavery, and that there will not fall on any one of us the ironical disaster of having discovered a truth only to disseminate a lie.

Blackfriars, Feb. 1923

The Catholic philosophy is a universal philosophy found to fit anywhere with human nature and the nature of things. But even when it does not fit in with human nature it is found in the long run to favour something yet more fitting. It generally suits us, but where it does not . . . we learn to suit it, so long as we are alive enough to learn anything. . . . Forbidden fruit is often more fruitful than the free. It is more fruitful in the sense of a fascinating botanical study of why it is really poisonous. . . . The Church is right in the main in being tolerant in the main; but . . . where she is intolerant she is most right and even most reasonable. Adam lived in a garden where a thousand mercies were granted to him; but the one inhibition was the greatest mercy of all.

The Catholic Church and Conversion, ch. 5

A man does not come an inch nearer to being a heretic by being a hundred times a critic. . . . He only becomes a heretic at the precise moment when he prefers his criticism to his Catholicism. That is, at the instant of separation in which he thinks the view peculiar to himself more valuable than the creed that unites him to his fellows. At any given moment the Catholic Church is full of people sympathizing with social movements or moral ideas, which may happen to have representatives outside the Church. For the Church is not a movement or a mood or a direction, but the balance of many movements and moods; and membership of it consists of accepting the ultimate arbitrament which strikes the balance between them, not in refusing to admit any of them into the balance at all . . . A Catholic did not come any nearer to being a Calvinist by dwelling on the omniscience of God and the power of Grace, any more than he came any nearer to being an atheist by saying that man possessed reason and freewill. What constituted a Calvinist was that he preferred his Calvinism to his Catholicism. And what constituted his Catholicism was that he accepted the ultimate arbitration which reconciled freewill and grace, and did not exclude either.

Chaucer, ch. 8

What Mahomet and Calvin and all those . . . breaking away from the dying civilization did not realize, is the curious fact that it is a dying civilization that never dies. . . . It is unwise to desert this perpetually sinking ship, or betray this everlastingly dying creed and culture. . . . It was not wise to leave it, even for the Republic; it will not be wise to leave it, even for the Soviet.[1]

. . . Within the body of the Christian world, there was a perpetual and centripetal tendency towards the discovery of a just balance to all these ideas. All those who broke away were centrifugal and not centripetal; they went away into deserts to develop a solitary doctrine. But medieval philosophy and culture, with all the crimes and errors of its exponents, was always *seeking* equilibrium. It can be seen in every line of its rhythmic and balanced art; in every sentence of its carefully qualified and self-questioning philosophy. It was everywhere in the air, though it affected various people in various degrees now impossible to distinguish. But it was everywhere a movement towards civilization; towards the centre of ideas; whatever might be the wild decentralization of events.

Chaucer, ch. 9

To become a Catholic is not to leave off thinking, but to learn how to think. It is so in exactly the same sense in which to recover from palsy is not to leave off moving but to learn how to move. The Catholic convert has for the first time a starting-point for straight and strenuous thinking. He has for the first time a way of testing the truth in any

1. i.e. the French Republic and the Bolshevik Soviet Union.

question that he raises. . . . It is . . . the heathen and the heretics, who seem to have every virtue except the power of connected thought. . . . What is now called free thought is valued, not because it is free thought, but because it is freedom from thought; because it is free thought-lessness.

. . . The outsiders . . . see, or think they see, the convert entering with bowed head a sort of small temple which they are convinced is fitted up inside like a prison, if not a torture-chamber. . . . He does not want to go into a larger room, because he does not know of any larger room to go into. He knows of a large number of much smaller rooms, each of which is labelled as being very large; but he is quite sure he would be cramped in any of them. Each of them professes to be a complete cosmos or scheme of all things. . . . But each of these cosmic systems or machines seems to him much smaller and even much simpler than the broad and balanced universe in which he lives.

The Catholic Church and Conversion, ch. 4

It is a miracle in itself that anything so huge and historic in date and design [as the Church] should be so fresh in its affections. It is as if a man found his own parlour and fireside in the heart of the Great Pyramid. It is as if a child's favourite doll turned out to be the oldest sacred image in the world, worshipped in Chaldea or Nineveh. . . . Everything that men called sentimental in Roman Catholic religion, its keepsakes, its small flowers and almost tawdry trinkets, its figures with merciful gestures and gentle eyes, its avowedly popular pathos . . . – all this is a sign of sensitive and vivid vitality in anything so vast and settled and systematic. There is nothing quite like this warmth, as in the warmth of Christmas, amid ancient hills hoary with such snows of antiquity.

The Catholic Church and Conversion, ch. 3

Catholicism really is in the twentieth century what it was in the second century; it is the New Religion. Indeed its very antiquity preserves an attitude of novelty. I have always thought it striking and even stirring that in the venerable invocation of the *Tantum Ergo*[1] which for us seems to come loaded with accumulated ages, there is still the language of innovation; of the antique document that must yield to a new rite. For us the hymn is something of an antique document itself. But the rite is always new.

The Catholic Church and Conversion, ch. 2

---

1. The last two verses of Thomas Aquinas's hymn *Pange Lingua Gloriosa*, used at Benediction. Chesterton refers to the lines translated as: 'types and shadows have their ending, for the newer rite is here.'

Development is the unfolding of all the consequences and applications of an idea; but of something that is there, not of something that is not there. In this sense the Catholic Church is the one Christian body that has always believed in Evolution.

'Roman Catholicism', in *An Outline of Christianity*, ed. A.S. Peake, 1926

I do really believe that there is a need for the restatement of religious truth; but not the statement of something quite different, which I do not believe to be true. I believe there is a very urgent need for a verbal paraphrase of many of the fundamental doctrines; simply because people have ceased to understand them as they are traditionally stated. . . . I do think that the Catholic culture suffers very much from the popular misunderstanding of its original terminology. I do think that Catholics are themselves to blame, in many cases, for not realising that their doctrines need to be stated afresh, and not left in language that is intrinsically correct but practically misleading. . . . It is practically true that there are misunderstandings, and that we ought chiefly to desire to make people understand. . . . We do not allow enough, in justifying the words that we speak, for the difference in the words that they hear.

'Some of our Errors', in *The Thing*

It is startling to note how near Swedenborg[1] was to Catholicism – in his insistence on free will, for instance, on the humanity of the incarnate God, and on the relative and mystical view of the Old Testament.

William Blake (1920), p. 125

It is a fundamental dogma of the Faith that all human beings without any exception whatever, were specially made, were shaped and pointed like shining arrows, for the end of hitting the mark of Beatitude. . . . That conviction does make every human face, every human feature, a matter of mystical poetry.

'Is Humanism a Religion?', in *The Thing*

[St. Thomas Aquinas] had from the first that full and final test of truly orthodox Catholicity: the impetuous, impatient, intolerant passion for the poor; and even that readiness to be rather a nuisance to the rich, out of a hunger to feed the hungry.

St. Thomas Aquinas, ch. 5

As compared with nearly all other cosmic philosophies, [Catholicism] primarily asserts a good Creator of a good Creation, in which the natural law and life of things is the general guide.

G.K.'s Weekly, 1 Mar. 1934

1. Emanuel Swedenborg founded his own church.

Nobody will begin to understand the Thomist philosophy,[1] or indeed the Catholic philosophy, who does not realise that the primary and fundamental part of it is entirely the praise of Life; the praise of Being; the praise of God as the Creator of the World. Everything else follows a long way after that, being conditioned by various complications like the Fall. . . . The trouble occurs because the Catholic mind moves upon two planes; that of the Creation and that of the Fall.

St. Thomas Aquinas, ch. 4

Heaven has *descended* into the world of matter; the supreme spiritual power is now operating by the machinery of matter, dealing miraculously with the bodies and souls of men. It blesses all the five senses; as the senses of the body are blessed at a Catholic christening. It blesses even material gifts and keepsakes, as with relics or rosaries. It works through water or oil or bread or wine. . . . The Incarnation is as much a part of that idea as the Mass; and . . . the Mass is as much a part of that idea as the Incarnation. A Puritan may think it blasphemous that God should become a wafer. A Moslem thinks it blasphemous that God should become a workman in Galilee. . . . But if the Moslem has a principle, the Protestant has only a prejudice. That is, he has only a fragment; a relic; a superstition. If it be profane that the miraculous should descend to the plane of matter, then certainly Catholicism is profane; and Protestantism is profane; and Christianity is profane. Of all human creeds or concepts, in that sense, Christianity is the most utterly profane. But why a man should accept a Creator who was a carpenter, and then worry about holy water, why he should accept a local Protestant tradition that God was born in some particular place mentioned in the Bible, merely because the Bible had been left lying about in England, and then say it is incredible that a blessing should linger on the bones of a saint, why he should accept the first and most stupendous part of the story of Heaven on Earth, and then furiously deny a few small but obvious deductions from it – that is a thing I do not understand.

'The Protestant Superstitions', in *The Thing*

When people ask me, . . . "Why did you join the Church of Rome?" the first essential answer . . . is, "To get rid of my sins." For there is no other religious system that does *really* profess to get rid of people's sins.

Autobiography, ch. 16

1. i.e. the philosophy of St. Thomas Aquinas and his school.

Will made the world; Will wounded the world; the same Divine Will
gave to the world for the second time its chance; the same human Will
can for the last time make its choice. That is the real outstanding
peculiarity, or eccentricity, of the peculiar sect called Roman Catholics.
. . . It is [the Catholic's] whole hope and glory that he is not at one with
the universal life; but stands out from it, an exception and even a miracle.

'The Outline of Liberty', in *The Common Man*

A man like Chaucer would most certainly have been a furious Papist, if
he had thought that the alternative was to be a Puritan. But he lived in
a world which had not yet even seen a real Puritan. In that world, in
that sense, and in that sense alone, we may say that such a man felt
himself rather as a Catholic than as a Papist.

Chaucer, ch. 2

[To a Protestant] it is the Papacy that makes the Papist. . . . Even if
democracy were applicable to a revelation, there could not really be a
democratic tribunal which should be deciding all the time and democratic
all the time. It would not be the millions of poor and humble Catholics
who would rule; it would be the officials if it were not the official. It
would be a Holy Synod. Now every popular instinct Catholics possess
seems to them to say that rather than have merely an official order –
that is, an oligarchy – it is far more human to have a monarchy – that is,
a man. It is indeed remarkable that those who broke with this purely
moral monarchy generally set up a material and a rather immoral
monarchy. The first great schism in the East was made by men who
turned from the Popes to bow down to the Caesars – and the Tsars.
The last great schism in the West was made by men who attributed
divine right to Henry VIII, not to mention Charles I.

'Roman Catholicism', in *An Outline of Christianity*, ed. A.S. Peake, 1926

The [mediaeval] Papacy stood, of course, for the international ideal. . .
. The international ideal, which seems so very modern to the moderns,
was . . . very ancient to the Popes. They had originally risen in a
cosmopolitan community, covering the civilized world, and their real
mistake was that they thought the world was more international than it
was. But this is not a mistake of barbaric bigotry; it rather amounted to
thinking the world more enlightened than it was.

Chaucer, ch. 2

It will be found again and again, in ecclesiastical history, that the new
departure, the daring innovation, the progressive party, depended directly
on the Pope. . . . Whenever there appeared, in Catholic history, a new

and promising experiment, . . . that movement always came to be identified with the Papacy; because the Papacy alone upheld it against the resisting social medium which it rent asunder. So . . . it was really the Pope who upheld St. Francis and the popular movement of the Friars. So, in the sixteenth century, it was really the Pope who upheld St. Ignatius Loyola and the great educational movement of the Jesuits. . . . The Pope was often very much in advance of the Church, as the Encyclical on Labour of Pope Leo XIII[1] would have been very much in advance of many reactionary bishops and priests of his time.

Chaucer, ch. 2

OTHER DENOMINATIONS

Catholic history contains much more of Protestantism than Protestant history does of Catholicism.

The Resurrection of Rome (1930), p. 165

Protestants are Catholics gone wrong; that is what is really meant by saying they are Christians.

The Catholic Church and Conversion, ch. 4

Nine times out of ten a man's broad-mindedness is necessarily the narrowest thing about him. . . . His vision of his own nation may have a rough resemblance to the reality. But his vision of the world is probably smaller than the world. His vision of the universe is certainly much smaller than the universe. Hence he is never so inadequate as when he is universal; he is never so limited as when he generalizes. This is the fallacy in the many modern attempts at a creedless creed, at something variously described as essential Christianity or undenominational religion or a world faith to embrace all the faiths in the world. It is that every sectarian is more sectarian in his unsectarianism than he is in his sect. The emancipation of a Baptist is a very Baptist emancipation. The charity of a Buddhist is a very Buddhist charity, and very different from Christian charity. When a philosophy embraces everything it generally squeezes everything, and squeezes it out of shape; when it digests it necessarily assimilates. When a theosophist absorbs Christianity it is rather as a cannibal absorbs Christian missionaries.

What I Saw in America, ch. 18, 'The Spirit of England'

1. *Rerum Novarum* (1891), which Chesterton strongly espoused.

A . . . heresy is the exaltation of something which, even if true, is secondary or temporary in its nature against those things which are essential and eternal, those things which always prove themselves true in the long run. In short, it is the setting up of the mood against the mind.

William Blake (1920), pp. 167-8

[Heresies] sometimes even look very true; they sometimes even are very true, in the limited sense of a truth that is less than the Truth. . . . A heresy is a truth that hides all the other truths.

'St. Thomas More', in *The Well and the Shallows*

Those who . . . accept the final effect of the Reformation will none the less face the fact, that it was [St. Thomas Aquinas] who was the Reformer; and that the later Reformers were by comparison reactionaries. . . . For instance, they riveted the mind back to the literal sufficiency of the Hebrew Scriptures; when St. Thomas had already spoken of the Spirit giving grace to the Greek philosophies. He insisted on the social duty of works; they only on the spiritual duty of faith. It was the very life of the Thomist teaching that Reason can be trusted: it was the very life of the Lutheran teaching that Reason is utterly untrustworthy.

St. Thomas Aquinas, ch. 1

The Protestant theology of Martin Luther was a thing that no modern Protestant would be seen dead in a field with. . . . That Protestantism was pessimism; it was nothing but a bare insistence on the hopelessness of all human virtue, as an attempt to escape hell.

St. Thomas Aquinas, ch. 8

The sixteenth-century schism was really a belated revolt of the thirteenth-century pessimists. It was a backwash of the old Augustinian Puritanism against the Aristotelian liberality.

St. Thomas Aquinas, Introductory Note

PURITANISM AND CALVINISM

The instant a breach, or even a crack, had been made in the dyke of Catholicism, there poured through it the bitter sea of Calvinism, . . . of a very cruel form of fatalism. Since that time, it has taken the much duller form of Determinism.

'The Outline of Liberty', in *The Common Man*

A Calvinist is a Catholic obsessed with the Catholic idea of the sovereignty of God. But when he makes it mean that God wishes particular people to be damned, we may say with all restraint that he has become a rather morbid Catholic. . . . Every step he takes back towards humanity is a step back towards Catholicism.

The Catholic Church and Conversion, ch. 4

The Calvinists took the Catholic idea of the absolute knowledge and power of God; and treated it as a rocky irreducible truism so solid that anything could be built on it, however crushing or cruel. They were so confident in their logic, and its one first principle of predestination, that they tortured the intellect and imagination with dreadful deductions about God, that seemed to turn Him into a demon.

'Is Humanism a Religion?', in *The Thing*

The Calvinist was a Catholic whose imagination had been in some way caught and overpowered by the one isolated theological truth of the power and knowledge of God; and he offered to it human sacrifice, not only of every human sentiment, but of every other divine quality. Something in that bare idea of all-seeing, all-searching and pitiless power intoxicated and exalted certain men for a certain period, as certain men are intoxicated by a storm of wind or some terrible stage tragedy.

'The Idols of Scotland', in *The Thing*

The . . . Puritan . . . possessed himself of a first principle which is one of the three or four alternative first principles which are possible to the mind of man . . . that the mind of man can alone directly deal with the mind of God. It may shortly be called the anti-sacramental principle. . . . It equally applies . . . to art, to letters, to the love of locality, to music, and even to good manners. The phrase about no priest coming between a man and his Creator is but an impoverished fragment of the full philosophic doctrine; the true Puritan was equally clear that no singer or story-teller or fiddler must translate the voice of God to him into the tongues of terrestrial beauty. . . . His individual reason, cut loose from instinct as well as tradition, taught him a concept of the omnipotence of God which meant simply the impotence of man. In Luther, the earlier and milder form of the Protestant process only went so far as to say that nothing a man did could help him except his confession of Christ; with Calvin it took the last logical step and said that even this could not help him, since Omnipotence must have disposed of all his destiny beforehand; that men must be created to be lost and saved. . . . Some great Romanists doubtfully followed it. . . . It was the spirit of the age, and should be a permanent warning against mistaking the spirit of the age for the immortal spirit of man. . . .

The synod or conventicle tended to be a small republic, but unfortunately to be a very small republic. In relation to the street outside the conventicle was not a republic but an aristocracy. It was the most awful of all aristocracies, that of the elect; for it was not a right of birth but a right before birth, and alone of all nobilities it was not laid level in the dust.

A Short History of England, ch. 13

The essence of Calvinism was certainty about salvation; the essence of Catholicism is uncertainty about salvation. The modern and materialised form of that certainty is superiority; the belief of a man in a fixed moral aristocracy of men like himself. . . . I doubt if this extreme school of Protestants believe in Christian humility even as an ideal. . . . There is here [in the north of Ireland] a school of thought and sentiment that does definitely regard self-satisfaction as a strength, as against the strong Christian tradition in the rest of [Ireland] that does as definitely regard it as a weakness.

'Belfast and the Religious Problem', in *Irish Impressions*

In the days when . . . the Covenanters were fighting with the Cavaliers, a fine old Cavalier of the Episcopalian persuasion made a rather interesting remark; that the change he really hated was represented by saying 'The Lord' instead of 'Our Lord.' The latter implied affection, the former only fear; indeed he described the former succinctly as the talk of devils. And this is so far true that the very eloquent language in which the name of 'The Lord' has figured has generally been the language of might and majesty and even terror. And there really was implied in it in varying degrees the idea of glorifying God for His greatness rather than His goodness. And again there occurred the natural inversion of ideas. Since the Puritan was content to cry with the Moslem: 'God is great,' so the descendant of the Puritan is always a little inclined to cry with the Nietzschean: 'Greatness is God.'

Robert Louis Stevenson, ch. 5

Puritanism made a man too individual, and had its horrible outcome in Individualism.

'On Loneliness', in *Come to Think of It*

This temptation of [John D. Rockefeller] to combine business brazenly with piety, to regard riches as a form of Divine approval, to be a plutocrat openly and with unction – this is, and has always been, the peculiar temptation of that type of Protestant individualist religion to which Mr. Rockefeller belongs.

. . . The real change wrought in the long run by Puritan morals was this: it was not so much that men began to say that lust and gluttony were deadly sins; it was that they began to say, for the first time, that pride and avarice were not deadly sins. Of course, they did not put it in those words. But I can tell you the words they did put it in: "The Industrious Apprentice," "Self-Help,"[1] "The Self-made Man," "Not slothful in business, serving the Lord," "Ever remember, my dear Dan, that you may some day be the head of that concern." I am certain that no honest modern Puritan will deny that from the middle of the seventeenth to the middle of the nineteenth century at least, the arresting feature of Puritan ethics was the vague association between being regular at chapel and being regular at the bank. . . . Avarice is a sin of Christians; it is an ideal of individualists. Hence the indisputable fact that millionaire worship is as much a mark of a Protestant country as Ancestor worship of China.

Letter to The Nation, *1 July 1909*

In most cases the Puritans lost their religion and retained their morality.

'On the Fossil of a Fanatic', in *Avowals and Denials*

Puritanism is only a paralysis; which stiffens into Stoicism when it loses religion.

Autobiography, ch. 15

The Puritan is only strong enough to stiffen; the Catholic is strong enough to relax.

George Bernard Shaw (1914), p. 107

This power of knowing a thing without feeling it, this power of believing a thing without experiencing it, this is an old Catholic complexity, and the Puritan has never understood it.

George Bernard Shaw (1914), p. 108

The Kirk . . . had no cult of the Holy Child, no feast of the Holy Innocents, no tradition of the Little Brothers of St. Francis, nothing that could in any way *carry on* the childish enthusiasm for simple things, and link it up with a lifelong rule of life.

Robert Louis Stevenson, ch. 3

. . . the essential Puritan idea, that God can only be praised by direct contemplation of Him. You must praise God only with your brain; it is wicked to praise Him with your passions or your physical habits or your gesture or instinct of beauty.

George Bernard Shaw (1914), pp. 43-4

---

1. The Scottish writer Samuel Smiles wrote the celebrated *Self-Help* in 1859, and *Thrift* in 1875.

The difference between Puritanism and Catholicism is not about whether some priestly word or gesture is significant and sacred. It is about whether any word or gesture is significant and sacred. To the Catholic every other daily act is a dramatic dedication to the service of good or of evil. To the Calvinist no act can have that sort of solemnity, because the person doing it has been dedicated from eternity, and is merely filling up his time until the crack of doom.

What's Wrong with the World, Part 4, sec. 1

The Manichean philosophy has had many forms. . . . But it is always in one way or another a notion that nature is evil; or that evil is at least rooted in nature. . . . Later, . . . it took the form of Calvinism, which held that God had indeed made the world, but in a special sense, made the evil as well as the good: had made an evil will as well as an evil world. . . . The old Manicheans taught that Satan originated the whole work of creation commonly attributed to God. The new Calvinists taught that God originated the whole work of damnation commonly attributed to Satan. One looked back to the first day when a devil acted like a god; the other looked forward to a last day when a god acted like a devil. But both had the idea that the creator of the earth was primarily the creator of the evil, whether we call him a devil or a god.

St. Thomas Aquinas, ch. 4

John Knox achieved that queer Puritan paradox, of combining the same concentrated invocation of Christ with an inhuman horror and loathing for all the signs and forms and traditions generally characteristic of Christians. He combined . . . the adoration of the Cross with the abomination of the Crucifix.

'The Religion of Fossils', in *The Well and the Shallows*

Puritanism was an honourable mood; it was a noble fad. In other words, it was a highly creditable mistake. We have all felt the frame of mind in which one wishes to smash golden croziers and mitres merely because they are golden. We all know how natural it is at certain moments to feel a profound thirst to kick clergymen simply because they are clergymen. But if we seriously ask ourselves whether in the long run humanity is not happier with gold in its religion rather than mere drab, then we come to the conclusion that the gold on cross or cope does give more pleasure to most men than it gives pain, for a moment, to us. If we really ask ourselves if religions do not work better with a definite priesthood to do the drudgery of religion, we come to the conclusion that they do work better. Anti-clericalism is a generous and ideal mood; clericalism is a permanent and practical necessity.

William Blake (1920), p. 171

ANGLICANISM

The quarrel in the Church of England is not about what it shall do; it is about what it shall be – indeed, about what it has been. Does its whole authority lie in being a branch of the Catholic Church? Or does its whole authority lie in being a protest, a part of the great sixteenth-century protest, against that Catholic Church?

Illustrated London News, 14 July 1906

It would be easy, and in a sense only too true, to call [Anglicanism] a piece of English half-conscious hypocrisy; the attempt to remedy a mistake without admitting it. Nor do I deny that there are High Churchmen who provoke and perhaps deserve this tone, by talking as if Catholicism had never been betrayed and oppressed. To them indeed one is tempted to say that St. Peter denied his Lord; but at least he never denied that he had denied Him.

Blackfriars, Dec. 1922

If it is true that the Church is simply the religion of the State, we have got precious near to saying that it is simply the irreligion of the State.

'The Erastian on the Establishment', in *The Common Man*

The more moderate Protestants, the Anglicans and to a large extent the Lutherans, had something of the same queer feeling [as the Calvinists had about the power of God] about the King. Hence came the Cavalier doctrine of Divine Right – and the court chaplains of Prussia. Nothing is more intriguing and challenging to the imagination than the necessity of trying to understand how men in the sixteenth and early seventeenth centuries felt a sort of abstract altruistic joy in the mere might and triumph of the Prince; in the mere autocracy of the earthly ruler.

'The Idols of Scotland', in *The Thing*

This power of resurrection in the Church does depend on this possession of reserves in the Church. To have this power, it is necessary to possess the whole past of the religion, and not merely those parts of it that seemed obviously needed in the nineteenth century by the men of the Oxford Movement, or in the twentieth century by the men of the Anglo-Catholic Congress. . . . They took their pick in the fields of Christendom, but they did not possess the fields; and, above all, they did not possess the fallow fields. They could not have all the riches, because they could not have all the reserves of the religion. . . . The Church . . . is prepared for problems which are utterly different from the problems of to-day. Now I think the truth about the man who calls himself, as I did, an Anglo-Catholic, may . . . be stated thus. . . . He is not . . . founding a heresy of the moment. But he is merely *fighting* a heresy at the moment. Even when he is defending orthodoxy, as he so often is, he is only defending it upon certain points against certain fallacies. But the fallacies are merely fashions, and the next fashion will be quite different. And then *his* orthodoxy will be old-fashioned, but not ours.

Blackfriars, Dec. 1922

The Book of Common Prayer is the masterpiece of Protestantism. . . . It is the one positive possession and attraction; the one magnet and talisman for people even outside the Anglican Church, as are the great Gothic cathedrals for people outside the Catholic Church. . . . The only thing that can produce any sort of nostalgia or romantic regret, any shadow of homesickness in one who has in truth come home, is the rhythm of Cranmer's prose. . . . The English Litany, the music and the magic of the great sixteenth-century style – *that* does call a man backwards like the song of the sirens; as Virgil and the poets might have called to a Pagan who had entered the Early Church. . . . The Anglicans cannot do the trick now, any more than anybody else. Modern prayers, and theirs perhaps more than any, seem to be perfectly incapable of avoiding journalese. . . . But *why* has the old Protestant Prayer-Book a power like that of great poetry? . . . It has tradition; it has religion; it was written by apostate Catholics. It is strong, not in so far as it is the first Protestant book, but in so far as it was the last Catholic book.

'The Prayer-Book Problem', in *The Well and the Shallows*

OTHERS

Eastern Christianity flattened everything, as it flattened the faces of the images into icons. It became a thing of patterns rather than pictures; and it made . . . war upon statues. . . . The East was the land of the Cross and the West was the land of the Crucifix. The Greeks were being dehumanised by a radiant symbol; while the Goths were being humanised by an instrument of torture. . . . The Greek element in Christian theology tended more and more to be a sort of dried up Platonism; a thing of diagrams and abstractions; to the last indeed noble abstractions, but not sufficiently touched by that great thing that is by definition almost the opposite of abstractions: Incarnation. Their Logos was the Word; but not the Word made Flesh.

St. Thomas Aquinas, ch. 3

[The Salvation Army's] methods are admirable. Their methods are the methods of all intense and hearty religions; they are popular like all religion, military like all religion, public and sensational like all religion. . . . [The Army] are really the old voice of glad and angry faith, hot as the riots of Dionysius, wild as the gargoyles of Catholicism, not to be mistaken for a philosophy. Professor Huxley, in one of his clever phrases, called the Salvation Army "corybantic Christianity." Huxley was the last and noblest of those Stoics who have never understood the Cross. If he had understood Christianity he would have known that there never has been, and never can be, any Christianity that is not corybantic.

Heretics, ch. 6

A Quaker is a Catholic obsessed with the Catholic idea of gentle simplicity and truth. But when he made it mean that it is a lie to say "you" and an act of idolatry to take your hat off to a lady, it is not too much to say that whether or not he had a hat off, he certainly had a tile loose. . . . Every step he takes back towards common sense is a step back towards Catholicism.

The Catholic Church and Conversion, ch. 4

Of all conceivable forms of enlightenment the worst is what [Quakers] . . . call the Inner Light. Of all horrible religions the most horrible is the worship of the god within. Any one who knows any body knows how it would work. . . . That Jones shall worship the god within him turns out ultimately to mean that Jones shall worship Jones. . . . Christianity came into the world firstly in order to assert with violence that a man had not only to look inwards, but to look outwards, to behold with astonishment and enthusiasm a divine company and a divine captain. The only fun of being a Christian was that a man was not left alone with the Inner Light, but definitely recognised an outer light, fair as the sun, clear as the moon, terrible as an army with banners.

Orthodoxy, ch. 5

The essential difference between Mrs. Eddy's[1] creed and mine is that she anchors [hope] in the air, while I put an anchor where the groping race of men have generally put it, in the ground. . . . The popular religious sense of mankind . . . has flowed from spirit to flesh, and not from flesh to spirit. . . . The first and last blunder of Christian Science is that it is a religion claiming to be purely spiritual. Now, being purely spiritual is opposed to the very essence of religion.

'Christian Science', in *The Uses of Diversity*

1. Mary Baker Eddy founded Christian Science, a doctrine of healing, based on the illusory nature of matter, sin and suffering, and the power of mind, or spirit, to control the conditions of life.

Part 6

The Christian Disposition

WONDER AND GRATITUDE

Witness, O Sun that blinds our eyes,
Unthinkable and unthankable King,
That though all other wonder dies
I wonder at not wondering.

From 'The Mystery', in *The Collected Poems of G.K. Chesterton*

We all go on every day, unless we are continually goading ourselves into gratitude and humility, seeing less and less of the significance of the sky or the stones.

'The Twelve Men', in *Tremendous Trifles*

Human beings are happy so long as they retain the receptive power and the power of reaction in surprise and gratitude to something outside . . . a something that is present in childhood and which can still preserve and invigorate manhood.

'If I had only one sermon to preach', in *The Common Man*

I do not . . . believe that a baby gets his best physical food by sucking his thumb; nor that a man gets his best moral food by sucking his soul, and denying its dependence on God or other good things. I would maintain that thanks are the highest form of thought; and that gratitude is happiness doubled by wonder. . . . This [is a] faith in receptiveness, and in respect for things outside oneself. . . . The mediaeval spirit loved its part in life as a part, not a whole; its charter for it came from something else . . . and *Benedictus benedicat*[1] is very precisely the motto of the earliest mediaevalism. I mean that everything is blessed from beyond, by something which has in its turn been blessed from beyond again; only the blessed bless.

A Short History of England, ch. 6

1. A blessing: 'May the Blessed bless [you]': 'God bless'.

We hear strangely little of the real merits of animals; and one of them surely is this innocence of all boredom; perhaps such simplicity is the absence of sin. I have some sense myself of the sacred duty of surprise; and the need of seeing the old road as a new road.

The New Jerusalem (1920), p. 2

Grass and children
There seems no end to them.
But if there were but one blade of grass
Men would see that it is fairer than lilies,
And if we saw the first child
We should worship it as the God come on earth.

Notebook, cited in Ward, *Gilbert Keith Chesterton*, p. 210

By the Babe Unborn

If trees were tall and grasses short,
As in some crazy tale,
If here and there a sea were blue
Beyond the breaking pale,

If a fixed fire hung in the air
To warm me one day through,
If deep green hair grew on great hills,
I know what I should do.

In dark I lie: dreaming that there
Are great eyes cold or kind,
And twisted streets and silent doors,
And living men behind.

Let storm-clouds come: better an hour,
And leave to weep and fight,
Than all the ages I have ruled
The empires of the night.

I think that if they gave me leave
Within the world to stand,
I would be good through all the day
I spent in fairyland.

They should not hear a word from me
Of selfishness or scorn,
If only I could find the door,
If only I were born.

From *The Collected Poems of G.K. Chesterton*

Astonishment at the universe is not mysticism, but a transcendent common sense.

'A Defence of Baby-Worship', in *The Defendant*

The function of imagination is not to make strange things settled, so much as to make settled things strange; not so much to make wonders facts as to make facts wonders.

'A Defence of China Shepherdesses', in *The Defendant*

[A man] sees more of the things themselves when he sees more of their origin; for their origin is a part of them and indeed the most important part of them. Thus they become more extraordinary by being explained. He has more wonder at them but less fear of them; for a thing is really wonderful when it is significant and not when it is insignificant. . . . The mystic will have nothing to do with mere mystery.

St. Francis of Assisi, ch. 5

Religion has for centuries been trying to make men exult in the 'wonders' of creation, but it has forgotten that a thing cannot be completely wonderful so long as it remains sensible. So long as we regard a tree as an obvious thing, naturally and reasonably created for a giraffe to eat, we cannot properly wonder at it. . . . This simple sense of wonder at the shapes of things, and at their exuberant independence of our intellectual standards and our trivial definitions, is the basis of spirituality as it is the basis of nonsense [verse]. Nonsense and faith . . . are the two supreme symbolic assertions of the truth that to draw out the soul of things with a syllogism is as impossible as to draw out Leviathan with a hook.

'A Defence of Nonsense', in *The Defendant*

Long before I came to accept any spiritual system, I had . . . a notion about that point at which extremes meet, and the most common thing becomes a cosmic and mystical thing. I did not want so much to alter the place and use of things as to weight them with a new dimension; to deepen them by going down to the potential nothing; to lift them to infinity by measuring from zero. The most logical form of this is in thanks to a Creator; but at every stage I felt that such praises could never rise too high; because they could not even reach the height of our own thanks for unthinkable existence, or horror of more unthinkable non-existence. And the commonest things, as much as the most complex, could thus leap up like fountains of praise. . . . All that new culture was very clean and very vacuous. There was nothing in it to make common life interesting; that could only be done by making common things interesting. And that can be done by imagination but not by invention; by festivals, traditions, images, legends, patron-saints or household-gods; but not by gadgets. . . . We have to tell [the people] how to enjoy enjoyment.

G.K.'s Weekly, 13 Dec. 1934

'CHRISTIAN HUMANISM'

The humanising of divinity is actually the strongest and starkest and most incredible dogma in the Creed. St. Francis [of Assisi] was becoming more like Christ, and not merely more like Buddha, when he considered the lilies of the field or the fowls of the air; and St. Thomas [Aquinas] was becoming more of a Christian, and not merely more of an Aristotelian, when he insisted that God and the image of God had come in contact through matter with a material world. These saints were, in the most exact sense of the term, Humanists; because they were insisting on the immense importance of the human being in the theological scheme of things. But they were not Humanists marching along a path of progress that leads to Modernism and general scepticism; for in their very Humanism they were affirming a dogma now often regarded as the most superstitious Superhumanism. They were strengthening that staggering doctrine of Incarnation, which the sceptics find it hardest to believe. . . . These men became more orthodox, when they became more rational or natural.

St. Thomas Aquinas, ch. 1

In the . . . words of Joinville's Chronicle, 'There was a great disputation between clergy and Jews at the Monastery of Cluny.'[1] . . . All the arabesque of Rabbinical riddle and commentary referred eventually to the ultimate Jewish idea; the idea of the awful distance between man and God. All the roaring and grinding syllogisms of the Schoolmen were tools and symbols of the awful union of God and man. The Jewish angel had ten eyes or twelve wings to express the idea that if ever we saw the beauty and wisdom of God it would seem to us outrageous or frightful. The Christian angel often had two wings only, in addition to eyes and two arms; to show that human beauty and dignity were divine realities which would survive and break the doors of death. Two sublime creeds were in collision; the creed that flesh is grass and the creed that flesh was God.

'An Anecdote of Persecution',
in *G.K. Chesterton: The Apostle and the Wild Ducks*

A really human human being would always put the spiritual things first.
'In Topsy-Turvy Land', in *Tremendous Trifles*

---

1. Jean de Joinville, *The Life of St. Louis*, Part 1, ch. 1.

There is something spiritually suffocating about our life. . . . With us the super-human is the only place where you can find the human. Human nature is hunted, and has fled into sanctuary.

'The Little Birds who Won't Sing', in *Tremendous Trifles*

All the noble necessities of man talk the language of eternity. When man is doing the three or four things that he was sent on this earth to do, then he speaks like one who shall live for ever.

'Questions of Divorce', in *The Uses of Diversity*

When I say that religion and marriage and local loyalty are permanent in humanity, I mean that they recur when humanity is most human; and only comparatively decline when society is comparatively inhuman. They have declined in the modern world. They may return through the war;[1] but anyhow, where we have the small farm and the free man and the fighting spirit, there we shall have the salute to the soil and the roof and to the altar.

'Ego et Shavius Meus', in *The Uses of Diversity*

> Man is a spark flying upwards. God is everlasting.
> Who are we, to whom this cup of human life has
> been given, to ask for more? Let us love mercy
> and walk humbly.[2] What is man, that thou regardest him?[3]
> Man is a star unquenchable. God is in him incarnate.
> His life is planned upon a scale colossal, of which he
> sees glimpses. Let him dare all things, claim all
> things: he is the son of Man, who shall come in the clouds of glory.
> I saw these two strands mingling to make the religion of man.

Notebook, cited Ward, *Gilbert Keith Chesterton*, p. 61

The meanest man is immortal and the mightiest movement is temporal, not to say temporary.

Blackfriars, Jan. 1923

A conception of the divinity of human life, as the last astounding biological product, is quite sufficient to base a faith on if we really believe in it as a fact, and not as a phrase. . . . If we believe in the sanctity of human life, it must be really a sanctity; we must make sacrifices for it, as the old creeds made for their sanctities. . . . The faithful of the ancient creeds gave up for the sake of their sanctities the ultimate and imperious cravings of human nature, the desire of love and liberty and home. We profess to believe in the divinity of life, and we cannot give up for it a few grimy political advantages, and a few

1. World War I.   2. Micah 6.8.   3. Psalm 8.4.

sullen psychological moods. They gave up their joys, and we cannot even surrender our lamentations. They denied themselves even the virtues of common men, and we cling openly, in art and literature, to the vices which are not even common. In this mood we are not likely to open a new era.

'A Wild Reconstruction', in *Lunacy and Letters*

> But now a great thing in the street
> Seems any human nod,
> Where shift in strange democracy
> The million masks of God.

From 'Gold Leaves', in *The Collected Poems of G.K. Chesterton*

Charity, as applied to humanity, means a more or less mystical realisation of the value and even the virtue of humanity; even if it be hidden virtue. . . . The Christian has to use his brain to see the hidden good of humanity; just as much as the detective has to use his brain to see the hidden evil of humanity. . . . To see good is to see God.

'Reflections on Charity', in *The Listener*, 4 Jan. 1933

When we really see men as they are, we do not criticise, but worship; and very rightly. For a monster with mysterious eyes and miraculous thumbs, with strange dreams in his skull, and a queer tenderness for this place or that baby, is truly a wonderful and unnerving matter. It is only the . . . habit of comparison with something else which makes it possible to be at our ease in front of him. A sentiment of superiority keeps us cool and practical; the mere facts would make our knees knock under us with religious fear. It is the fact that every instant of conscious life is an unimaginable prodigy. It is the fact that every face in the street has the incredible unexpectedness of a fairy-tale.

Heretics, ch. 4

Man is something more awful than men; something more strange. The sense of the miracle of humanity itself should be always more vivid to us than any marvels of power, intellect, art, or civilization.

Orthodoxy, ch. 4

God! shall we ever honour what we are . . . ?

From 'King's Cross Station', in *The Collected Poems of G.K. Chesterton*

The moment any matter has passed through the human mind it is finally and for ever spoilt for all purposes of science. It has become a thing incurably mysterious and infinite; this mortal has put on immortality.[1]

---

1. I Cor. 15.51.

Even what we call our material desires are spiritual, because they are human. Science can analyse a pork-chop, and say how much of it is phosphorous and how much is protein; but science cannot analyse any man's wish for a pork-chop, and say how much of it is hunger, how much custom, how much nervous fancy, how much a haunting love of the beautiful. The man's desire for the pork-chop remains literally as mystical and ethereal as his desire for heaven. . . . You can no more be certain in economic history that a man's desire for money was merely a desire for money than you can be certain in hagiology that a saint's desire for God was merely a desire for God.

Heretics, ch. 11

I did not really understand what I meant by Liberty, until I heard it called by the new name of Human Dignity. It was a new name to me; though it was part of a creed nearly two thousand years old.

Autobiography, ch. 16

The lowest part of man is that which he does in accordance with law, such as eating, drinking, growing a beard, or falling over a precipice. The highest part of him is that which is most lawless: spiritual movements, passionate attachment, art.

'The Poetic Quality in Liberalism', in *The Independent Review*, Feb. 1905

In its primary spiritual sense, liberty is the god in man, or, if you like the word, the artist.

'The Free Man', in *A Miscellany of Men*

A child is the very sign and sacrament of personal freedom. He is a fresh free will; . . . he is something that his parents have freely chosen to produce and which they freely agree to protect. . . . He has been born without the intervention of any master or lord. He is a creation and a contribution; he is their own creative contribution to creation. . . . People who prefer the mechanical pleasures, to such a miracle, are jaded and enslaved. They are preferring the very dregs of life to the first fountains of life.

'Babies and Distributism', in *The Well and the Shallows*

Lost somewhere in the enormous plains of time, there wanders a dwarf who is the image of God, who has produced on a yet more dwarfish scale an image of creation. The pigmy picture of God we call Man; the pigmy picture of creation we call Art. . . . [The artist's] business (as something secondary but divine) is to make the world over again. . . . Even if he tries to paint things as they are he will, of course, inevitably paint them as they ought to be. . . . He will by instinct humanise the most inhuman monster and domesticate the most wild of the wild beasts. Of his own nature he will try to understand a horse better than the horse understands himself. . . . Of his own nature he will see birds and beasts as omens rather than animals.

'The Mirror', in *Lunacy and Letters*

The principle of progress in which all sane men believe is mainly this: that we are engaged and ought to be engaged in a persistent effort to change the external world into the image of something that is within ourselves; to turn what is, as far as we are concerned, a chaos into what shall be, as far as we are concerned, a cosmos. God did not give us a universe, but rather the materials of a universe. The world is not a picture, it is a palette. . . . Heaven gave us this splendid chaos of colours and materials. Heaven gave us a few instinctive rules of practice and caution corresponding to 'do not put the brush in the mouth'. And Heaven gave us a vision. . . . It may be that we shall never reach perfection, but we may continue to approach it. But even if we only approach it, we must believe that it exists, we must believe that there is some comprehensible statement of what it is and where it is.

Daily News, 15 Sept. 1906

We must be fond of this world, even in order to change it. . . . We must be fond of another world . . . in order to have something to change it to. . . . Progress should mean that we are always changing the world to suit the vision. Progress does mean (just now) that we are always changing the vision. . . . As long as the vision of heaven is always changing, the vision of earth will be exactly the same.

Orthodoxy, ch. 7

Some portion at least of the sacredness of the dead man belongs to the sleeping man. . . . The greatest act of faith that a man can perform is the act that we perform every night. We abandon our identity, we turn our soul and body into chaos and old night. We uncreate ourselves as if at the end of the world: for all practical purposes we become dead men, in the sure and certain hope of a glorious resurrection. After that it is in vain for us to call ourselves pessimists when we have this trust in the laws of nature, when we let them keep an armed and omnipotent watch over our cradle. It is in vain for us to say that we think the ultimate power evil when every twelve hours or so we give our soul and body back to God without security. This is the essential sanctity of sleep, and the sound and sufficient reason why all tribes and ages have found in it and its phenomena a source of religious speculation.

'The Meaning of Dreams', in *Lunacy and Letters*

Sleep is . . . some mysterious pleasure which is too perfect to be remembered. It must be some drawing on our divine energies, some forgotten refreshment at the ancient fountains of life. If this is not so, why do we cling to sleep when we have already had enough of it; why does waking up always seem like descending from heaven upon earth? I believe that sleep is a sacrament; or, what is the same thing, a food.

'On Keeping a Dog', in *Lunacy and Letters*

In resisting this horrible theory of the Soul of the Hive, we of Christendom stand not for ourselves, but for all humanity; for the essential and distinctive human idea, that one good and happy man is an end in himself, that a soul is worth saving.

What's Wrong with the World, Part 5

If any man really fails to understand the mystical dogma of the equality of man, he can immediately test it by thinking of two men, of totally different types and fortunes, falling on the same field at some terrible crisis in the war which saved our country. One might be . . . a gentleman, . . . fortunate in his friends, in his tastes, in his culture as well as his character. Another might be some stunted serf of our industrial slums, a man whom all modern life conspired to crush and deform. In the hour when the flag of England was saved, there was no man who dared to say, or would have dreamed of saying, that one death was less glorious than the other.

'The Unknown Warrior', in *Lunacy and Letters*

The French Revolution was the prodigal son of Christianity. It went into a far country and wasted its substance in riotous living, but it had most emphatically . . . the "blood of Christianity" in it, it had the idea that men . . . "are of a kind with men," that all men are brothers, that all men are equal before the moral law, that the intellect does not excuse sin, that the State . . . is the image of abstract right, that nothing can excuse injustice – all these ideas . . . are essentially Christian. . . . They are all based upon that general idea, that a certain morality dominates all politics, and that morality is that all men are of equal value.

'Vox Populi, Vox Dei', in *Preachers from the Pew,* ed. Rev. W. Henry Hunt (1906)

Democracies make great men. The other main factory of heroes besides a revolution is a religion. And a religion again, is a thing which, by its nature, does not think of men as more or less valuable, but of men as all intensely and painfully valuable. . . . For religion all men are equal, as all pennies are equal, because the only value in any of them is that they bear the image of the King. . . . It has often been said, very truly, that religion is the thing that makes the ordinary man feel extraordinary; it is an equally important truth that religion is the thing that makes the extraordinary man feel ordinary. . . . The error of Diogenes lay in the fact that he omitted to notice that every man is both an honest man and a dishonest man. Diogenes looked for his honest man inside every crypt and cavern; but he never thought of looking inside the thief. And that is where the Founder of Christianity found the honest man; He found him on a gibbet and promised him Paradise. . . . [Democracy] was full of a faith in the infinity of human souls, which is in itself not only Christian but orthodox. . . . Christianity said that any man could be a saint if he chose; democracy, that any man could be a citizen if he chose.

Charles Dickens, ch. 1

HUMILITY

Strange crawling carpets of the grass,
Wide windows of the sky:
So in this perilous grace of God
With all my sins go I:
And things grow new though I grow old,
Though I grow old and die.

From 'A Second Childhood', in *The Collected Poems of G.K. Chesterton*

No Catholic thinks he is a good Catholic; or he would by that thought become a bad Catholic.

'The Don and the Cavalier', in *The Well and the Shallows*

When in the near future the real collision comes between Christianity and the genuine forces opposed to it, the central symbol and standard round which the whole battle will rage will be the problem of the thing called Humility. . . . [The moderns] will be able plausibly and defensibly, and with an air of modern intelligence, to deny that humility is a virtue at all. There they have on their side some pagan and some Eastern examples of virtue; and there they have on their side (or appear to have on their side) all that instinctive and even admirable rhetoric of vainglory and self-exaltation which has made so much of the poetry and oratory of mankind. Yet this doctrine of pagan pride will break down as it broke down before.

'The Paradox of Humility', in *Lunacy and Letters*

Humility was largely meant as a restraint upon the arrogance and infinity of the appetite of man. He was always outstripping his mercies with his own newly invented needs. . . . If a man would make his world large, he must be always making himself small.

Orthodoxy, ch. 3

Humility . . . is said both by its upholders and opponents to be the peculiar growth of Christianity. . . . Nietzsche . . . admitted that the philosophy of self-satisfaction led to looking down upon the weak, the cowardly, and the ignorant. Looking down on things may be a delightful experience, only there is nothing, from a mountain to a cabbage, that is really *seen* when it is seen from a balloon. The philosopher of the ego sees everything, no doubt, from a high and rarefied heaven; only he sees everything foreshortened or deformed.

Now if we imagine that a man wished truly, as far as possible, to see everything as it was, he would certainly proceed on a different principle. He would seek to divest himself for a time of those personal peculiarities which tend to divide him from the thing he studies. . . . The student of birds will eliminate his arms; the frog-lover will with one stroke of the imagination remove all his teeth, and the spirit wishing to enter into all the hopes and fears of jelly-fish will simplify his personal appearance to a really alarming extent. It would appear, therefore, that this great body of ours and all its natural instincts . . . is rather an encumbrance at the moment when we attempt to appreciate things as they should be appreciated. We do actually go through a process of mental asceticism, a castration of the entire being, when we wish to feel the abounding good in all things. It is good for us at certain times that ourselves should be like a mere window – as clear, as luminous, and as invisible.

. . . Humility is the . . . art of reducing ourselves to a point, . . . to a thing with no size at all, so that to it all the cosmic things are what they really are – of immeasurable stature. . . . To the spirit which has stripped off for a moment its own idle temporal standards the grass is an everlasting forest, with dragons for denizens.

'A Defence of Humility', in *The Defendant*

'Humility is the mother of giants. One sees great things from the valley; only small things from the peak.'

'The Hammer of God', in *The Innocence of Father Brown*

[Humility is] a virtue . . . obviously and historically connected with Christianity. . . . It has been the boast of hundreds of the champions of Christianity. . . . Civilization discovered Christian humility for the same urgent reason that it discovered faith and charity – that is, because Christian civilization had to discover it or die. . . . The psychological discovery is merely this, that whereas it had been supposed that the fullest possible enjoyment is to be found by extending our ego to infinity, the truth is that the fullest possible enjoyment is to be found by reducing our ego to zero.

Humility is the thing which is for ever renewing the earth and the stars. . . . The curse that came before history has laid on us all a tendency to be weary of wonders. If we saw the sun for the first time it would be the most fearful and beautiful of meteors. . . . Humility is perpetually putting us back in the primal darkness. There all light is lightning, startling and instantaneous. Until we understand that original dark, in which we have neither sight nor expectation, we can give no hearty and childlike praise to the splendid sensationalism of things. . . . The man who destroys himself creates the universe. To the humble man, and to the humble man alone, the sun is really a sun; to the humble man, and to the humble man alone, the sea is really a sea. When he looks at all the faces in the street, he does not only realize that men are alive, he realizes with a dramatic pleasure that they are not dead. . . . Humility is a permanent necessity as a condition of effort and self-examination.

Heretics, ch. 12

There are no things for which men will make such herculean efforts as the things of which they know they are unworthy. . . . The whole secret of the practical success of Christendom lies in the Christian humility. . . . For with the removal of all question of merit or payment, the soul is suddenly released for incredible voyages. If we ask a sane man how much he merits, his mind shrinks instinctively and instantaneously. It is doubtful whether he merits six feet of earth. But if you ask him what he can conquer – he can conquer the stars. Thus comes the thing called Romance, a purely Christian product. A man cannot deserve adventures. . . . The mediaeval Europe which asserted humility gained Romance; the civilization which gained Romance has gained the habitable globe.

Heretics, ch. 5

> He that has been a servant
> Knows more than priests and kings. . . .
> From *The Ballad of the White Horse*, Book IV

All genuine appreciation rests on a certain mystery of humility and almost of darkness. The man who said, "Blessed is he that expecteth nothing, for he shall not be disappointed,"[1] put . . . [it] falsely. The truth is, "Blessed is he that expecteth nothing, for he shall be gloriously surprised." The man who expects nothing sees redder roses than common men can see, and greener grass, and a more startling sun. Blessed is he that expecteth nothing, for he shall possess the cities and the mountains; blessed is the meek, for he shall inherit the earth. Until

---

1. Alexander Pope, letter to Gay, 6 Oct. 1727.

we realize that things might not be, we cannot realize that things are. Until we see the background of darkness we cannot admire the light as a single and created thing. . . . Until we picture nonentity we underrate the victory of God. . . . It is one of the million wild jests of truth that we know nothing until we know nothing.

Heretics, ch. 4

Christianity had taught men to be humble that they might realise how bad things were. Francis was the first (after Christ himself) to teach men to be humble that they might realise how good things were. Pride is not only an enemy to instruction. Pride is an enemy to amusement. The main lesson of St. Francis of Assisi is this idea of an almost fantastic self-effacement corresponding to an almost fantastic pleasure. Matthew Arnold expressed distress and disapproval when Francis referred to his own body as "my brother the donkey".[1] It was exactly because Matthew Arnold thought more of Matthew Arnold than Francis did of Francis that Francis was so much the jollier of the two. Arnold could never have written the Canticle of the Creatures with its roaring fraternity of the universe. It is only he who can say "my brother the donkey" who can feel "my brother the sun". . . . The later pagan had worshipped himself. The earlier Christian had been forced to revile himself. When he had begun to revile himself he began to forget himself. When he had begun to forget himself he began to enjoy himself.

'The Paradox of Humility', in *Lunacy and Letters*

JOY AND SUFFERING

Joy is a far more elusive and elvish matter [than pain] since it is our reason for existing.

'A Defence of Farce', in *The Defendant*

Many of the most brilliant intellects of our time have urged us to the same self-conscious snatching at a rare delight. . . . It is the *carpe diem* religion . . . the religion . . . of very unhappy people. Great joy does not gather the rosebuds while it may; its eyes are fixed on the immortal rose which Dante saw. Great joy has in it the sense of immortality. . . . Suppose a man experiences a really splendid moment of pleasure . . . an almost painful happiness. A man may have, for instance, a moment

---

1. A reference to Arnold's essay 'Pagan and Mediaeval Religious Sentiment', in *Essays in Criticism First Series* (1865).

of ecstasy in first love. . . . The lover enjoys the moment, but precisely not for the moment's sake. He enjoys it for the woman's sake, or his own sake. . . . The lover thinks of his love as something that cannot end. These moments are filled with eternity; these moments are joyful because they do not seem momentary. . . . Man cannot love mortal things. He can only love immortal things for an instant.

Heretics, ch. 7

All the real argument about religion turns on the question of whether a man who was born upside down can tell when he comes right way up. The primary paradox of Christianity is that the ordinary condition of man is not his sane or sensible condition; that the normal itself is an abnormality. That is the inmost philosophy of the Fall. . . . And to question, "What is meant by the Fall?" I could answer with complete sincerity, "That whatever I am, I am not myself." This is the prime paradox of our religion; something that we have never in any full sense known, is not only better than ourselves, but even more natural to us than ourselves. . . .

It is said that Paganism is a religion of joy and Christianity of sorrow; . . . [but] Paganism is pure sorrow and Christianity pure joy. . . . The pagan was (in the main) happier and happier as he approached the earth, but sadder and sadder as he approached the heavens. . . . There was more cosmic contentment in the narrow and bloody streets of Florence than in the theatre of Athens. . . . Giotto lived in a gloomier town than Euripides, but he lived in a gayer universe.

The mass of men have been forced to be gay about the little things, but sad about the big ones. . . . Man is more himself, man is more manlike, when joy is the fundamental thing in him, and grief the superficial. . . . Praise should be the permanent pulsation of the soul. . . . Joy is the uproarious labour by which all things live. . . . Joy ought to be expansive; but for the agnostic it must be contracted, it must cling to one corner of the world. Grief ought to be a concentration; but for the agnostic its desolation is spread through an unthinkable eternity. This is what I call being born upside down. The sceptic may truly be said to be topsy-turvy; for his feet are dancing upwards in idle ecstacies, while his brain is in the abyss. . . . Christianity satisfies suddenly and perfectly man's ancestral instinct for being the right way up; satisfies it supremely in this; that by its creed joy becomes something gigantic and sadness something special and small. . . . The vault above us is not deaf because the universe is an idiot; the silence is not the heartless silence of an endless and aimless world. Rather the silence around us is a small and pitiful stillness like the prompt stillness in a sick room. We are perhaps permitted tragedy as a sort of merciful comedy: because the frantic energy of divine things would knock us down like a drunken farce. . . . So we sit perhaps in a starry chamber of silence, while the laughter of the heavens is too loud for us to bear.

Orthodoxy, ch. 9

We are to regard existence as a raid or great adventure; it is to be judged, therefore, not by what calamities it encounters, but by what flag it follows and what high town it assaults. The most dangerous thing in the world is to be alive; one is always in danger of one's life. But anyone who shrinks from this is a traitor to the great scheme and experiment of being.

T.P.'s Weekly, Christmas Number, 1910

St. Thomas [Aquinas], like other monks, and especially other saints, lived a life of renunciation and austerity; his fasts, for instance, being in marked contrast to the luxury in which he might have lived if he chose. This element stands high in his religion, as a manner of asserting the will against the power of nature, of thanking the Redeemer by partially sharing his sufferings, of making a man ready for anything as a missionary or martyr.

St. Thomas Aquinas, ch. 4

Pessimism is a thing which is learnt from books, as sorrow is a thing learnt from life. Sorrow can never be pessimistic, for it is founded upon the value of things.

Daily News, 13 June 1903

An automatic scheme of 'Karma'[1] or 'reaping what we sow' would be just as gross and material as sowing beans or reaping barley. . . . The one thing that would make suffering intolerable would be the thought that it was systematically inflicted upon sinners. . . . The doctrine which makes it most endurable is exactly the opposite doctrine, that life is a battle in which the best put their bodies in the front, in which God sends only his holiest into the hail of the arrows of hell. In the book of Job is foreshadowed that better doctrine, full of a dark chivalry, that he that bore the worst that man can suffer was the best that bore the form of man.

The Speaker, 9 Sept. 1905

1. The Hindu and Buddhist spiritual concept that a person's actions cumulatively determine their ultimate fate.

The book of Job is better worth hearing than any modern philosophical conversation. . . . From it the modern Christian may with astonishment learn Christianity; learn, that is, that suffering may be a strange honour and not a vulgar punishment; that the King may be conferring a decoration when he pins the man on the cross, as much as when he pins the cross on the man.

The Illustrated London News, 10 Feb. 1906

The Book of Job definitely asks, 'But what is the purpose of God?' Is it worth the sacrifice even of our miserable humanity? Of course it is easy enough to wipe out our own paltry wills for the sake of a will that is grander and kinder. But is it grander and kinder? Let God use His tools; let God break His tools. But what is He doing and what are they being broken for? . . . [Job] remonstrates with his Maker because he is proud of his Maker. . . . God . . . takes up the rôle of sceptic. . . . Job [is] suddenly satisfied with the mere presentation of something impenetrable. Verbally speaking the enigmas of Jehovah seem darker and more desolate than the enigmas of Job; yet Job was comfortless before the speech of Jehovah and is comforted after it. He has been told nothing, but he feels the terrible and tingling atmosphere of something which is too good to be told. The refusal of God to explain His design is itself a burning hint of His design. The riddles of God are more satisfying than the solutions of man.

. . . The mechanical optimist endeavours to justify the universe avowedly upon the ground that it is a rational and consecutive pattern. . . . God says, in effect, that if there is one fine thing about the world, as far as men are concerned, it is that it cannot be explained. He insists on the inexplicableness of everything. . . . God will make man see things, if it is only against the black background of nonentity. God will make Job see a startling universe if He can only do it by making Job see an idiotic universe. . . . The whole is a sort of psalm or rhapsody of the sense of wonder. The maker of all things is astonished at the things He has Himself made. . . . Job puts forward a note of interrogation; God answers with a note of exclamation. Instead of proving to Job that it is an explicable world, He insists that it is a much stranger world than Job ever thought it was. . . . [The author of the *Book of Job*] has contrived to let fall here and there . . . sudden and splendid suggestions that the secret of God is a bright and not a sad one – semi-accidental suggestions, like light seen for an instant through the cracks of a closed door. . . . For instance, . . . when God is speaking of snow and hail in the mere catalogue of the physical cosmos, He speaks of them as a treasury that He has laid up against the day of battle – a hint of some huge Armageddon in which evil shall be at last overthrown.

. . . Here in this Book the question is really asked whether God invariably punishes vice with terrestrial punishment and rewards virtue with terrestrial prosperity. . . . When once people have begun to believe that prosperity is the reward of virtue their next calamity is obvious. If prosperity is regarded as the reward of virtue it will be regarded as the symptom of virtue. Men will leave off the heavy task of making good men successful. They will adopt the easier task of making our successful men good. This, which has happened throughout modern commerce and journalism, is the ultimate Nemesis of the wicked optimism of the comforters of Job. If the Jews could be saved from it, the Book of Job saved them. The Book of Job is chiefly remarkable . . . for the fact that it does not end in a way that is conventionally satisfactory. Job is not told that his misfortunes were due to his sins or a part of any plan for his improvement. But in the prologue we see Job tormented not because he was the worst of men, but because he was the best. It is the lesson of the whole work that man is most comforted by paradoxes; and it is by all human testimony the most reassuring. I need not suggest what a high and strange history awaited this paradox of the best man in the worst fortune. I need not say that in the freest and most philosophical sense there is one Old Testament figure who is truly a type; or say what is pre-figured in the wounds of Job.

'The Book of Job', in *G.K.C. As M.C.*

FAITH AND HOPE

Belief in spirit, so far from being a morbid thing, is held by almost all people who are physically strong and live in the open air. Powerful peasants and farmers six feet high all believe in faeries. Rationalism is a disease of the towns, like the housing problem.

Daily News, 14 Mar. 1903

Faith means believing the incredible, or it is no virtue at all. . . . Faith . . . must always mean a certainty about something we cannot prove. Thus, for instance, we believe by faith in the existence of other people.

Heretics, ch. 12

The best way to see if a coat fits a man is not to measure both of them, but to try it on. It is the replacing of the very slow, logical method of accumulating, point by point, an absolute proof by a rapid, experimental and imaginative method which gives us, long before we can get absolute proof, a very good working belief. . . . What we know . . . are the fruits of the spirit. We know that with this idea once inside our heads a million things become transparent as if a lamp were lit behind them: we see the thing in the dog in the street, in the pear on the wall, in the book of history we are reading. . . . And the fulfilments pour in upon us in so natural and continual a cataract that at last is reached that paradox of the condition which is called belief.

Daily News, 14 Mar. 1903

The early Christian might be wrong in believing that by entering the brotherhood men could in a few years become perfect even as their Father in Heaven was perfect, but he believed it and acted flatly and fearlessly on the belief: this is the type of the higher visionary. . . . This then is [a] . . . moral virtue of the older school, an immense direct sincerity of action, a cleansing away, by the sweats of hard work, of all those subtle and perilous instincts of mere ethical castle-building which have been woven, like the spells of an enchantress, round so many of the strong men of our own time.

Cited in Ward, *Gilbert Keith Chesterton*, pp. 75, 76

"I tell you naught for your comfort,
   Yea, naught for your desire,
Save that the sky grows darker yet
   And the sea rises higher.

"Night shall be thrice night over you,
   And heaven an iron cope.
Do you have joy without a cause,
   Yea, faith without a hope?"

From *The Ballad of the White Horse*, Book I

Every man . . . who begins by worshipping success, must end in mere mediocrity. . . . A man may be a hero . . . for the sake of human sacrifice, but not for the sake of success. . . . When the test of triumph is men's test of everything, they never endure long enough to triumph at all. As long as matters are really hopeful, hope is a mere flattery or platitude; it is only when everything is hopeless that hope begins to be a strength at all. Like all the Christian virtues, it is as unreasonable as it is indispensable.

Heretics, ch. 8

Hope means hoping when things are hopeless, or it is no virtue at all. . . . Hope is the power of being cheerful in circumstances which we know to be desperate. . . . The virtue of hope exists only in earthquake and eclipse. . . . For practical purposes it is at the hopeless moment that we require the hopeful man, and the virtue either does not exist at all, or begins to exist at that moment. Exactly at the instant when hope ceases to be reasonable it begins to be useful.

Heretics, ch. 12

Faith, hope and charity, the three mystical virtues of Christianity, are also the gayest of the virtues. . . . Call it faith, call it vitality, call it the will to live, call it the religion of to-morrow morning, call it the immortality of man, call it self-love and vanity; it is the thing that explains why man survives all things. . . . If there be anywhere a man who has really lost it, . . . the man is dead.

G.F. Watts (1920), pp. 102, 103

To [Victor Hugo] delight in himself was the first condition of all optimism, and faith in himself the first condition of all faith. If a man does not enjoy himself whom he has seen, how shall he enjoy God whom he has not seen? To the great poet, as to the child, there is no hard-and-fast line drawn between the Ego and the Cosmos.

'Victor Hugo', in *A Handful of Authors*

APPROACHES TO OTHERS

[A Catholic's] whole religion is rooted in the unity of the race of Adam, the one and only Chosen Race. He is loyal to his own country; indeed he is generally ardently loyal to it, such local affection being in other ways very natural to his religious life, with its shrines and relics. . . . But the Protestant patriot really never thought of any patriotism except his own. . . . I cannot see how [patriotism] can be defended except as part of a larger morality; and the Catholic morality happens to be one of the very few large moralities now ready to defend it. But the Church defends it as one of the duties of men and not as the whole duty of man.

The Catholic Church and Conversion, ch. 2

[A good social order cannot be achieved by] a mere improvement in social machinery, or the establishment of Bureaus for Everything. I think it happens only when there is a strong sense of duty and dignity implanted in people, not by any government or even any school, but by something which they recognize as making a secret call upon a solitary soul.

'On the Next Hundred Years', in *Avowals and Denials*

No one worth calling a man allows his moods to change his convictions; but it is by moods that we understand other men's convictions. The bigot is not he who knows he is right; every sane man knows he is right. The bigot is he whose emotions and imagination are too cold and weak to feel how it is that other men go wrong.

'The Anarchist', in *Alarms and Discursions*

The Earth's Shame

Name not his deed: in shuddering and in haste
We dragged him darkly o'er the windy fell:
That night there was a gibbet in the waste,
And a new sin in hell.

Be his deed hid from commonwealths and kings,
By all men born be one true tale forgot;
But three things, braver than all earthly things,
Faced him and feared him not.

Above his head and sunken secret face
Nested the sparrow's young and dropped not dead.
From the red blood and slime of that lost place
Grew daisies white, not red.

And from high heaven looking upon him,
Slowly upon the face of God did come
A smile the cherubim and seraphim
Hid all their faces from.

From *The Collected Poems of G.K. Chesterton*

Charity . . . means one of two things – pardoning unpardonable acts, or loving unlovable people. . . . Christianity . . . divided the crime from the criminal. The criminal we must forgive unto seventy times seven.[1] The crime we must not forgive at all. It was not enough that slaves who stole wine inspired partly anger and partly kindness. We must be much more angry with theft than before, and yet much kinder to thieves than before. There was room for wrath and love to run wild. . . . Those underrate Christianity who say that it discovered mercy; any one might discover mercy. . . . But to discover a plan for being merciful and also severe – *that* was to anticipate a strange need of human nature. For no one wants to be forgiven for a big sin as if it were a little one.

Orthodoxy, ch. 6

Contemplating the sort of philanthropist who is also an egoist, I am tempted to . . . say to him . . . do not be kind merely to exhibit your own kindness; for that is an insult that is never forgiven. When you are helping people, pray for a spirit of humility; I had almost said, when you are helping them, pray for an appearance of helplessness.

'On Bright Old Things – and other things',
in *Sidelights on New London and Newer York*

1. Mat. 18.22.

Now just as that vague hope that we call romance or poetry points to a paradise even if it be called elf-land, so this vague charity or sense of sacred human values really points to a higher standard of sacredness. We have to look at men in a certain light in order to love them all; and the most agnostic of us know that it is not exactly identical with the light of common day. But the mystery is immediately explained when we turn towards that light itself; which is the light that lighteth every man that cometh into the world.[1] Ordinary men find it difficult to love ordinary men; at least in an ordinary way. But ordinary men can love the love of ordinary men. They can love the lover of ordinary men, who loves them in an extraordinary way. . . . Men can admire perfect charity before they practise even imperfect charity; and that is by far the most practical way of getting them to practise it. It is not to leave men merely staring at each other and standing face to face to criticize and grow weary; it is rather to see them standing side by side and looking out together at a third thing; the world's desire and the love-affair of all humanity; which is really a human sun that can shine upon the evil and the good.

'Utopias', in *G.K.C. as M.C.*

1. John 1.9.

Part 7

Christian Spirituality

SPIRITUALITY

[St. Thomas Aquinas] insured that the main outline of the Christianity that has come down to us should be supernatural but not anti-natural; and should never be darkened with a false spirituality to the oblivion of the Creator and the Christ who was made Man.

St. Thomas Aquinas, ch. 8

The human soul is the only thing that we cannot properly study, because it is at once both the study and the student. We can analyse a beetle by looking through a microscope, but we cannot analyse a beetle by looking through a beetle.

'The Meaning of Dreams', in *Lunacy and Letters*

It seems to be the sceptic who really thinks of the soul superstitiously, as a separate and secret animal with wings; who considers the soul quite apart from the self.

'The Optimist as a Suicide', in *The Thing*

It might reasonably be maintained that the true object of all human life is play. Earth is a task garden; heaven is a playground. To be at last in such secure innocence that one can juggle with the universe and the stars, to be so good that one can treat everything as a joke – that may be, perhaps, the real end and final holiday of human souls. When we are really holy we may regard the Universe as a lark.

'Oxford from Without', in *All Things Considered*

Religion [tends] to take some one thing or other out of the stress of time, from under the tyranny of circumstances, and give it that liberty which is only another name for sanctity. For liberty is altogether a mystical thing.

'The Poetic Quality in Liberalism', in *The Independent Review*, Feb. 1905

The sentiment of [*A Midsummer Night's Dream*] . . . is the mysticism of happiness . . . the conception that as man lives upon a borderland he may find himself in the spiritual or supernatural atmosphere, not only through being profoundly sad or meditative, but by being extravagantly happy. The soul might be rapt out of the body in an agony of sorrow, or a trance of ecstasy; but it might also be rapt out of the body in a paroxysm of laughter.

'A Midsummer Night's Dream', in *The Common Man*

To this day I cannot see certain things such as a white horse or wood painted white, without a pang of pleasure going through me stronger than sex or the fear of death. And unlike sex and death, it does not concentrate; for an instant, like a lost lightning flash, it has spread over the whole world, full of too many wonders to be wondered at.

The New Witness, 17 June 1921

It may seem a paradox to say that a man may be transported with joy to discover that he is in debt. But this is only because in commercial cases the creditor does not generally share the transports of joy; especially when the debt is by hypothesis infinite and therefore unrecoverable. . . . The parallel of a natural love-story of the nobler sort disposes of the difficulty in a flash. There the infinite creditor does share the joys of the infinite debtor; for indeed they are both debtors and both creditors. . . . Debt and dependence do become pleasures in the presence of unspoilt love; . . . here the word . . . is the key of asceticism. It is the highest and holiest of the paradoxes that the man who really knows he cannot pay his debt will be for ever paying it. He will be for ever giving back what he cannot give back, and cannot be expected to give back. He will be always throwing things away into a bottomless pit of unfathomable thanks. . . . We are not generous enough to be ascetics. . . . A man must have magnanimity of surrender, of which he commonly only catches a glimpse in first love, like a glimpse of our lost Eden. . . .

Men will ask what selfish sort of woman it must have been who ruthlessly exacted tribute in the form of flowers, or what an avaricious creature she can have been to demand solid gold in the form of a ring; just as they ask what cruel kind of God can have demanded sacrifice and self-denial. They will have lost the clue to all that lovers have meant by love; and will not understand that it was because the thing was not demanded that it was done.

St. Francis of Assisi, ch. 5

You say grace before meals.
All right.
But I say grace before the play and the opera,
And grace before the concert and pantomime,
And grace before I open a book,
And grace before sketching, painting,
Swimming, fencing, boxing, walking, playing, dancing;
And grace before I dip the pen in the ink.

Notebook, cited Ward, *Gilbert Keith Chesterton*, p. 59

The mystic is not a man who reverences large things so much as a man who reverences small ones, who reduces himself to a point, without parts or magnitude, so that to him the grass is really a forest and the grasshopper a dragon. Little things please great minds.

The Speaker, 15 Dec. 1900

I do not think there is anyone who takes quite such a fierce pleasure in things being themselves as I do. The startling wetness of water excites and intoxicates me: the fieriness of fire, the steeliness of steel, the unutterable muddiness of mud. It is just the same with people. . . . When we call a man "manly" or a woman "womanly" we touch the deepest philosophy.

Letter of July 1899, cited Ward, *Gilbert Keith Chesterton*, p. 97

MYSTICISM

Mysticism . . . celebrates personality, positive variety, and special emphasis: just as in broad fact the mystery of dissolution is emphasized and typified in the East, so in practice the mystery of concentration and identity is manifest in the historic churches of Christendom. Even the foes of Christianity would readily agree that Christianity is "personal" in the sense that a vulgar joke is "personal": that is corporeal, vivid, perhaps ugly. . . . [William Blake] was on the side of historic Christianity on the fundamental question on which it confronts the East; the idea that personality is the glory of the universe and not its shame; that creation is higher than evolution, because it is more personal; that pardon is higher than Nemesis, because it is more personal; that the forgiveness of sins is essential to the communion of saints; and the resurrection of the body to the life everlasting.

William Blake (1920), pp. 204, 209

What makes a real religion mystical . . . is that it claims . . . to be hiding a beauty that is more beautiful than any that we know, or perhaps an evil that is more evil. This gives another sort of intensity to common things.

'On Egyptian Influence', in *Generally Speaking*

The mystic is one who will serve something invisible for his own reasons. The materialist is one who will serve anything visible for no reason.

'On Flocking', in *All is Grist*

The Mystics can be represented as men who maintain that the final fruition or joy of the soul is rather a sensation than a thought. The motto of the Mystics has always been, "Taste and see."[1] Now St. Thomas [Aquinas] also began by saying, "Taste and see"; but he said it of the first rudimentary impressions of the human animal. It might well be maintained that the Franciscan [St. Bonaventure] puts Taste last and the Dominican [Aquinas] puts it first. It might be said that the Thomist begins with something solid like the taste of an apple, and afterwards deduces a divine life for the intellect; while the Mystic exhausts the intellect first, and says finally that the sense of God is something like the taste of an apple. A common enemy might claim that St. Thomas begins with the taste of fruit and St. Bonaventure ends with the taste of fruit. But they are both right; if I may say so, it is a privilege of people who contradict each other in their cosmos to be both right. The Mystic is right in saying that the relation of God and Man is essentially a love-story; the pattern and type of all love-stories. The Dominican rationalist is equally right in saying that the intellect is at home in the top-most heavens; and that the appetite for truth may outlast and even devour all the duller appetites of man.

St. Thomas Aquinas, ch. 3

The best and last word of mysticism is an almost agonising sense of the preciousness of everything, the preciousness of the whole universe, which is like an exquisite and fragile vase.

'Sherlock Homes', in *A Handful of Authors*

[The mystic] does really praise creation, in the sense of the act of creation. He praises the passage or transition from nonentity to entity; there falls here also the shadow of that archetypal image of the bridge, which has given to the priest his archaic and mysterious name. The mystic who passes through the moment when there is nothing but God does in some sense behold the beginningless beginnings in which there was really nothing else. He not only appreciates everything but the nothing of which everything was made. In a fashion he endures and answers even the earthquake irony of the Book of Job; in some sense he is there when the foundations of the world are laid, with the morning stars singing together and the sons of God shouting for joy.[2]

St. Francis of Assisi, ch. 5

---

1. Psalm 34.8: 'O taste and see that the Lord is good.'   2. Job 38.7.

All good things are one thing. . . . One thing is always walking among us in fancy-dress, in the grey cloak of a church or the green cloak of a meadow. He is always behind, His form makes the folds fall so superbly. . . . The Greeks and Norsemen and Romans saw the superficial wars of nature and made the sun one god, the sea another, the wind a third. They were not thrilled, as some rude Israelite was, one night in the wastes, alone, by the sudden blazing idea of all being the same God.

> Letter of July 1899, cited Ward, *Gilbert Keith Chesterton*, pp. 99-100

No true mystic ever loved darkness rather than light. No pure mystic ever loved mere mystery. The mystic does not bring doubts or riddles: the doubts and riddles exist already. We all feel the riddle of the earth without anyone to point it out. . . . We have grown accustomed to the unaccountable. Every stone or flower is a hieroglyphic of which we have lost the key; with every step of our lives we enter into the middle of some story which we are certain to misunderstand. The mystic is not the man who makes mysteries but the man who destroys them. The mystic is one who offers an explanation which may be true or false, but which is *always* comprehensible – by which I mean, not that it is always comprehended, but that it always can be comprehended, because there is always something to comprehend.

> *William Blake* (1920), pp. 131-2

. . . a mystic, a man who finds a meaning in everything.

> 'Victor Hugo', in *A Handful of Authors*

. . . mysticism – the belief that logic is misleading, and that things are not what they seem.

> In *Leo Tolstoy*, by Chesterton, Perris and Garnett (1903)

Mysticism keeps men sane. As long as you have mystery you have health; when you destroy mystery you create morbidity. The ordinary man has always been sane because the ordinary man has always been a mystic. He has permitted the twilight. He has always had one foot in earth and the other in fairyland. He has always left himself free to doubt his gods; but . . . free also to believe in them. He has always cared more for truth than for consistency. If he saw two truths that seemed to contradict each other, he would take the two truths and the contradiction along with them. . . . The whole secret of mysticism is this: that man can understand everything by the help of what he does not understand. The morbid logician seeks to make everything lucid, and succeeds in making everything mysterious. The mystic allows one thing to be mysterious, and everything else becomes lucid. The determinist makes the theory of causation quite clear, and then finds that he cannot say "if you please" to the housemaid. The Christian permits free will to remain a sacred mystery; but because of this his relations with the housemaid become of a sparkling and crystal clearness. He puts the seed of dogma in a central darkness; but it branches forth in all directions with abounding natural health.

. . . The one created thing which we cannot look at is the one thing in the light of which we look at everything. Like the sun at noonday, mysticism explains everything else by the blaze of its own victorious invisibility.

Orthodoxy, ch. 2

What was the matter with [the Fraticelli][1] was that they were mystics; mystics and nothing else but mystics; mystics and not Catholics; mystics and not Christians; mystics and not men. They rotted away because . . . they would not listen to reason. And St. Francis [of Assisi], however wild and romantic his gyrations might appear to many, always hung on to reason by one invisible and indestructible hair.

St. Francis of Assisi, ch. 10

[Thomas] Carlyle was . . . a mystic, and mysticism was with him, as with all its genuine professors, only a transcendent form of common sense. Mysticism and common sense alike consist in a sense of the dominance of certain truths and tendencies which cannot be formally demonstrated or even formally named.

'Thomas Carlyle', in *Twelve Types*

The Prayer of a Man Resting

The twilight closes round me,
My head is bowed before the Universe.
I thank thee, O Lord, for a child I knew seven years ago
And whom I have never seen since.

Notebook, cited Ward, *Gilbert Keith Chesterton*, p. 59

1. Extremist, 'anti-material' mediaeval followers of St. Francis of Assisi.

SAINTS

All the evils which our Rationalist or Protestant tradition associates with the idolatrous veneration of sacred figures arises in the merely human atmosphere of literature and history. Every extravagance of hagiology can be found in hero-worship. Every folly alleged in the worship of saints can be found in the worship of poets. . . . There are people who have a vague idea that the worship of saints is worse than the imitation of sinners. There are some, like a lady I once knew, who think that hagiology is the scientific study of hags.

'Reprinted Pieces',
in *Appreciations and Criticisms of the Works of Charles Dickens*

The great conception at the back of the oldest religions in the world is, of course, the conception that man is of divine origin, a sacred and splendid heir, the eldest son of the universe. But humanity could not in practice carry out this conception that everyone was divine. The practical imagination recoils from the idea of two gods swindling each other over a pound of cheese. The mind refuses to accept the idea of sixty bodies, each filled with a blazing divinity, elbowing each other to get into an omnibus. This mere external difficulty causes men in every age to fall back upon the conception that certain men preserved for other men the sanctity of man. Certain figures were more divine because they were more human. . . . To the old Hebrews this sacred being was the prophet: to the men of the Christian ages it was the saint.

'The Heroines of Shakespeare', in *A Handful of Authors*

It is a real case against conventional hagiography that it sometimes tends to make all saints seem to be the same. Whereas in fact no men are more different than saints; not even murderers.

St. Thomas Aquinas, ch. 4

It is almost necessary to say nowadays that a saint means a very good man. The notion of an eminence merely moral, consistent with complete stupidity or unsuccess, is a revolutionary image grown unfamiliar by its very familiarity. . . . The materials of it were almost the same as those of labour and domesticity: it did not need the sword or sceptre, but rather the staff or spade. It was the ambition of poverty.

A Short History of England, ch. 7

A saint may be any kind of man; with an additional quality that is at once unique and universal. . . . The one thing which separates a saint from ordinary men is his readiness to be one with ordinary men. . . . A saint is long past any desire for distinction; he is the only sort of superior man who has never been a superior person.

St. Thomas Aquinas, ch. 5

Alone of all superiors, the saint does not depress the human dignity of others. He is not conscious of his superiority to them; but only more conscious of his inferiority than they are.

                                        A Short History of England, ch. 2

Every saint is a man before he is a saint; and a saint may be made of every sort or kind of man. . . . The saint is a medicine because he is an antidote. Indeed, that is why the saint is often a martyr; he is mistaken for a poison because he is an antidote. He will generally be found restoring the world to sanity by exaggerating whatever the world neglects, which is by no means always the same element in every age. Yet each generation seeks its saint by instinct; and he is not what the people want; but rather what the people need. This is surely the . . . meaning of those words to the first saints, "Ye are the salt of the earth,"[1] . . . salt seasons and preserves beef, not because it is like beef, but because it is very unlike it.

                                        St. Thomas Aquinas, ch. 1

I will not say that [Dr. Samuel Johnson] died alone with God, for each of us will do that; but he did in a doubtful and changing world, what in securer civilizations the saints have done. He detached himself from time as in an ecstasy of impartiality; and saw the ages with an equal eye. He was not merely alone with God; he even shared the loneliness of God, which is love.

                                        'Dr. Johnson', in *G.K.C. as M.C.*

M. Vianney[2] appeared in history at the supreme moment of the French Revolution. . . . And in the midst of all those thunders the Curé d'Ars stood calmly talking about something totally different. He was talking exactly as he would have talked if he had been a Celtic hermit of the Dark Ages talking to a savage tribe of Picts. At the very moment when the human world seemed to have been enlarged beyond all limits for all to see, he declared it to be quite small as compared with things that hardly anybody could see. At the moment when thousands thought they were reading a radiant and self-evident philosophy, proved quite clearly in black and white, he calmly called its black white and its white black. . . . It was in the dull daylight of the manufacturing and materialistic nineteenth century that the unearthly light shone from the cavern of Lourdes. And it was in the full sunrise of the secular age of reason introduced by the eighteenth century that a nimbus not of that age or of this world could be seen round the head of the Curé d'Ars.

                                        'The Challenge of the Curé d'Ars',
                                        in H. Ghéon *The Secret of the Curé D'Ars*

1. Mat. 5.13.
2. Jean-Baptiste Vianney (1786-1859), known as the Curé d'Ars, was canonized in 1925.

The transition from the good man to the saint is a sort of revolution; by which one for whom all things illustrate and illuminate God becomes one for whom God illustrates and illuminates all things. . . . For one the joy of life is a cause for faith, for the other rather a result of faith. . . . Being in some mystical sense on the other side of things, [the saint] sees things go forth from the divine as children going forth from a familiar and accepted home, instead of meeting them as they come out, as most of us do, upon the roads of the world. And it is the paradox that by this privilege he is more familiar, more free and fraternal, more carelessly hospitable than we.

St. Francis of Assisi, ch. 5

. . . The text was, "Precious in the sight of the Lord is the death of one of his saints."[1] . . . It is this passionate sense of the value of things: of the richness of the cosmic treasure: the world where every star is a diamond, every leaf an emerald, every drop of blood a ruby, it is this sense of *preciousness* that *is* really awakened by the death of His saints. Somehow we feel that even their death is a thing of incalculable value and mysterious sweetness: it is awful, tragic, desolating, desperately hard to bear – but still "precious."

Letter of 1899, cited in Ward, *Gilbert Keith Chesterton*, p. 101

When I was a boy a more Puritan generation objected to a statue upon a parish church representing the Virgin and Child. After much controversy, they compromised by taking away the Child. . . . You cannot chip away the statue of a mother from all round that of a new-born child. . . . Similarly, you cannot suspend the idea of a new-born child in the void or think of him without thinking of his mother. You cannot visit the child without visiting the mother; you cannot in common human life approach the child except through the mother. . . . We must either leave Christ out of Christmas, or Christmas out of Christ, or we must admit . . . that those holy heads are too near together for the haloes not to mingle and cross.

The Everlasting Man, Part 2, ch. 1

I never doubted that this figure [of Our Lady] was the figure of the Faith; that she embodied, as a complete human being still only human, all that this Thing [the Church] had to say to humanity.

'Mary and the Convert', in *The Well and the Shallows*

God is God, Maker of all things visible and invisible; the Mother of God is in a rather special sense connected with things visible; since she is of this earth, and through her bodily being God was revealed to the senses. In the presence of God, we must remember what is invisible, . . . intellectual. . . . But Our Lady, reminding us especially of God

1. Psalm 116.15: 'Precious in the sight of the Lord is the death of his saints.'

Incarnate, does in some degree gather up and embody all those elements of the heart and the higher instincts, which are the legitimate short cuts to the love of God.

'Mary and the Convert', in *The Well and the Shallows*

[St. Francis of Assisi] was always turning towards the centre and heart of the maze; he took the queerest and most zigzag short cuts through the wood, but he was always going home. . . . He was above all things a great giver; and he cared chiefly for the best kind of giving which is called thanksgiving. . . . He understood down to its very depths the theory of thanks; and its depths are a bottomless abyss. He knew that the praise of God stands on its strongest ground when it stands on nothing. He knew that we can best measure the towering miracle of the mere fact of existence if we realise that but for some strange mercy we should not even exist.

St. Francis of Assisi, ch. 10

It was in a wholly happy and enthusiastic sense that St. Francis said, "Blessed is he who expecteth nothing, for he shall enjoy everything." It was by this deliberate idea of starting from zero, from the dark nothingness of his own deserts, that he did come to enjoy even earthly things as few people have enjoyed them. . . . There is no way in which a man can earn a star or deserve a sunset. . . . The less a man thinks of himself, the more he thinks of his good luck and of all the gifts of God.

St. Francis of Assisi, ch. 5

St. Francis really meant what he said when he said he had found the secret of life in being the servant. . . . There was to be found ultimately in such service a freedom.

St. Francis of Assisi, ch. 5

[St. Francis] was a Lover. He was a lover of God and he was really and truly a lover of men; possibly a much rarer mystical vocation. A lover of men is very nearly the opposite of a philanthropist. . . . A philanthropist may be said to love anthropoids. But as St. Francis did not love humanity but men, so he did not love Christianity but Christ. Say, if you think so, that he was a lunatic loving an imaginary person; but an imaginary person, not an imaginary idea. . . . To this great mystic his religion was not a thing like a theory but a thing like a love-affair.

St. Francis of Assisi, ch. 1

St. Francis is the mirror of Christ rather as the moon is the mirror of the sun. The moon is much smaller than the sun, but it is also much nearer to us; and being less vivid it is more visible. Exactly in the same sense St. Francis is nearer to us, and being a mere man like ourselves is in that sense more imaginable.

. . . He said that in fasting or suffering humiliation he was but trying to do something of what Christ did. . . . The service to which St. Francis had committed himself was one which . . . he conceived more and more in terms of sacrifice and crucifixion. He was full of the sentiment that he had not suffered enough to be worthy even to be a distant follower of his suffering God. . . . St. Francis was not thinking of Martyrdom as a means to an end, but almost as an end in itself; in the sense that to him the supreme end was to come closer to the example of Christ.

St. Francis of Assisi, ch. 8

Perhaps it would sound too paradoxical to say that [St. Thomas Aquinas and St. Francis] saved us from Spirituality. . . . Perhaps it may be misunderstood if I say that St. Francis, for all his love of animals, saved us from being Buddhists; and that St. Thomas, for all his love of Greek philosophy, saved us from being Platonists. . . . They both reaffirmed the Incarnation, by bringing God back to earth.

St. Thomas Aquinas, ch. 1

St. Francis walked the world like the Pardon of God. I mean that his appearance marked the moment when men could be reconciled not only to God but to nature and, most difficult of all, to themselves. It was . . . his whole function to tell men to start afresh and, in that sense, to tell them to forget.

St. Francis of Assisi, ch. 10

It is not true to represent St. Francis as a mere romantic forerunner of the Renaissance and a revival of natural pleasures for their own sake. The whole point of him was that the secret of recovering the natural pleasures lay in regarding them in the light of a supernatural pleasure.

St. Francis of Assisi, ch. 5

The whole philosophy of St. Francis revolved round the idea of a new supernatural light on natural things, which meant the ultimate recovery not the ultimate refusal of natural things.

St. Francis of Assisi, ch. 4

St. Francis was not a lover of nature. . . . The phrase implies accepting the material universe as a vague environment, a sort of sentimental pantheism. . . . He saw everything as dramatic, distinct from its setting, not all of a piece like a picture but in action like a play. A bird went by him like an arrow; something with a story and a purpose, though it was a purpose of life and not a purpose of death.

. . . He wanted to see each tree as a separate and almost a sacred thing, being a child of God and therefore a brother or sister of man. . . . Everything would be in every sense a character. This is the quality in which, as a poet, he is the very opposite of a pantheist. He did not call nature his mother; he called a particular donkey his brother or a particular sparrow his sister. . . . They were particular creatures assigned by their Creator to particular places; not mere expressions of the evolutionary energy of things. That is where his mysticism is so close to the common sense of the child. . . . Francis was a mystic, but he believed in mysticism and not in mystification. . . . Francis was emphatically a realist, using the word realist in its much more medieval sense. In this matter he really was akin to the best spirit of his age, which had just won its victory over the nominalism[1] of the twelfth century. . . . He not only loved but reverenced God in all his creatures.

St. Francis of Assisi, ch. 6

To [St. Francis] a man was always a man and did not disappear in a dense crowd any more than in a desert. He honoured all men; that is, he not only loved but respected them all. . . . There was never a man who looked into those brown burning eyes without being certain that Francis Bernardone was really interested in *him*; in his own inner individual life from the cradle to the grave; that he himself was being valued and taken seriously, and not merely added to the spoils of some social policy or the names in some clerical document. Now for this particular moral and religious idea there is no external expression except courtesy. . . . He treated the whole mob of men as a mob of kings. And this was . . . the only attitude that will appeal to that part of man to which he wished to appeal. It cannot be done by giving gold or even bread. . . . No plans or proposals . . . will give back to a broken man his self-respect and sense of speaking with an equal. One gesture will do it.

St. Francis of Assisi, ch. 6

St. Francis had that liberating and humanising effect upon religion; though perhaps rather on the imagination than the intellect.

St. Thomas Aquinas, ch. 4

---

1. 'Nominalism' is the philosophy which tends to deny the objective reality of qualities, and hence to belittle the independent reality of things; which 'realism' controverted.

MIRACLES, ASCETICISM, MARTYRDOM

The good miracles, the acts of the saints, . . . are always acts of restoration. They give the victim back his personality; and it is a normal and not a super-normal personality. The miracle gives back his legs to the lame man; but it does not turn him into a large centipede. It gives eyes to the blind; but only a regular and respectable number of eyes. . . . Black magic is that which blots out or disguises the true form of a thing; while white magic, in the good sense, restores it to its own form and not another.

'Magic and fantasy in fiction', in *Sidelights on New London and Newer York*

The believers in miracles accept them (rightly or wrongly) because they have evidence for them. The disbelievers in miracles deny them (rightly or wrongly) because they have a doctrine against them.

Orthodoxy, ch. 9

The fixed points of faith and philosophy do indeed remain always the same. Whether a man believes that fire in one case could fail to burn, depends on why he thinks it generally does burn. If it burns nine sticks out of ten because it is its nature . . . to do so, then it will burn the tenth stick as well. If it burns nine sticks because it is the will of God that it should, then it might be the will of God that the tenth should be unburned. Nobody can get behind that fundamental difference about the reason of things; and it is as rational for a theist to believe in miracles as for an atheist to disbelieve in them. In other words there is only one intelligent reason why a man does not believe in miracles and that is that he does believe in materialism.

St. Francis of Assisi, ch. 9

Reform or . . . progress means simply the gradual control of matter by mind. A miracle simply means the swift control of matter by mind. . . . A miracle only means the liberty of God. . . . The Catholic Church believed that man and God both had a sort of spiritual freedom. Calvinism took away the freedom from man, but left it to God. Scientific materialism binds the Creator Himself. . . . It leaves nothing free in the universe.

Orthodoxy, ch. 8

The modern mind always mixes up two different ideas: mystery in the sense of what is marvellous, and mystery in the sense of what is complicated. That is half its difficulty about miracles. A miracle is startling; but it is simple. It is simple because it *is* a miracle. It is power coming directly from God (or the devil) instead of indirectly through nature or human wills.

'The Wrong Shape', in *The Innocence of Father Brown*

What I think you mean is that science has shown *miracles* to be untrue. But miracles are not ideas about the nature of the physical universe. They are ideas about the nature of a power capable of breaking through the nature of the physical universe. And science has not shown *that* to be untrue, for anybody who can think.

Letter to C.E.M. Joad, May 1930,
cited Ward, Gilbert Keith Chesterton, p. 511

There is no philosophical case against miracles. There are such things as the laws of Nature, rationally speaking. What everybody knows is this only, that there is repetition in nature. . . . Do you know why a pumpkin goes on being a pumpkin? If you do not, you cannot possibly tell whether a pumpkin could turn into a coach or couldn't. . . . You say, 'It is a law of nature that pumpkins should remain pumpkins'. That only means that pumpkins generally do remain pumpkins. . . . What Christianity says is . . . that this repetition in Nature has its origin, not in a thing resembling a law, but in a thing resembling a will. . . . It believes that a God who could do anything so extraordinary as making pumpkins go on being pumpkins is, like the prophet Habakkuk, *capable de tout.*[1] If you do not think it extraordinary that a pumpkin is always a pumpkin, think again. You have not yet even begun philosophy.

Daily News, 2 Sept. 1905

There are critics so shallow that they cannot see the quite fundamental difference between the Puritanism from which England is emerging at the present time and the Asceticism from which England was emerging in the time of Chaucer. . . . The roots are utterly distinct; even when there is in both a renunciation of the things of this world in the name of the other. . . . The older ascetic saw heaven as very bright, and this world as dark in comparison. But the later Puritan saw heaven itself as dark, in the sense of stern and rather stormy; and his genuine imagination exulted in the storm. For him the Lord was in the thunder, much more than in the still small voice; and he was thus at the opposite extreme to even the most extreme ascetic, . . . who wished the sound of lutes and viols to cease, so that the still small voice might be heard. . . . The old ascetic was looking for joy and beauty, whether we think his vision of joy and beauty impossible or merely invisible. But the true Puritan was not primarily looking for joy and beauty, but for strength and even violence.

. . . The contrast instantly appears . . . when the two creeds express themselves in externals. When once the ascetic was assured that certain things were dedicated to divine things, he wanted them to be

---

1. Attributed to Voltaire: *'Habacuc était capable de tout.'*

exceptionally brilliant and gorgeous things. He wanted the vestments of the priest to run through all the colours of the rainbow or the marbles of the shrine to mimic all the sunsets of the world. The Puritan insisted that the preacher should wear a black Geneva gown, . . . and that the chapel should be a shed or barn. . . . [Puritanism was] a howling to the gods of fear. . . . Now this note is *never* found in medieval asceticism. . . . These [medievals] . . . thought the supernatural more beautiful than the natural; not merely more naked or elemental or terrible . . . [and] the purely medieval artists always represented heavenly beings as gay and happy, and attributed sorrow only to the lost.

Chaucer, ch. 8

Asceticism, or the war with the appetites, is itself an appetite. It can never be eliminated from among the strange ambitions of Man. But it can be kept in some reasonable control; and it is indulged in much saner proportion under Catholic Authority than in Pagan or Puritan anarchy. . . . The whole of this ideal, though an essential part of Catholic idealism . . . is in some ways entirely a side issue. . . . It is only a particular deduction from Catholic ethics. . . . Any extreme of Catholic asceticism is a wise, or unwise, precaution against the evil of the Fall; it is *never* a doubt about the good of the Creation.

St. Thomas Aquinas, ch. 4

To most ordinary Roman Catholics, who are not called upon to practise special austerities, those examples [of asceticism] are valuable not only as examples of heroism, but as very vivid evidences of the reality of religious hopes. Granted that for us the divine light is valued as a daily light, brightening our daily and normal affairs, yet it would not brighten them at all if we did not believe that the light was really divine. If we only believed that religion was useful, it would be of no use. Now nothing could better prove the light divine than that some should live on it as on a food; nothing could more clearly show religion to be real than that for some people it can be a substitute for other realities.

'Roman Catholicism',
in *An Outline of Christianity*, ed. A.S. Peake (1926)

[It is suggested that] there is some abstract divine standard in [lawn tennis], to which it is everybody's duty to rise, at any sacrifice of pleasure or affection. When Christians say this of the sacrifices made for Christ, it sounds rather a hard saying. But when tennis-players say it about the sacrifices demanded by tennis, it sounds quite ordinary and casual in the confusion of current thought and expression. And nobody notices that a sort of human sacrifice is being offered to a sort of new and nameless god.

'Logic and Lawn Tennis', in *The Thing*

A martyr is a man who cares so much for something outside him, that he forgets his own personal life. . . . The martyr is noble, exactly because (however he renounces the world or execrates all humanity) he confesses this ultimate link with life; he sets his heart outside himself: he dies that something may live.

Orthodoxy, ch. 5

CONVERSION, REPENTANCE, DEATH

Conversion calls on a man to stretch his mind, as a man awakening from a sleep may stretch his arms and legs. It calls on the imagination to stretch itself, for instance, over a wider area than England, and a longer period than English history. . . . The great difficulty is whether a man can stretch his mind . . . enough to see the need for an eternal Church.

'The Last Turn', in *The Well and the Shallows*

Truth is a magnet, with the powers of attraction and repulsion. . . . It is impossible to be just to the Catholic Church. The moment men cease to pull against it they feel a tug towards it. The moment they cease to shout it down they begin to listen to it with pleasure. The moment they try to be fair to it they begin to be fond of it. But when that affection has passed a certain point it begins to take on the tragic and menacing grandeur of a great love affair.

The Catholic Church and Conversion, ch. 3

Christianity is the religion of repentance; it stands against modern fatalism and pessimistic futurism mainly in saying that a man can go back.

Letter of Feb. 1923, cited in Ward, *Gilbert Keith Chesterton*, p. 390

So far from interruptions being in their nature bad for our aesthetic feelings, an interruption is in its nature good. . . . Such a sudden check would bring all our impressions into an intense and enjoyable compass. . . . God . . . has . . . put the perfect artistic limit – death.
. . . When we see the Old Year out, we . . . die temporarily. Whenever we admit that it is Tuesday we fulfil St. Paul, and die daily.[1] I doubt if the strongest stoic that ever existed on earth could endure the idea of a Tuesday following on a Tuesday, and a Tuesday on that. . . .
The divisions of time are arranged so that we may have a start or shock at each reopening of the question. The object of a New Year is not that

1. 2 Cor. 4.11.

we should have a new year. It is that we should have a new soul . . . and
new eyes. It is that we should look out instantaneously on an impossible
earth; that we should think it very odd that grass should be green instead
of being reasonably purple; that we should think it almost unintelligible
that a lot of straight trees should grow out of the round world instead
of a lot of round world growing out of the straight trees. The object
of the cold and hard definitions of time is almost exactly the same as
those of the cold and hard definitions of theology; it is to wake people
up. Unless a particular man made New Year resolutions, he would make
no resolutions. Unless a man starts afresh about things, he will certainly
do nothing effective. Unless a man starts on the strange assumption
that he has never existed before, it is quite certain that he will never
exist afterwards. Unless a man be born again, he shall by no means
enter into the Kingdom of Heaven.[1]

'January One', in *Lunacy and Letters*

When we have satisfied men about the problem of their living, we shall
then be instantly challenged to satisfy them about the problem of their
life. Indeed, their depression will not be finally dealt with till we also
satisfy them about the problem of their death. . . . Those who fear death
most and feel most the mutability of things and find their pleasures most
poisoned by pessimism are often the most wealthy and luxurious people
in the world. They quite frequently fear death, but they not infrequently
hate life; and jump off liners or blow out their brains with revolvers.

New York American, 1 Apr. 1933

A fierce sense of the value of things lies at the heart . . . of tragedy; for if
lives were not valuable, tragedies would not be tragic. . . . It may be that
this is indeed the whole meaning of death; that heaven, knowing how we
tire of our toys, forces us to hold this life on a frail and romantic tenure.

'The Poetic Quality in Liberalism', in *The Independent Review*, Feb. 1905

It is the point of all deprivation that it sharpens the idea of value; and,
perhaps, this is, after all, the reason of the riddle of death. In a better
world, perhaps, we may permanently possess, and permanently be
astonished at possession. In some strange estate beyond the stars we
may manage at once to have and to enjoy. But in this world, through
some sickness at the root of psychology, we have to be reminded that a
thing is ours by its power of disappearance. With us the prize of life is
one great, glorious cry of the dying; it is always "morituri te salutant".[2]

1. John 3.3.
2. 'Those who are about to die salute you': the salutation of gladiators entering the
Roman arena: '*Ave Caesar, morituri te salutamus*'.

At the four corners of our human temple of happiness stand a lame man pointing to one road, and a blind man worshipping the sun, a deaf man listening for the birds, and a dead man thanking God for his creation.

'On Being Moved', in *Lunacy and Letters*

The spectacle of a God dying is much more grandiose than the spectacle of a man living for ever. The former suggests that awful changes have really entered the alchemy of the universe; the latter is only vaguely reminiscent of hygienic octogenarians and Eno's Fruit Salts.[1] . . . To talk (as some modern theosophists do) about death being nothing, the mere walking into another room, to talk like this is not only prosaic and profoundly un-Christian; it is decidedly vulgar. It is against the whole trend of the secret emotions of humanity. It is indecent, like persuading a decent peasant to go without clothes. . . . There is more real mysticism in nailing down a coffin lid than in pretending, in mere rhetoric, to throw open the doors of death.

William Blake (1920), pp. 179-180

1. A popular cure-all.

Part 8

Christian History and its Biblical Origin

THE DIFFERENCE MADE BY THE CHURCH

The Christian ideal has not been tried and found wanting. It has been found difficult; and left untried.[1]

What's Wrong with the World, Part 1, sec. 5

If the Church had not entered the world then, it seems probable that Europe would be now very much what Asia is now. . . . There would still be Pythagoreans teaching reincarnation, as there are still Hindus teaching reincarnation. There would still be Stoics making a religion out of reason and virtue, as there are still Confucians making a religion out of reason and virtue. There would still be Neo-Platonists studying transcendental truths, . . . as the Buddhists still [do]. . . . There would still be crowds of people attending the popular feasts of the gods, in pagan Europe as in pagan Asia. . . . There would still be a great deal of . . . black magic. . . . All these things . . . would have an indescribable air of being too old to die. None of these things occupying Europe in the absence of Christendom would bear the least likeness to Christendom.

The Everlasting Man, Part 2, ch. 5

Slavery was for the Church not a difficulty of doctrine, but a strain on the imagination. Aristotle and the pagan sages who had defined the servile or "useful" arts, had regarded the slave as a tool, an axe to cut wood or whatever wanted cutting. The Church did not denounce the cutting; but she felt as if she was cutting glass with a diamond. She was haunted by the memory that the diamond is so much more precious than the glass.

A Short History of England, ch. 2

---

1. John O'Connor claimed to have said something similar: *Father Brown on Chesterton* (1938), pp. 54-5. Cf. John Morley, *Critical Miscellanies* (1886), vol. II, p. 336: 'Christianity, according to a well-known saying, has been tried and failed; the religion of Christ remains to be tried.'

[In the ancient pagan world] religion was a social function. . . . What was individual was not really religion, but rather speculation. The speculator was separated from social religion. . . . What Christianity did was to combine these two things in a third thing that had never existed before; a public worship that could be believed, and a private conviction that could be shared. It took the popular superstitions very sympathetically; but it grouped them round something that could also be taken seriously. It made a creed that was more than a cult and was also a culture. . . . This change was one of the few giant strides made by man.

'On Egyptian Influence', in *Generally Speaking*

Paganism . . . is an attempt to reach the divine reality through the imagination alone; in its own field reason does not restrain it at all. It is vital to the view of all history that reason is something separate from religion even in the most rational of these [ancient] civilisations. . . . The rivers of mythology and philosophy run parallel and do not mingle till they meet in the sea of Christendom. Simple secularists still talk as if the Church had introduced a sort of schism between reason and religion. The truth is that the Church was actually the first thing that ever tried to combine reason and religion. There had never before been any such union of the priests and the philosophers.

The Everlasting Man, Part 1, ch. 5

Christianity, so far from belonging to the dark ages, was the one path across the dark ages that was not dark. It was a shining bridge connecting two shining civilisations. If anyone says that the faith arose in ignorance and savagery the answer is simple: it didn't. It arose in the Mediterranean civilisation in the full summer of the Roman Empire. The world was swarming with sceptics, and pantheism was as plain as the sun, when Constantine nailed the cross to the mast. It is perfectly true that afterwards the ship sank; but it is far more extraordinary that the ship came up again: repainted and glittering, with the cross still at the top. . . . The ark lived under the load of waters; after being buried under the débris of dynasties and clans, we arose and remembered Rome. . . . The Christian Church was the last life of the old society and was also the first life of the new.

Orthodoxy, ch. 9

It was no flock of sheep the Christian shepherd was leading, but a herd of bulls and tigers, of terrible ideals and devouring doctrines, each one of them strong enough to turn to a false religion and lay waste the world. . . . The idea of birth through a Holy Spirit, of the death of a divine being, of the forgiveness of sins, or the fulfilment of prophecies, are ideas which . . . need but a touch to turn them into something blasphemous or ferocious. . . .

This is the thrilling romance of Orthodoxy. . . . It was the equilibrium of a man behind madly rushing horses, seeming to stoop this way and to sway that, yet in every attitude having the grace of statuary and the accuracy of arithmetic. . . . She left on one hand the huge bulk of Arianism, buttressed by all the worldly powers to make Christianity too worldly. The next instant she was swerving to avoid an orientalism, which would have made it too unworldly. The orthodox Church never took the tame course or accepted the conventions; the orthodox Church was never respectable. It would have been easier to have accepted the earthly power of the Arians. It would have been easy, in the Calvinistic seventeenth century, to fall into the bottomless pit of predestination. It is easy to be a madman: it is easy to be a heretic. It is always easy to let the age have its head; the difficult thing is to keep one's own. . . . It is always simple to fall; there are an infinity of angles at which one falls, only one at which one stands.

Orthodoxy, ch. 6

The world, especially the modern world, has reached a curious condition of ritual or routine; in which we might almost say that it is wrong even when it is right. It continues to a great extent to do the sensible things. It is rapidly ceasing to have any of the sensible reasons for doing them. It is always lecturing us on the deadness of tradition; and it is living entirely on the life of tradition. It is always denouncing us for superstition; and its own principal virtues are now almost entirely superstitious. . . . All such social sanities are now the traditions of old Catholic dogmas. . . . In most modern people there is a battle between the new opinions, which they do not follow out to their end, and the old traditions, which they do not trace back to their beginning. If they followed the new notions forward, it would lead them to Bedlam. If they followed the better instincts backward, it would lead them to Rome.

'The Roots of Sanity', in *The Thing*

THE MIDDLE AGES

At the beginning of the Dark Ages the great pagan cosmopolitan society now grown Christian was as much a slave state as old South Carolina. By the fourteenth century it was almost as much a state of peasant proprietors as modern France. . . . This startling and silent transformation is perhaps the best measure of the pressure of popular life in the Middle Ages, of how fast it was making new things in its spiritual factory. . . . The conscious and active emancipators everywhere were the parish priests and the religious brotherhoods. . . . The Catholic type of Christianity was not merely an element, it was a climate; and in that climate the slave would not grow. . . . Over a great part . . . of the whole territory, the lords were abbots, magistrates elected by a mystical communism and themselves often of peasant birth. . . . The slave was long in the intermediate status of a serf. . . . At the end [of the medieval process] he had really become a small landlord. . . . The mediaevals, except when they were monks, were none of them Communists; but they were all, as it were, potential Communists. . . . Mediaevalism believed in mending its broken men; and as the idea existed in the communal life for monks, it existed in the communal land for peasants. . . . These provisions for a healthier distribution of property would by themselves show any man of imagination that a real moral effort had been made towards social justice. . . . Mediaeval men [were] busy upon a social scheme which points . . . to pity and a craving for equality. . . . The aim of the Guild charities was the same as the aim of the Common Land. It was to resist inequality. . . . Religion ran like a rich thread through the rude tapestry of these popular things while they were still merely popular; and many a trade society must have had a patron saint long before it had a royal seal.

A Short History of England, ch. 8

Our world . . . cannot understand St. Thomas [Becket], any more than St. Francis [of Assisi], without accepting very simply a flaming and even fantastic charity, by which the great Archbishop undoubtedly stands for the victims of this world, where the wheel of fortune grinds the faces of the poor.

A Short History of England, ch. 7

The mediaeval Christian insisted that God gave man a charter, . . . a gift of liberties and not of laws.

'The Chartered Libertine', in *A Miscellany of Men*

Christianity [in the Middle Ages] did *not* conceive Christian virtues as tame, timid, and respectable things. It *did* conceive of these virtues as vast, defiant, and even destructive things, scorning the yoke of this world, dwelling in the desert, and seeking their meat from God.

'Monsters and the Middle Ages', in *The Common Man*

Chivalry might be called the baptism of Feudalism. It was an attempt to bring the justice and even the logic of the Catholic creed into a military system which already existed; to turn its discipline into an initiation and its inequalities into a hierarchy. To the comparative grace of the new period belongs . . . that considerable cultus of the dignity of woman, to which the word "chivalry" is often narrowed, or perhaps exalted. This also was a revolt against one of the worst gaps in the more polished civilization of the Saracens. Moslems denied even souls to women; perhaps from the same instinct which recoiled from the sacred birth, with its inevitable glorification of the mother.

A Short History of England, ch. 6

What St. Benedict had stored St. Francis [of Assisi] scattered; . . . in the world of spiritual things what had been stored into the barns like grain was scattered over the world as seed. The servants of God who had been a besieged garrison became a marching army.

St. Francis of Assisi, ch. 6

The end of the Dark Ages was not merely the end of a sleep. . . . It was the end of a penance; or, if it be preferred, a purgation. It marked the moment when a certain spiritual expiation had been finally worked out and certain spiritual diseases had been finally expelled from the system. They had been expelled by an era of asceticism, which was the only thing that could have expelled them. Christianity had entered the world to cure the world; and she had cured it in the only way in which it could be cured. . . .

Now the historic importance of St. Francis [of Assisi] and the transition from the twelfth to the thirteenth century, lies in the fact that they marked the end of this expiation. . . . [Christianity's] counsels of perfection had always taken the form of vows of chastity and poverty and obedience. With these unworldly aims it had long ago civilised a great part of the world. The monks had taught people to plough and sow as well as to read and write; indeed they had taught the people nearly everything that the people knew. But . . . the monks were severely practical, in the sense that they were not only practical but also severe. . . . Gradually against this grey background beauty begins to appear. . . . Love returning is no longer what was once called platonic but what is still called chivalric love. The flowers and stars have recovered their first innocence. Fire and water are felt to be worthy to be the brother and sister of a saint. The purge of paganism is complete at last. . . . Neither the universe nor the earth have now any longer the old sinister significance. . . . They await a new reconciliation with man, but they are already capable of being reconciled. Man has stripped from his soul the last rag of nature-worship, and can return to nature.

St. Francis of Assisi, ch. 2

[The writer on St. Francis of Assisi] may describe this divine demagogue as being, as he probably was, the world's one quite sincere democrat. . . . He may say . . . that St. Francis anticipated all that is most liberal and sympathetic in the modern mood; the love of nature; the love of animals; the sense of social compassion; the sense of spiritual dangers of prosperity and even of property. All those things that nobody understood before Wordsworth were familiar to St. Francis. All those things that were first discovered by Tolstoy had been taken for granted by St. Francis. He could be presented, not only as a human but a humanitarian hero; indeed as the first hero of humanism. He has been described as a sort of morning star of the Renaissance. . . . The writer might describe . . . the whole of that great Franciscan inspiration that was felt in the painting of Giotto, in the poetry of Dante, in the miracle plays that made possible the modern drama.

St. Francis of Assisi, ch. 1

When modern humanitarians talk of international solidarity and the need for a United States of Europe, I do not notice that they give much praise to the Popes . . . who so nearly made it a reality.

'The Religious Aspect of Westminster Abbey', in *The Spice of Life*

What was the meaning of all that whisper of fear that ran round the West under the shadow of Islam? . . . [Many] probably believed in their hearts that Islam would conquer Christendom; that Averroes[1] was more rational than Anselm; that the Saracen culture was really, as it was superficially, a superior culture. . . . We should probably find a whole generation, the older generation, very doubtful and depressed and weary. The coming of Islam would only have been the coming of Unitarianism a thousand years before its time. To many it may have seemed quite reasonable . . . and quite likely to happen. If so, they would have been surprised at what did happen. What did happen was a roar like thunder from thousands and thousands of young men, throwing all their youth into one exultant counter-charge; the Crusades.

The Everlasting Man, Part 2, ch. 6

[St. Francis of Assisi's] idea . . . was to bring the Crusades in a double sense to their end; that is, to reach their conclusion and to achieve their purpose. Only he wished to do it by conversion and not by conquest. . . . It was . . . simply the idea that it is better to create Christians than to destroy Moslems. If Islam had been converted, the world would have been immeasurably more united and happy; for one thing, three quarters of the wars of modern history would never have taken place.

St. Francis of Assisi, ch. 8

---

1. A twelfth-century Arab-Islamic philosopher, who studied reason in the classical writers.

REFORMATION

The English Reformers were Capitalists. . . . That which was death to Catholicism was actually the birth of Capitalism. . . . The distinguishing mark of the Reformers was a profound respect for the powers that be, but an even profounder respect for the wealth that was to be; and a really unfathomable reverence for the wealth that was to be their own. Some people like that spirit, and regard it as the soundest foundation of stable government. . . . It is, broadly speaking, what is regarded as respectability by all those who have nothing else to respect. . . . Capitalism . . . set up a class to be worshipped openly and frankly because of its wealth. . . . Such wealth was the abuse of the monks and abbots; it was the use of the merchants and the squires. The avaricious abbot violated his ideals. The avaricious employer had no ideals to violate. For there never has been, properly speaking, such a thing as the ideal good of Capitalism; though there are any number of good men who are Capitalists following other ideals. The Reformation, especially in England, was above all the abandonment of the attempt to rule the world by ideals, or even by ideas. . . . The English Reformers did not really set up an opposite ideal or an alternative set of ideas. . . . They set up certain very formidable things called facts. They set out . . . to rule . . . by facts; by the fact that somebody called Russell had two hundred times more money than any of his neighbours; by the fact that somebody called Cecil[1] had obtained the power of having any of his neighbours hanged. Facts are at least solid while they last; but the fatal thing about them is that they do not last. It is only the ideas that last.

'The Revolt Against Ideas', in The Thing

It was an abominable abuse that the corruption of the monasteries sometimes permitted a rich noble to play the patron and even play at being the Abbot, or draw on the revenues supposed to belong to a brotherhood of poverty and charity. But all that the Reformation did was to allow the same rich noble to take over *all* the revenue, to seize the whole house and turn it into a palace or a pig-sty, and utterly stamp out the last legend of the poor brotherhood.

'Why I am a Catholic', in The Thing

It was only the Roman Catholic Church that saved the Protestant truths. It may be right to rest on the Bible; but there would be no Bible if the Gnostics had proved that the Old Testament was written by the devil,

---

1. The Russells and the Cecils were aristocratic families whose fortunes were promoted during the Reformation era.

or had littered the world with Apocryphal Gospels. It may be right to say that Jesus alone saves from sin; but nobody would be saying it if a Pelagian movement[1] had altered the whole notion of sin. Even the very selection of dogmas which the reformers decided to preserve had only been preserved for them by the authority which they denied.

'Roman Catholicism', in *An Outline of Christianity* (1926), ed. A.S. Peake

The whole social substance of Christianity changed with the divorce of Henry VIII. . . . The externals remained for a time and some of them remain still. Some divorced persons, who can be married quite legally by a registrar, go on complaining bitterly that they cannot be married by a priest. They regard a church as a peculiarly suitable place in which to make and break the same vow at the same moment. . . . The psychological substance of the whole thing has altered; the marble has turned to ice; and the ice has melted with most amazing rapidity. The Church was right to refuse even the exception. The world has admitted the exception; and the exception has become the rule.

'The Surrender Upon Sex', in *The Well and the Shallows*

All our [cultural] expansion since [the Reformation] . . . has not been an expansion, but the closing in of a prison, so that less and less beautiful and humane things have been permitted. The Puritans destroyed images; the Rationalists forbade fairy tales.

What's Wrong with the World, Part 4, sec. 6

With the religious schism, . . . a deeper and more inhuman division appeared. . . . There entered with the religious wars the idea which modern science applies to racial wars; the idea of *natural* wars, not arising from a special quarrel but from the nature of the people quarrelling. The shadow of racial fatalism first fell across our path, and far away in distance and darkness something moved that men had almost forgotten. . . .

The august accident of that Spanish [Armada] defeat may perhaps have coincided only too well with [the Puritan] concentration on the non-Christian parts of Scripture. It may have satisfied a certain Old Testament sentiment of the election of the English being announced in the stormy oracles of air and sea, which was easily turned into that heresy of a tribal pride that took even heavier hold upon the Germans. It is by such things that a civilized state may fall from being a Christian nation to being a Chosen People.

A Short History of England, chapters 12, 13

---

1. Pelagianism was a heresy which thrived in the late fourth and early fifth centuries: it tended to make man more responsible for his salvation by marginalizing the doctrine of Original Sin.

THE WORLD AND THE CHURCH

It was difficult for many not to think that one might be as good or bad as the other when they saw the Protestant and the Catholic go up and down on the see-saw of the Thirty Years War. Many were disposed to suspect that it was six to one and half-a-dozen to the other. This addition involved an immense subtraction; and the two religions came to much less than one. Many began to think that, as they could not both be true, they might both be false. When that thought had crossed the mind the reign of the rationalist had begun.

'Anti-Religious Thought in the Eighteenth Century', in *The Spice of Life*

Now the eighteenth century was primarily the release (as its leaders held) of reason and nature from the control of the Church. But when the Church was once really weakened, it was the release of many other things. It was not the release of reason only, but of a more ancient unreason. It was not the release of the natural, but also of the supernatural, and also, alas! of the unnatural. The heathen mystics hidden for two thousand years came out of their caverns – and Freemasonry was founded. It was entirely innocent in the manner of its foundation; but so were all the other resurrections of this ancestral occultism.

William Blake (1920), p. 123

Christendom has had a series of revolutions and in each one of them Christianity has died. Christianity has died many times and risen again; for it had a god who knew the way out of the grave. . . . Europe has been turned upside down over and over again; and . . . at the end of each of these revolutions the same religion has again been found on top. The Faith is always converting the age, not as an old religion but as a new religion.

The Everlasting Man, Part 2, ch. 6

Conversion [to Catholicism] consists very largely, on its intellectual side, in the discovery that all that picture of equal creeds inside an indifferent cosmos is quite false. It is not a question of comparing the merits and defects of the Quaker meeting-house set beside the Catholic cathedral. It is the Quaker meeting-house that is inside the Catholic cathedral; it is the Catholic cathedral that covers everything like the vault of the Crystal Palace. . . . Quakerism is but a temporary form of Quietism which has arisen technically outside the Church as the Quietism of Fénelon[1] appeared technically inside the Church. . . . The principle of

---

1. François Fénelon, Archbishop of Cambrai, was implicated in Quietism in the later seventeenth century, Quietism emphasizing the ineffectuality of man's spiritual efforts.

life in all these variations of Protestantism . . . consists of what remained in them of Catholic Christendom; and to Catholic Christendom they have always returned to be recharged with vitality. . . . The return of Catholic ideas to the separated parts of Christendom was often indeed indirect. But though the influence came through many centres, it always came from one. It came through the Romantic Movement, a glimpse of the mere picturesqueness of medievalism; but it is something more than an accident that Romances, like Romance languages, are named after Rome. Or it came through the instinctive reaction of old-fashioned people like [Dr] Johnson or [Sir Walter] Scott or [William] Cobbett, wishing to save old elements that had originally been Catholic against a progress that was merely Capitalist. But it led them to denounce that Capitalist progress and become, like Cobbett, practical foes of Protestantism without being practising followers of Catholicism. Or it came from the Pre-Raphaelites or the opening of continental art and culture by Matthew Arnold and [William] Morris and [John] Ruskin and the rest. But examine the actual make-up of the mind of a good Quaker or Congregational minister at this moment, and compare it with the mind of such a dissenter in the Little Bethel before such culture came. And you will see how much of his health and happiness he owes to Ruskin and what Ruskin owed to Giotto; to Morris and what Morris owed to Chaucer; to fine scholars of his own school like Philip Wicksteed, and what they owe to Dante and St. Thomas [Aquinas]. Such a man will still sometimes talk of the Middle Ages as the Dark Ages. But the Dark Ages have improved the wallpaper on his wall and the dress on his wife and all the whole dingy and vulgar life which he lived in the days of Stiggins and Brother Tadger.[1]

The Catholic Church and Conversion, ch. 4

Every man of us to-day is three men. There is in every modern European three powers so distinct as to be almost personal, the trinity of our earthly destiny. The three may be rudely summarised thus. First and nearest to us is the Christian, the man of the historic church, of the creed that must have coloured our minds incurably whether we regard it . . . as the crown and combination of the other two, or whether we regard it as an accidental superstition which has remained for two thousand years. . . . Behind him comes the Roman, the citizen of that great cosmopolitan realm of reason and order in the level and equality of which Christianity rose. He is the stoic who is so much sterner than the anchorites. He is the republican who is so much prouder than kings. He it is that makes straight roads and clear laws, and for whom good

1. Dissenting characters in Charles Dickens's *Pickwick Papers.*

sense is good enough. And the third man – he is harder to speak of. He has no name, and all true tales of him are blotted out; yet he walks behind us in every forest path and wakes within us when the wind wakes at night. He is the origins – he is the man in the forest. . . . The chief claim of Christianity is . . . that it revived the pre-Roman madness, yet brought it into the Roman order. The gods had really died long before Christ was born. What had taken their place was simply the god of government – Divus Caesar. . . . It is said that when Christ was born the cry went through the world that Pan was dead. The truth is that when Christ was born Pan for the first time began to stir in his grave. The pagan gods had become pure fables when Christianity gave them a new lease of life as devils. . . . Christianity called to a kind of clamorous resurrection all the old supernatural instincts of the forests and the hill. But it put upon this occult chaos the Roman idea of balance and sanity. Thus, marriage was a sacrament, but mere sex was not a sacrament as it was in many of the frenzies of the forest. Thus wine was a sacrament with Christ; but drunkenness was not a sacrament as with Dionysus. In short, Christianity (merely historically seen) can best be understood as an attempt to combine the reason of the market-place with the mysticism of the forest. It was an attempt to accept all the superstitions that are necessary to man and to be philosophic at the end of them. Pagan Rome has sought to bring order or reason among men. Christian Rome sought to bring order and reason among gods.

William Blake (1920), pp. 106-8

THE BIBLE

[Catholicism] does not, in the conventional phrase, believe what the Bible says, for the simple reason that the Bible does not say anything. You cannot put a book in the witness-box and ask it what it really means. The Fundamentalist controversy itself destroys Fundamentalism. The Bible by itself cannot be a basis of agreement when it is a cause of disagreement; it cannot be the common ground of Christians when some take it allegorically and some literally. The Catholic refers it to something that can say something; to [a] living, consistent and continuous mind.

'Why I am a Catholic', in *Twelve Modern Apostles and Their Creeds* (1926)

Most Fundamentalists are not Fundamentalists. For whatever we think of the thing now called Fundamentalism, it is not fundamental. It is not particularly fundamental to throw a big Bible at people's heads (or

rather, a particular translation of the Bible, with a lot of books left out
as Apocrypha) any more than to throw the Encyclopaedia Britannica
or the Institutes of Calvin. Even if it be a truth, it is not a first principle.

'William Penn and His Royalist Friends',
in *G.K. Chesterton: The Apostle and the Wild Ducks*

Christians are not constrained, and least of all Christians of my own
confession, to treat Genesis with the heavy verbalism of the Puritan –
the Hebraiser who knows no Hebrew.

'If Don John of Austria had Married Mary Queen of Scots',
in *The Common Man*

Mr. Bernard Shaw has written a very Protestant tract, on the paramount
duty of reading the Bible, . . . of course in the light of Private Judgment.
For Private Judgment is never wrong, just as Private Property is never
right.[1] . . . Like every other sectarian "Scripture reader," Mr. Shaw re-
reads the Bible and finds something different from what the last sectarian
found.

'The Scripture Reader', in *The Well and the Shallows*

Protestant Christianity believes that there is a Divine record in a book;
. . . that everyone who gets hold of it can save his soul by it, whether he
finds it in a library or picks it off a dustcart. Catholic Christianity believes
that there is a Divine . . . league . . . called the Church; that any man
who joins it can save his soul by it without ever opening any of the old
books of the Church at all. The Bible is only one of the institutions of
Catholicism, like its rites or its priesthood; it thinks the Bible only
efficient when taken as part of the Church.

Letter to *Daily News*, 1902, cited Ward, *Gilbert Keith Chesterton*, p. 249

[Fr Brown is explaining the battlefield death of General St Clare (an
evangelical Puritan) amidst his crimes of treachery and murder.] 'St Clare
. . . was a man who read his Bible. That was what was the matter with
him. When will people understand that it is useless for a man to read his
Bible unless he also reads everybody else's Bible? A printer reads a Bible
for misprints. A Mormon reads his Bible and finds polygamy; a Christian
Scientist reads his and finds we have no arms and legs. St Clare was an
old Anglo-Indian Protestant soldier. Now, just think what that might mean;
and for Heaven's sake, don't cant about it. It might mean a man physically
formidable living under a tropic sun in an Oriental society, and soaking
himself without sense or guidance in an Oriental book. Of course, he
read the Old Testament rather than the New. Of course, he found in the
Old Testament anything that he wanted – lust, tyranny, treason. . . .

1. Shaw campaigned against private property.

In each of the hot and secret countries to which that man went he kept a harem, he tortured witnesses, he amassed shameful gold; but certainly he would have said with steady eyes that he did it to the glory of the Lord. My own theology is sufficiently expressed by asking which Lord?'

'The Sign of the Broken Sword', in *The Innocence of Father Brown*

The tradition of Israel . . . had one of the colossal corner-stones of the world: the Book of Job . . . [which] avowedly only answers mystery with mystery. Job is comforted with riddles; but he is comforted. . . . When he who doubts can only say, 'I do not understand,' it is true that he who knows can only reply,. . . . 'You do not understand.' And under that rebuke there is always a sudden hope in the heart; and the sense of something that would be worth understanding.

The Everlasting Man, Part 1, ch. 4

Those . . . who complain of the atrocities and treacheries of the judges and prophets of Israel have really got a notion in their head that has nothing to do with the subject. They are too Christian. They are reading back into the pre-Christian scriptures a purely Christian idea – the idea of saints, the idea that the chief instruments of God are very particularly good men. . . . They fancy that the patriarchs must be meant for patterns. . . . That is not the atmosphere of the Old Testament at all. The heroes of the Old Testament are not the sons of God, but the slaves of God. . . . The central idea of the great part of the Old Testament may be called the idea of the loneliness of God. God is not only the chief character of the Old Testament; God is properly the only character in the Old Testament. . . . All the patriarchs and prophets are merely His tools or weapons. . . . The book is so intent upon asserting the personality of God that it almost asserts the impersonality of man.

'The Book of Job', in *G.K.C. As M.C.*

The whole point of the spiritual revolt, dealt with in the Bible, is that it is always a revolt against good conditions. . . . The point of the story of Satan is not that he revolted against being in hell, but that he revolted against being in heaven. The point about Adam is not that he was discontented with the conditions of the earth, but that he was discontented with the conditions of the earthly paradise. That is a totally different idea . . . than the obvious reasonableness of revolt against gross tyranny. And until it is understood once more, people will go on being discontented even with contentment. The rich will be even more discontented than the poor. They will explain that theirs is a divine discontent; and divine discontent is the very devil.

New York American, 15 Dec. 1932

[Men] gained their morality by guarding their religion. They fought for the shrine, and found they had become courageous. . . . They purified themselves for the altar, and found that they were clean. . . . The Ten Commandments . . . were merely military commands . . . issued to protect a certain ark across a certain desert. Anarchy was evil because it endangered the sanctity. And only when they made a holy day for God did they find they had made a holiday for men.

Orthodoxy, ch. 5

The grinding power of the plain words of the Gospel story is like the power of mill-stones; and those who can read them simply enough will feel as if rocks had been rolled upon them.

The Everlasting Man, Part 2, ch. 3

Christianity, whatever else it is, is an explosion. . . . Unless it is sensational there is simply no sense in it. Unless the Gospel sounds like a gun going off it has not been uttered at all.

'The Theology of Christmas Presents', in *Contemporary Review*, Jan. 1910

Instead of looking at books and pictures about the New Testament I looked at the New Testament. There I found an account, not in the least of a person with his hair parted in the middle or his hands clasped in appeal, but of an extraordinary being with lips of thunder and acts of lurid decision, flinging down tables, casting out devils, passing with the wild secrecy of the wind from mountain isolation to a sort of dreadful demagogy; a being who often acted like an angry god – and always like a god.

Orthodoxy, ch. 9

A man reading the New Testament frankly and freshly would *not* get the impression of what is now meant by a human Christ. The merely human Christ is a made-up figure, a piece of artificial selection, like the merely evolutionary man. Moreover there have been too many of these human Christs found in the same story. . . . The first rational explanation of his life was that he never lived. And this in turn gave an opportunity for three or four different explanations; as that he was a sun-myth or a corn-myth. . . . In my youth it was the fashion to say that he was merely an ethical teacher in the manner of the Essenes, who had apparently nothing very much to say that Hillel[1] or a hundred other Jews might not have said. . . . Then somebody said he was a madman with a Messianic delusion. Then others said he was indeed an original teacher because he cared about nothing but Socialism; or (as others said) about nothing but Pacifism. . . .

1. The Essenes were a Jewish sect; Hillel was a teacher in the Holy Land at the time of Christ

There must surely have been something not only mysterious but many-sided about Christ if so many smaller Christs can be carved out of him. If the Christian Scientist is satisfied with him as a spiritual healer and the Christian Socialist is satisfied with him as a social reformer, so satisfied that they do not even expect him to be anything else, it looks as if he really covered rather more ground than they could be expected to expect. And it does seem to suggest that there might be more than they fancy in these other mysterious attributes of casting out devils or prophesying doom.

The Everlasting Man, Part 2, ch. 2

The freethinker frequently says that Jesus of Nazareth was a man of his time, . . . and that we cannot accept his ethics as final for humanity. . . . But the Zealots and the Legionaries did not turn the other cheek any more than we do. . . . The Jewish traders and Roman tax-gatherers took thought for the morrow as much as we. . . . We cannot pretend to be abandoning the morality of the past for one more suited to the present. It is certainly not the morality of another age, but it might be of another world. . . .

These ideals are impossible in themselves. Exactly what we cannot say is that they are impossible for us. They are rather notably marked by a mysticism which, if it be a sort of madness, would always have struck the same sort of people as mad. Take, for instance, the case of marriage. . . . It might rationally be expected that a man in the time of Tiberius would have advanced a view conditioned by the time of Tiberius; but he did not. What he advanced was something quite different; something very difficult; but something no more difficult now than it was then. . . . Jews and Romans and Greeks did not believe, and did not even understand enough to disbelieve, the mystical idea that the man and the woman had become one sacramental substance. We may think it an incredible or impossible ideal; but we cannot think it any more incredible or impossible than they would have thought it. In other words, whatever else is true, it is not true that the controversy has been altered by time. . . . It is emphatically not true that the ideas of Jesus of Nazareth were suitable to his time, but are no longer suitable to our time. Exactly how suitable they were to his time is perhaps suggested in the end of his story. . . . It is extraordinary how very little there is in the recorded words of Christ that ties him at all to his own time. . . . He never used a phrase that made his philosophy depend even upon the very existence of the social order in which he lived. He spoke as one conscious that everything was ephemeral. . . . 'Heaven and earth shall pass away; but my words shall not pass away.'[1]

The Everlasting Man, Part 2, ch. 2

1. Mat. 24.35.

We have all heard people say . . . that the Jesus of the New Testament is indeed a most merciful and humane lover of humanity, but that the Church has hidden this human character in repellent dogmas . . . till it has taken on an inhuman character. . . . The truth is that it is the image of Christ in the churches that is almost entirely mild and merciful. It is the image of Christ in the Gospels that is a good many other things as well. . . . There is something insupportable . . . in the idea of turning the corner of a street . . . to meet the petrifying petrifaction of *that* figure as it turned upon a generation of vipers, or that face as it looked at the face of a hypocrite. . . . A man simply taking the words of the [New Testament] story as they stand would form . . . an impression full of mystery and possibly of inconsistency. . . . It is full of sudden gestures . . . of enigmatic silences; of ironical replies. The outbreaks of wrath, like storms above our atmosphere, do not seem to break out exactly where we should expect them, but to follow some higher weather-chart of their own. . . .

There are a great many things about it which nobody would have invented, . . . things which . . . have remained rather as puzzles. . . . It is anything but what these people talk of as a simple Gospel. Relatively speaking, it is the Gospel that has the mysticism and the Church that has the rationalism. . . . It is the Gospel that is the riddle and the Church that is the answer. . . .

The morality of most moralists, ancient and modern, has been one solid and polished cataract of platitudes flowing for ever and ever. That would certainly not be the impression of the imaginary independent outsider studying the New Testament. . . . He would find a number of strange claims; . . . a number of very startling pieces of advice; a number of stunning rebukes; a number of strangely beautiful stories. He would see some very gigantesque figures of speech about the impossibility of threading a needle with a camel or the possibility of throwing a mountain into the sea. He would see a number of very daring simplifications of the difficulties of life; like the advice to shine upon everybody indifferently as does the sunshine or not to worry about the future any more than the birds. He would find on the other hand some passages of almost impenetrable darkness, . . . such as the moral of the parable of the Unjust Steward. . . . He would not find the ordinary platitudes in favour of peace. He would find several paradoxes in favour of peace. He would find several ideals of non-resistance, which taken as they stand would be rather too pacific for any pacifist. . . .

The blessing upon the meek would seem to be a very violent statement; in the sense of doing violence to reason and probability. . . . Something of the same thing may be said about the incident of Martha and Mary. . . . If in Mary the mystic and child of love Christ was guarding the seed of something more subtle, who was likely to understand it at the time?. . . . It is so in another way with that magnificent menace about bringing into the world a sword to sunder and divide. Nobody could have guessed then either how it could be fulfilled or how it could be justified. . . . The point here is that if we *could* read the Gospel reports as things as new as newspaper reports, they would puzzle us and perhaps terrify us much *more* than the same things as developed by historical Christianity.

The Everlasting Man, Part 2, ch. 2

If I say 'Suppose the Divine did really walk and talk upon the earth, what should we be likely to think of it?' . . . I think we should see in such a being exactly the perplexities that we see in the central figure of the Gospels: I think he would seem to us extreme and violent; because he would see some further development in virtue which would be for us untried. I think he would seem to us to contradict himself; because, looking down on life like a map, he would see a connection between things which to us are disconnected. I think, however, that he would always ring true to our own sense of right, but ring (so to speak) too loud and too clear. He would be too good but never too bad for us: 'Be ye perfect.' I think there would be, in the nature of things, some tragic collision between him and the humanity he had created, culminating in something that would be at once a crime and an expiation. I think he would be blamed as a hard prophet for dragging down the haughty, and blamed also as a weak sentimentalist for loving the things that cling in corners, children or beggars. I think, in short, that he would give us a sensation that he was turning all our standards upside down, and yet also a sensation that he had undeniably put them the right way up.

Hibbert Journal, July 1909

The life of Jesus went as swift and straight as a thunderbolt. It was above all things dramatic; it did above all things consist in doing something that had to be done. . . . It is a journey with a goal and an object, like Jason going to find the Golden Fleece. . . . The gold that he was seeking was death. The primary thing that he was going to do was to die. . . . We are meant to feel that Death was the bride of Christ as Poverty was the bride of St. Francis. We are meant to feel that his life was in that sense a sort of love-affair with death, a romance of the pursuit of the ultimate sacrifice. From the moment when the star goes up like a birthday rocket to the moment when the sun is extinguished like a funeral torch, the whole story moves on wings with the speed and direction of a drama, ending in an act beyond words. . . .

As kings and philosophers and the popular element had been symbolically present at his birth, so they were more practically concerned in his death; and with that we come face to face with the essential fact to be realised. All the great groups that stood about the Cross represent in one way or another the great historical truth of the time; that the world could not save itself. Man could do no more. Rome and Jerusalem and Athens and everything else were going down like a sea turned into a slow cataract. . . . In this story of Good Friday it is the best things in the world that are at their worst. . . . In the lightning flash of this incident, we see great Rome . . . going down. . . . Scepticism has eaten away even the confident sanity of the conquerors of the world. He who is enthroned to say what is justice can only ask, 'What is truth?' . . . There too were the priests of that pure and original truth . . . and even that could not save the world. . . . The Jewish priests had guarded it jealously in the good and the bad sense. They had kept it as a gigantic secret. . . . They were proud that they alone could look upon the blinding sun of a single deity; and they did not know that they had themselves gone blind. . . . The populace . . . showed also the weaknesses that were dissolving the world. . . . There was present in this ancient population an evil . . . the soul of the hive. . . . The cry of this spirit also was heard in that hour, 'It is well that one man die for the people.' . . . The mob went along with the Sadducees and the Pharisees, the philosophers and the moralists. It went along with the imperial magistrates and the sacred priests, the scribes and the soldiers, that the one universal human spirit might suffer a universal condemnation; that there might be one deep, unanimous chorus of approval and harmony when Man was rejected of men. . . .

And if there be any sound that can produce a silence, we may surely be silent about the end and the extremity; when a cry was driven out of that darkness in words . . . which man shall never understand in all the eternity they have purchased for him; and for one annihilating instant an abyss that is not for our thoughts had opened even in the unity of the absolute; and God had been forsaken of God.

They took the body down from the cross and one of the few rich men among the first Christians obtained permission to bury it in a rock tomb. . . . In that second cavern the whole of that great and glorious humanity which we call antiquity . . . was buried . . . On the third day the friends of Christ coming at daybreak to the place found the grave empty and the stone rolled away. . . . But even they hardly realised that the world had died in the night. What they were looking at was the first day of a new creation, with a new heaven and a new earth; and in a semblance of the gardener God walked again in the garden, in the cool not of the evening but the dawn.

The Everlasting Man, Part 2, ch. 3

Part 9

Christian Life

TRADITION

Great tales are told of dead men gone
   And all men live by tales
And glory be to the endless tale
   Whose old news never fails.
From 'The Ballad of King Arthur', in *The Queen of Seven Swords*

All the men in history who have really done anything with the future have had their eyes fixed upon the past. . . . So the modern Catholic movement has looked back to patristic times. . . . For some strange reason man must always thus plant his fruit trees in a graveyard. Man can only find life among the dead.

What's Wrong with the World, Part 1, sec. 4

I have never been able to understand where people got the idea that democracy was in some way opposed to tradition. It is obvious that tradition is only democracy extended through time. It is trusting to a consensus of common human voices rather than to some isolated or arbitrary record. . . . Tradition means giving votes to the most obscure of all classes, our ancestors. It is the democracy of the dead.

Orthodoxy, ch. 4

A thing can be a superstition and still be true. Ten thousand people may recite a thing as a lie, and it may still be a truth, in spite of their saying it. Thus Liberalism is true; but many Liberals are mere myths. Christianity can be believed; but some Christians are quite incredible. A hypocrite can hand on truth. . . . The fashionable French priests of the later eighteenth century handed on the tradition of Catholicism, though there was hardly one of them who was not an atheist. . . . When the Catholic revival came, it was glad the French clergy had kept the tradition of St. Louis.

'Tommy and the Traditions', in *Lunacy and Letters*

CULTURE

Art could not exist apart from, still less in opposition to, life; especially
the life of the soul, which is salvation.

'Milton and Merry England', in *Fancies Versus Fads*

There are . . . certain real advantages in pictorial symbols, and one of them is
that everything that is pictorial suggests, without naming and defining. There
is a road from the eye to the heart that does not go through the intellect.

'A Defence of Heraldry', in *The Defendant*

The artist is not so much to copy the works of God as to copy the
work of God, in the sense of the working of God; or the way in which
God works. . . . It is a principle which liberates the artist from the
trivial tyranny of mere mimicry. . . . It is consonant with that original
and heroic doctrine of Christianity, which distinguishes the son from
the slave, and salutes in his free will the highest crest and signal of his
divine origin. God created . . . a creative creature.

. . . Mr. [Eric] Gill[1] says, "Look inside you, for the wonderful plastic
powers that God has given you." [John] Ruskin said, "Look outside
you, for the wonderful sea and birds that God has made." But is it so
absolutely certain that the sea and birds are outside you? Are not the
sea and birds you really look at, when you recall them artistically, things
already soaked in your own mystical nature, reshaped and simplified by
your own instinct for symbol and design; so that being true to that
truth is not merely photographic, but something which quacks call
psychological, and sensible men call spiritual?

'Eric Gill and No Nonsense', in *A Handful of Authors*

The supreme and most practical value of poetry is this, that in poetry,
as in music, a note is struck which expresses beyond the power of
rational statement a condition of mind, and all actions arise from a
condition of mind.

Robert Browning (1903), p. 185

Every great literature has always been allegorical – allegorical of some
view of the whole universe. The *Iliad* is only great because all life is a
battle, . . . the Book of Job because all life is a riddle.

'A Defence of Nonsense', in *The Defendant*

Progress is superiority to oneself, and it is stopped dead by superiority
to others. . . . The more we attempt to analyse that strange element of
wonder, which is the soul of all the arts, the more we shall see that it

1. A Roman Catholic sculptor and engraver, who wrote on aesthetics and knew
Chesterton.

must depend on some subordination of the self to a glory existing beyond it, and even in spite of it. Man always feels as a creature when he acts as a creator. When he carves a cathedral, it is to make a monster that can swallow him. But the Nietzschean nightmare of swallowing the world is only a sort of yawning.

Irish Impressions (1919), p. 233

The baby has known the dragon intimately ever since he had an imagination. What the fairy tale provides for him is a St. George to kill the dragon. Exactly what the fairy tale does is this: it accustoms him by a series of clear pictures to the idea that these limitless terrors have a limit, that these shapeless enemies have enemies, that these infinite enemies of man have enemies in the knights of God, that there is something in the universe more mystical than darkness, and stronger than strong fear.

'The Red Angel', in *Tremendous Trifles*

Religion . . . must answer that deep and mysterious human demand for something as distinct from the demand for everything, even if the nature of that demand be too deep to be easily defined in logic. It will never cease to be described in poetry. . . . Even when you have only natural religion, you will still have supernatural poetry. And it will be poetic because it is particular, not because it is general. . . . Now if this particularism always stubbornly recurs even in poetry, how can it be left out of philosophy? What is the *meaning* of this incurable itch to give to airy nothing, or still more airy everything, a local habitation and a name? Why is it always something at once odd and objective, a precious fruit or a flying cup or a buried key, that symbolizes the mystery of the world? . . . *Why* are all mysteries concerned with the notion of finding a particular thing in a particular place?

New Witness, 15 July 1921

Man has always had the instinct that to isolate a thing was to identify it. . . . For all human imaginative and artistic purposes nothing worse could be said of a work of beauty than that it is infinite; for to be infinite is to be shapeless, and to be shapeless is to be something more than mis-shapen. No man really wishes a thing which he believes to be divine to be in this earthly sense infinite. . . . This is surely the reason that men have pursued towards the idea of holiness, the course that they have pursued; that they have marked it out in particular spaces, limited it to particular days, worshipped an ivory statue, worshipped a lump of stone. They have desired to give to it the . . . dignity of definition, they have desired to save it from the degradation of infinity. . . . No man wishes the thing he loves to grow, for he does not wish it to alter.

'The Philosophy of Islands', in *The Spice of Life*

A man who is only a Medievalist is very much broadened by becoming a Catholic. . . . I am a much more . . . moderate Medievalist than I was when I was only a Medievalist. For instance, I felt it necessary to be perpetually pitting Gothic architecture against Greek architecture, because it was necessary to back up Christians against pagans. But now I am in no such fuss and I know what Coventry Patmore[1] meant when he said calmly that it would have been quite as Catholic to decorate his mantelpiece with the Venus of Milo as with the Virgin.

The Catholic Church and Conversion, ch. 3

It is perfectly natural that the boy should find the church a bore. But why are we bound to treat what is natural as something actually superior to what is supernatural; as something which is . . . super-supernatural?

'Shocking the Modernists', in *The Well and the Shallows*

[Hardship led the medieval community to see that ugliness and deformity play their part in worshipping God.] The sun . . . gives life to all those earthly things that are full of ugliness and energy. . . . The ugly animals praise God as much as the beautiful. . . . Under the new inspiration they planned a gorgeous cathedral in the Gothic manner, with all the animals of the earth crawling over it, and all the possible ugly things making up one common beauty, because they all appealed to God. . . . This was Gothic, this was romantic, this was Christian art; this was the whole advance of Shakespeare upon Sophocles.

'Introductory: On Gargoyles', in *Alarms and Discursions*

A great deal has been said by Protestants, naturally enough, and not a little even by Catholics, about the danger of displaying before the world a pomp and triumph that may easily be called worldly. . . . Art . . . can . . . express actualities that are at once too large and too elusive to be expressed in words. St. Mark's Cathedral at Venice . . . does look like a thing coloured with the sunrise and the sunset, in touch with the very ends of the earth; open like a harbour and full of popular poetry like a fairy-palace. That is, it does express the first essential fact that Catholicism is not a narrow thing; that it knows more than the world knows about the potentialities and creative possibilities of the world, and that it will outlast all the worldly and temporary expressions of the same culture.

'The Church and Agoraphobia', in *The Well and the Shallows*

The cathedrals bear witness not to ambitions but to ideals; and to ideals that are still alive. They are more than alive, indeed they are immortal because they are ideals that no man has ever been able either to frustrate or to fulfil. . . .

1. A Victorian Catholic poet.

A Christian cathedral was more than an aspiration, it was a proclamation. It was not addressed only to the ultimate reality above us all; it was also addressed, in a very definite and a very detailed way, to us also; that is, to the ordinary, emotional and exasperated race of men. The spired minster was not merely meant to strike the stars like an arrow; it was also meant to shake the earth like an explosion.

If anyone wishes to know why the Gothic architecture was among all architectures unprecedentedly alive, luxuriant, exciting, complicated and comic, the answer is in one word; because it was didactic. It had to be interesting as a schoolmaster has to be interesting. It had to be exciting as a demagogue has to be exciting. All architectures, presumably, must have taught; but this was the one that talked.

'The Riddle of Restoration', in *Lunacy and Letters*

We joke about death-beds, but not at death-beds. We play the fool on the subject of the Church; we do not play the fool in the church. This is because such special times are dedicated by human instinct to the brief but direct consideration of the fact that life is serious. Life is serious all the time; but living cannot be serious all the time. That is the whole human use and meaning of a church: that we enter a small building in order to see for the first time the universe outside. A church acts precisely as a camera obscura. It tightens up our varied experiences and makes them our pictures. By making life small it makes it serious. All men tend to take seriously the low arches and the little lamps. All men tend to take frivolously, to take recklessly, to take with entire levity, the terrible universe outside, the infinite heavens and the stars. The physical universe is at once shapeless and slippery; it eludes our grasp; it is all over the place; it is everywhere and nowhere. Nature is too large to be taken seriously.

'A Charge of Irreverence', in *Lunacy and Letters*

What is it . . . which gives us a vague feeling of discontent in listening to the individual who is commonly called the popular preacher? He is logical, eloquent, scientific, convincing, no one cares what. The essential and damning point is that he is not – in the true and forcible meaning of the phrase – he is not in church. A church represents a certain feeling which is an integral and perfectly natural part of an ordinary man – the feeling of sanctity. We do not care in the least in comparison which rites or what dogmas the Church professes; we do care very much that it should be a Church. The instant it is turned into a moral lecture room; that instant we desert it and walk into the nearest Roman Catholic or Salvation Army chapel. A church is nothing if it is not a sanctity.

'The Meaning of the Theatre', in *Lunacy and Letters*

The ruder savages . . . are poets. . . . All that they say about their totems, their taboos, their dances, and services to the dead must be understood with a certain poetic sympathy, as meant to be weird, glorious, shocking, or even impossible. They are the abrupt expressions of unique spiritual experiences, quiet and queerly coloured moods; dreams and glimpses that do really lie on the border-line between this existence and some other. . . . The idolater adoring the stone, the sage choosing his star, the patriot dying for a boundary, all do unmistakably mean something – something far down in the abysses of the universe and the soul. Do they mean that everything is sacred? Or do they perhaps mean that *something* is sacred – something they have not found?

'Something', in *G.K. Chesterton: The Apostle and the Wild Ducks*

A mystical materialism marked Christianity from its birth; the very soul of it was a body. Among the stoical philosophies and oriental negations that were its first foes it fought fiercely . . . for a supernatural freedom to cure concrete maladies by concrete substances. Hence the scattering of relics was everywhere like the scattering of seed. All who took their mission from the divine tragedy bore tangible fragments which became the germs of churches and cities. St. Joseph carried the cup which held the wine of the Last Supper and the blood of the Crucifixion to that shrine in Avalon which we now call Glastonbury; and it became the heart of a whole universe of legends and romances, not only for Britain but for Europe.

A Short History of England, ch. 3

In the last resort all men talk by signs.

'An Essay on Two Cities', in *All Things Considered*

I once heard in a railway-train a farmer's family of the Puritan sort discussing with a Nonconformist minister the action of a boy, at the front in the Great War, who had occupied himself in hospital with carving a wooden cross and sent it home to his family. His family was pained but apologetic. Their remarks had a continual chorus of, 'He didn't mean anything by it.' This extraordinary state of mind intrigued me so much that I listened to the rest of the conversation; at intervals of which the minister repeated firmly that we didn't want that sort of thing; what we wanted was a living Christ. And it never seemed to occur to this reverend gentleman that he was at that moment at war with every living as well as every Christian thing; with the creative instinct, with the desire for form, with the love of family, with the impulse to send signals and messages, with humour, with pathos, with the virility of martyrdom and the vividness of exile. It was in truth the carver of the cross who was bearing witness to a living Christ and the partisan of a living Christ who was repeating a dead form.

Robert Louis Stevenson, ch. 10

There is one element always to be remarked in the true mystic [who is an artist], however disputed his symbolism, and that is its brightness of colour and clearness of shape. I mean that we may be doubtful about the significance of a triangle or the precise lesson conveyed by a crimson cow. But in the work of a real mystic the triangle is a hard mathematical triangle not to be mistaken for a cone or a polygon. The cow is in colour a rich incurable crimson, and in shape unquestionably a cow, not to be mistaken for any of its evolutionary relatives, such as the buffalo or the bison. This can be seen very clearly, for instance, in the Christian art of illumination as practised at its best in the thirteenth and fourteenth centuries. The Christian decorators, being true mystics, were chiefly concerned to maintain the reality of objects. For the highest dogma of the spiritual is to affirm the material. By plain outline and positive colour those pious artists strove chiefly to assert that a cat was truly in the eyes of God a cat and that a dog was pre-eminently doggish.

. . . [The point resides in] the difference . . . between the old meaning and the new meaning of the word "Realist." In modern fiction and science a Realist means a man who begins at the outside of a thing: sometimes merely at the end of a thing, knowing the monkey only by its tail or the motor by its smell. In the twelfth century a Realist meant exactly the opposite; it meant a man who began at the inside of a thing. The mediaeval philosopher would only have been interested in a motor because it moved. He would have been interested (that is) only in the central and original idea of a motor – in its ultimate motorishness. . . . If he saw an elephant . . . he would merely see an essence of elephant . . . the shadow of an eternal elephant, conceived and created by God.

. . . A white cow at one particular instant of the evening light may be gold on one side and violet on the other. . . . The essence of mysticism is to insist that there is a white cow, however veiled with shadow or painted with sunset gold. Blessed are they who have seen the violet cow and who yet believe in the white one. To the mystic a white cow has a sort of solid whiteness, as if the cow were made out of frozen milk. . . . The cow's whiteness is more important than anything except her cowishness.

. . . In the ordinary modern meaning [William] Blake's symbols are not symbols at all. They are not allegories. An allegory nowadays means taking something that does not exist as a symbol of something that does exist. . . . So we make the unreal dragon an allegory of the real sin. But that is not what Blake meant when he made the lamb the symbol of innocence. He meant that there really is behind the universe an eternal image called the Lamb, of which all living lambs are merely copies or the approximation. He held that eternal innocence to be an actual and even an awful thing. He would not have seen anything comic, any more than the Christian Evangelist saw anything comic, in talking about the Wrath of the Lamb. . . . Blake did not mean that meekness was true and the lamb only a pretty fable. If anything he meant that meekness was a mere shadow of the everlasting lamb. The distinction is essential to anyone at all concerned for this rooted spirituality which is the only enduring sanity of mankind. The personal is not a mere figure for the impersonal; rather the impersonal is a clumsy term for something more personal than common personality. God is not a symbol of goodness. Goodness is a symbol of God.

William Blake (1920), pp. 132-142

[In the best of the Middle Ages there was] the idea of the great levellers, luck and laughter; the idea of a sense of humour defying and domesticating hell.

'A Drama of Dolls', in *Alarms and Discursions*

Perspective is really the comic element in everything . . . as if on the ultimate horizon of the world everything was sardonically doomed to stand up laughable and little against heaven.

'The Triumph of the Donkey', in *Alarms and Discursions*

It is absolutely useless and absurd to tell a man that he must not joke about sacred subjects . . . because there are no subjects that are not sacred subjects. Every instant of human life is awful. Every step, every stirring of a finger, is full of an importance so huge and even so horrible that a man might go mad if he thought of it. . . . If it is wrong to joke about a dying man it is wrong to joke about any man. For every man is a dying man; a man dying slow or fast. In short, if we say that we must not jest about solemn subjects, what we really mean or ought to mean is that we must not jest at all. . . . Life is too uniformly serious not to be joked about. . . .

Observe and imitate the admirable Scotch nation. They joke about their religion; but they never joke about their golf. You cannot be too solemn about golf to be a good golfer; you can be a great deal too solemn about Christianity to be a good Christian. You may safely put into your neckties solemnity, and nothing but solemnity, because neckties are not the whole of your life – at least, I hope not. But in anything that does cover the whole of your life – in your philosophy and your religion – you must have mirth. If you do not have mirth you will certainly have madness.

'A Charge of Irreverance', in *Lunacy and Letters*

THE CULT

Man found it natural to worship. . . . He not only felt freer when he bent; he actually felt taller when he bowed. Henceforth anything that took away the gesture of worship would stunt and even maim him for ever. Henceforth being merely secular would be a servitude and an inhibition. If man cannot pray he is gagged; if he cannot kneel he is in irons.

The Everlasting Man, Part 1, ch. 5

. . . the great virtue of reverence which is at the heart of ceremonial religion.

Robert Browning (1903), p.88

Man, savage or civilised, simple or complex, always desires to see his own soul outside himself; in some material embodiment.

'The Poetry of the Revolution', in *Utopia of Usurers*

Religious services, the most sacred of all things, have always been held publicly. . . . The record of the great spiritual movements of mankind is dead against the idea that spirituality is a private matter.

'A Defence of Publicity', in *The Defendant*

Ritual is really much older than thought; it is much simpler and much wilder than thought. A feeling touching the nature of things does not only make men feel that there are certain proper things to say; it makes them feel that there are certain proper things to do. . . . Everywhere the religious dance came before the religious hymn, and man was a ritualist before he could speak.

Heretics, ch. 6

I realized the origin and essence of all ritual. That in the presence of those sacred riddles about which we can say nothing it is often more decent merely to do something. And I realized that ritual will always mean throwing away something; *destroying* our corn or wine upon the altar of our gods.

'The Secret of a Train', in *Tremendous Trifles*

There is an instinctive movement of the body towards better and nobler things, as in the text that said, 'I will lift up mine eyes to the hills', or in that divine command of liberation that took the form of 'Stretch forth thine hand'.[1] The old ceremonial gestures of the human body are necessary to the health of the human soul: the gesture that pledged [i.e. 'toasted'] the guest in the goblet; that strewed the flowers upon the grave; that drew the sword for the

1. Psalm 121.1, and Mat. 12.13.

salute or set up the candle before the shrine. In that sense a man actually can think with his muscles; he can pray with his muscles; he can love with his muscles and lament with his muscles. All religion that is without that gesture, all Puritan or purely Intellectualist religion that rages at ritual, is raging at human nature.

'On the Behaviourist', in *All is Grist*

That indestructibility of religion, and even of ritualism, which puzzles the poor old rationalist so much, is not a little due to the fact that in ritual, for the first time, modern men see forms and colours placed where they mean something. Anybody can see why the priest's vestments on common days is green like the common fields, and on martyrs' days red as blood.

The Coloured Lands (1938), p. 110

The ritual which is comparatively rude and straightforward is the ritual which people call "ritualistic." It consists of plain things like bread and wine and fire, and men falling on their faces. But the ritual which is really complex . . . and needlessly formal, is the ritual which people enact without knowing it. It consists not of plain things like wine and fire, but of . . . things like door-mats, and door-knockers, and electric bells, and silk hats, and white ties, and shiny cards, and confetti. . . . In the case of these old and mystical formalities we can at least say that the ritual is not mere ritual; that the symbols employed are in most cases symbols which belong to a primary human poetry. . . . But white ties in the evening are ritual, and nothing else but ritual. . . . [The ordinary modern man] may think . . . that men give too much incense and ceremonial to their adoration of the other world. But nobody thinks that he can give too much incense and ceremonial to the adoration of this world. All men, then, are ritualists, but are either conscious or unconscious ritualists.

Heretics, ch. 18

[The early Church] was as ritualistic as the seven-branched candlestick, and the candles it carried were considerably more than were probably permitted by the first prayer-book of Edward the Sixth. It might well be asked, indeed, why any one accepting the Bethlehem tradition should object to golden or gilded ornament since the Magi themselves brought gold; why he should dislike incense in the church since incense was brought even to the stable.

The Everlasting Man, Part 2, ch. 4

I do not think . . . that the Papacy was wrong then, having once decided to meet human nature on the subject of ceremonial, [that] it made it a very gorgeous ceremonial. I can see no good at all in it having made it a mean or doubtful or third-rate or threadbare ceremonial. . . . Rome had to decide whether it would express the simplicity of Christ in simplicity or the glory of God in glory.

The Resurrection of Rome (1930), pp. 167, 169

To find expression in emblem and established ritual for feelings that are most difficult to express in words is not merely a salute to the departed; it is also a liberating gesture for the living. It is even especially an expression of the life of the living. The practical alternative to it is not speech but silence; not simplicity, but merely embarrassment. Not one man in a thousand ever *says* anything worthy of the dead, or even at all adequate to his own emotions about the dead. It is a far fuller release for his feelings to do something; and especially something that is not too unusual or unnatural to do. The motions that men have always made, uncovering, bowing the head, scattering flowers on the grave, are in the real sense individual actions. They are not only more dignified, but more direct than official speech or extempore prayer. They are not only more serious, but more spontaneous than the ghastly mummery of 'saying a few appropriate words'. A man would be more likely to do such things than to say such things even if he were left entirely to himself, without tradition or culture, even if he were a savage or an utterly unlettered peasant. Ritualism is more natural than rationalism about these things. It is a living necessity for those who survive; sometimes almost a necessity to enable them to survive. It is almost the first gesture of awakening, by which they show that they have not also been struck by the thunderbolt. 'Funeral ceremonies are not a tribute to the dead, but to the living.'[1]

'The Rights of Ritual', in *The Glass Walking-Stick*

The sacramental system is . . . based on the idea that certain material acts are mystical acts; are events in the spiritual world. This mystical materialism does divide us from all those forms of idealism that hold all good to be inward and invisible and matter to be unworthy to express it.

'Roman Catholicism', in *An Outline of Christianity*, ed. A.S. Peake (1926)

We have got to explain somehow that the great mysteries like the Blessed Trinity or the Blessed Sacrament are the starting-points for trains of thought far more stimulating, subtle and even individual, compared with which all that sceptical scratching is as thin, shallow and dusty as a

---

1. This echoes St. Augustine remarking in *The City of God* that funerals are more a consolation to the living than a service to the dead.

nasty piece of scandalmongering in a New England village. . . . To exalt
the Mass is to enter into a magnificent world of metaphysical ideas,
illuminating all the relations of matter and mind, of flesh and spirit, of
the most impersonal abstractions as well as the most personal affections.
To set out to belittle and minimise the Mass, by talking ephemeral back-
chat about what it had in common with Mithras or the Mysteries, is to
be in altogether a more petty and pedantic mood.

'What we think about', in *The Thing*

The Mass is exactly the opposite of a Man seeking to be a God. It is a
God seeking to be a Man; it is God giving his creative life to mankind
as such, and restoring the original pattern of their manhood; making
not gods, nor beasts, nor angels; but, by the original blast and miracle
that makes all things new, turning men into men.

'Magic and fantasy in fiction', in *Sidelights on New London and Newer York*

The word Eucharist is but a verbal symbol, we might say a vague verbal
mask, for something so tremendous that the assertion and the denial
of it have alike seemed a blasphemy; a blasphemy that has shaken the
world with the earthquake of two thousand years.

Cited in Ward, *Gilbert Keith Chesterton*, p. 530

In dreams is revealed the elemental truth that it is the spiritual essence
behind a thing that is important, not its material form. Spiritual forces,
abroad in the world, simply disguise themselves under material forms.
A good force disguises itself as a rose in bloom, a bad force disguises
itself as an attack of chicken-pox. But in the world of subconscious
speculation, where all superficial ornaments are shattered and only the
essentials remain intact, everything but the ultimate meaning is altered.
The spiritual forces, in their nocturnal holiday, have, like lovers on a
Bank Holiday, changed hats.

All the outrageous topsy-turvydom of dreams is sufficiently
represented by saying that angel and devil have changed hats, or, to
speak more accurately, have changed heads. In a dream we love pestilence
and hate the sunrise. . . . There is something mystical and undefined
behind all the things which we love and hate, which makes us love and
hate them. The metaphysicians of the Middle Ages . . . had a theory
that every object had two parts: its accidents and its substance. Thus a
pig was not only fat and four-legged and grunting . . . – beyond all this
he was a pig. . . . The medieval doctors . . . applied this principle . . . to
the idea of Transubstantiation, maintaining that a thing might be in its
accidents bread, while being in its substance divine. Whether it be
reasonable or not for a waking man to worship a wafer of bread, it is

quite certain that a dreaming man would worship a wafer of bread, or a pair of boots, or a sack of potatoes. . . . It all depends upon what disguise the highest spiritual power took in appearing to him, the incognito in which the King chose to travel.

'The Meaning of Dreams', in *Lunacy and Letters*

Of all the sacraments [Confession] is, in the modern jargon, the most psychological. And the proof of it is that even the people who abolished it a few centuries ago found that they had to invent a new imitation of it a few years ago. They told the people to go to a new priest, often without credentials, and make confession generally without absolution, and they called it psycho-analysis.

'Roman Catholicism', in *An Outline of Christianity*, ed. A.S. Peake

According to [a modern critic], it is morbid to confess your sins. I should say that the morbid thing is not to confess them . . . to conceal your sins and let them eat your heart out, which is the happy state of most people in highly civilized communities.

Daily News, 18 Jan. 1908

Confession . . . is the end of mere solitude and secrecy.

Autobiography, ch. 16

[The Church has] claimed to be a divine detective who helped the criminal to escape by a plea of guilty.

A Short History of England, ch. 7

When a Catholic comes from Confession, he does truly, by definition, step out again into that dawn of his own beginning. . . . He believes that in that dim corner, and in that brief ritual, God has really re-made him in His own image. He is now a new experiment of the Creator. . . . The Sacrament of Penance gives a new life, and reconciles a man to all living, but it does not do it as the optimists and the hedonists and the heathen preachers of happiness do it. The gift is given at a price, and is conditioned by a confession. In other words, the name of the price is Truth, which may also be called Reality; but it is facing the reality about oneself.

Autobiography, ch. 16

There is nothing but nonsense . . . in all pretences that the mere round of Nature itself is the source of our highest hopes or could by itself have evolved all that is meant by Resurrection. It is the soul that has received an unspeakable secret from heaven which it can only express in images of the earth, and naturally expresses in terms of the temporary resurrections of the earth. In other words, it uses Spring as a symbol

of Easter; not Easter as a symbol of Spring. . . . The very task before us
is enough to prove that things begin in the mind and that the spirit
must blow its trumpet before any resurrection. For we are trying to
bring back a Spring that as yet only exists in the spirit; to create grass
and green things which must exist in a dream before they can exist in a
landscape; the growth of which will be a miracle in the sense of
something turning back the whole trend and movement of the earth. A
Revolution is a mild thing compared with a Resurrection; and nothing
less can raise us from the dead.

G.K.'s Weekly, 26 March 1932

The first thing that [modernists] will probably tell you today is that
Christmas is really a Pagan festival; because many traditional features
of it were taken from Pagans . . . [who] knew that such a ritual must be
old, that it must be religious, that it must be concerned fundamentally
with simple elements like wood or water or fire, but that it must also
be, in a queer way of its own, revolutionary: exalting the humble or
putting down the mighty from their seat. That was expressed in a
hundred ways, both among heathens and Christians. The Saturnalia[1]
was made for a society of slaves; but it gave one wild holiday to those
slaves. The medieval Christmas had to exist in a feudal society; but all
its carols and legends told again and again a story in which angels spoke
to shepherds and a devil inspired a king. An ancient revolt is enshrined
in an ancient ritual. Now the reason why Christianity found it quite
easy to absorb these Pagan customs is that they were in this way almost
Christian customs. The man who does not see that the Saturnalia was
almost Christian is a man who has never read the Magnificat.[2]

'The Winter Feast', in G.K. Chesterton: The Apostle and the Wild Ducks

All the old Carols, from the Dark Ages downwards, have been soaked
in a purely Christian spirit of holy poverty and the overwhelming
conception of the humility of God.

G.K.'s Weekly, 13 Dec. 1934

Christmas has been a family festival. . . . It was concerned with a happy
family because it was consecrated to the Holy Family. . . . Christmas is
built upon a beautiful and intentional paradox; that the birth of the
homeless should be celebrated in every home. . . . Christmas occurs in
the winter. . . . The old and healthy idea of such winter festivals was

1. The ancient Roman festival celebrated on 19 December, marked by freedom from
   restraint, especially for slaves.
2. The Virgin's prayer – Luke 1.46-55 – celebrating God's 'preferential option for the
   poor'.

this; that people being shut in and besieged by the weather were driven back on their own resources; or, in other words, had a chance of showing whether there was anything in them. . . . Christmas might be creative. . . . I would have the doors shut at Christmas, or at least just before Christmas; and then the world shall see what we can do. . . . Let there be one night when things grow luminous from within: and one day when men seek for all that is buried in themselves; and discover, where she is indeed hidden, behind locked gates and shuttered windows, and doors thrice barred and bolted, the spirit of liberty.

'The Spirit of Christmas', in *The Thing*

Part 10

The Church and Society

AUTHORITY

Is God compatible with Church Government? Why should He be? It is the other things that have to be compatible with God. A Church can only be a humble effort to utter God.

> Letter of 1911, cited Ward, *Gilbert Keith Chesterton*, p. 275

Even if [a man] is so ill-advised as to consult a medical work of reference for the proper proportions of hyoscine for the poisoning of an aunt, he must be so far in a pious and respectful attitude and accepting something upon a sort of authority.

I remember a man who told me he never accepted anything on any sort of authority; I also remember asking him whether he ever consulted Bradshaw,[1] or whether he insisted on travelling by every train first, to see whether it was safe to travel by it. The journey itself might be highly private, . . . but he would not evolve a railway train entirely out of his private judgment.

But a work of reference works in another way also. It reminds the traveller in the train that there are a good many other trains full of travellers. It reminds the neoethical nephew that there are a good many different words in the dictionary. In his search for hyoscine he will pass carelessly over the honey of Hymettus, and think it needless to dwell on the life of Heliogabalus or the science of hydraulics. And thus he will learn the same lesson in another way; the somewhat difficult lesson that he is nobody except himself.

. . . My own thought, when it was not yet Catholic, was often blasted with the name of Optimist. . . . It was an attempt to hold on to religion by the thread of thanks for our creation; by the praise of existence and of created things. . . . I found that this piece of private judgment, or private nonsense, was really much more true than I ever thought it was; and yet, if

_____
1. A railway timetable.

that truth were left to stand alone, it would be a complete falsehood. . . .

In the very act of understanding my own little private problem, I understood the public authority which I have compared to an encyclopaedia. Here there were thousands of other private problems solved for thousands of other private persons; masses of them had nothing to do with my own case at all; but one of them turned and confronted my own case in a curious way. I began to realize that it would not do to act as so many of the most brilliant men of my time had acted. It was not enough for a man to value a truth merely because he had picked it up by himself; to take it away with him and turn it into a private system; at the best into a philosophy and at the worst into a sect. He was very proud of answering his own question without the help of an encyclopaedia; but he did not even pretend to answer all the other questions in the encyclopaedia.

'Consulting the Encyclopaedia', in *The Common Man*

The Gospel Jesus [is] too shadowy to be all-sufficient; that is the argument for a Church.

Hibbert Journal, July 1909

I could never . . . tolerate any Utopia which did not leave to me the liberty for which I chiefly care, the liberty to bind myself. Complete anarchy would not merely make it impossible to have any discipline or fidelity; it would also make it impossible to have any fun. . . . The perils, rewards, punishments, and fulfilments of an adventure must be *real*, or the adventure is only a shifting and heartless nightmare. If I bet I must be made to pay, or there is no poetry in betting. . . . If I vow to be faithful I must be cursed when I am unfaithful, or there is no fun in vowing. . . . For the purpose even of the wildest romance, results must be real; results must be irrevocable. Christian marriage is the great example of a real and irrevocable result.

Orthodoxy, ch. 7

When people begin to say that the material circumstances have alone created the moral circumstances, then they have prevented all possibility of serious change. For if my circumstances have made me wholly stupid, how can I be certain even that I am right in altering those circumstances? The man who represents all thought as an accident of environment is simply smashing and discrediting all his own thoughts – including that one. To treat the human mind as having an ultimate authority is necessary to any kind of thinking, even free thinking. And nothing will ever be reformed in this age or country unless we realize that the moral fact comes first.

'The Wind and the Trees', in *Tremendous Trifles*

The human intellect is free to destroy itself. . . . There is a thought that
stops thought. That is the only thought that ought to be stopped. That is
the ultimate evil against which all religious authority was aimed. . . . The
creeds and the crusades, the hierarchies and the horrible persecutions
were not organized . . . for the suppression of reason. They were organized
for the difficult defence of reason. . . . The authority of priests to absolve,
the authority of popes to define the authority, even of inquisitors to
terrify: these were all only dark defences erected round one central
authority, more undemonstrable, more supernatural than all – the authority
of a man to think. . . . We can hear scepticism crashing through the old
ring of authorities, and at the same moment we can see reason swaying
upon her throne. In so far as religion is gone, reason is going. For they
are both of the same primary and authoritative kind. They are both
methods of proof which cannot themselves be proved.

Orthodoxy, ch. 3

The world will more and more find itself in a position in which even
politicians . . . will find themselves saying, "If the Pope had not existed,
it would be necessary to invent him." . . . Men will attempt to put some
sort of moral power out of the reach of material powers. It is the
weakness of many worthy and well-meaning attempts at international
justice . . . that the international council can hardly help being merely a
microcosm or model of the world outside it. . . . I do not see how
Europe can ever escape from that logical dilemma, except by discovering
again an authority that is purely moral and is the recognised custodian
of a morality. . . .

Again and again in history . . . the Papacy has intervened in the
interests of peace and humanity. . . . But if there had been no Papacy
and no saints and no Catholic Church at all, the world left to itself
would certainly not have substituted social abstractions for theological
creeds. As a whole, humanity has been far from humanitarian. If the
world had been left to itself . . . in the age of feudalism, all the decisions
would have been rigidly and ruthlessly on the lines of feudalism. There
was only one institution in that world that had existed before
feudalism. . . . If the world had been left to itself in the time of the
Renaissance and the Italian statecraft of the Prince,[1] it would have been
arranged entirely in the current fashion of the glorification of princes.
There was only one institution that could at any moment be moved to
repeat, "Put not your trust in princes."[2] Had it been absent, the only
result would have been that the famous settlement of *cujus regio ejus*

---

1. Alluding to both Machiavelli's *The Prince* (1513) and the culture of princely rule.
2. Psalm 146.3.

religio[1] would have been all *regio* with precious little *religio*. And so, of course, our own day has its unconscious dogmas and its universal prejudices; and it needs a special, a sacred and what seems to many an inhuman separation to stand above them or to see beyond.

. . . The thing of which I speak is purely moral and cannot exist without a certain moral loyalty; it is a thing of atmosphere and even in a sense of affection. . . . I see no prospect of any such positive nucleus of amity except in some positive enthusiasm for something that moves the deepest parts of man's moral nature; something which can unite us not . . . by being entirely international, but by being universally human. Men cannot agree about nothing any more than they can disagree about nothing. And anything wide enough to make such an agreement must itself be wider than the world.

'Peace and the Papacy', in *The Thing*

Over the ship which sailed to found the free Catholic colony of Maryland were written the words: 'Where is the spirit of God, there is Liberty.'

'Friends, Romans, Countrymen', in *G.K.C. As M.C.*

CREED AND DOGMA

Philosophy and theology . . . are democratic to the point of being vulgar. . . . They alone admit all matters; they alone lie open to all attacks. . . . There is no fact of life, from the death of a donkey to the General Post Office, which has not its place to dance and sing in, in the glorious Carnival of theology.

G.F. Watts (1920), pp. 167-8

The more I considered Christianity, the more I found that while it had established a rule and order, the chief aim of that order was to give room for good things to run wild.

Orthodoxy, ch. 6

Mental and emotional liberty are not so simple as they look. Really they require almost as careful a balance of laws and conditions as do social and political liberty. . . . By defining its main doctrine, the Church not only kept seemingly inconsistent things side by side, but, what was more, allowed them to break out in a sort of artistic violence. . . . Meekness

---

1. A principle of the Peace of Augsburg (1555) by which each German prince was to settle the religion of his own state: whether Catholic or Lutheran. Chesterton translated it as 'Let every State establish its State Church'; but retranslated it as 'Let the Prince do what he likes': *The Spice of Life* (1964), p. 92.

grew more dramatic than madness. Historic Christianity rose into a high and strange *coup de théatre* of morality. . . . Doctrines had to be defined within strict limits, even in order that man might enjoy general human liberties. The Church had to be careful, if only that the world might be careless.

Orthodoxy, ch. 6

A fixed creed is absolutely indispensable to freedom. For while men are and should be various, there must be some communication between them if they are to get any pleasure out of their variety. [If dogma is rejected] not only does the individual become narrow, but he spreads narrowness across the world like a cloud. . . . Instead of the liberty of dogma, you have the tyranny of taste. . . . Once break the bond of doctrine which alone holds these [varied types of] people together and each will gravitate to his own kind outside the group.

'The Sectarian Society', in *A Miscellany of Men*

If dogma is incredible, it is because it is incredibly liberal. . . . If man has a primary power of choice, he has in that fact a supernatural power of creation, as if he could raise the dead or give birth to the unbegotten. . . . Anybody who believes at all in God must believe in the absolute supremacy of God. But in so far as that supremacy does allow of any degrees that can be called liberal or illiberal, it is self-evident that the illiberal power is the deity of the rationalists and the liberal power is the deity of the dogmatists. . . . It is precisely the unknown God of the scientist, with his impenetrable purpose and his inevitable and unalterable law, that reminds us of a Prussian autocrat . . . moving mankind like machinery. It is precisely the God of miracles and of answered prayers who reminds us of a liberal and popular prince, receiving petitions, . . . and considering the cases of a whole people. . . .

The denouncer of dogma . . . means that dogma is too liberal to be likely. Dogma gives man too much freedom when it permits him to fall. Dogma gives even God too much freedom when it permits him to die. . . . [The sceptics] mean that the universe is itself a universal prison; that existence itself is a limitation and a control; and it is not for nothing that they call causation a chain. . . . We say . . . that the truth has made us free. . . . To them it is like believing in fairyland to believe in such freedom as we enjoy. It is like believing in men with wings to entertain the fancy of men with wills.

The Everlasting Man, Part 2, ch. 5

. . . the provincial stupidity of those who object to what they call "creeds and dogmas." It was precisely the creed and dogma that saved the sanity of the world. These people generally propose an alternative religion of intuition and feeling. If, in the really Dark Ages, there had been a religion of feeling, it would have been a religion of black and suicidal feeling. It was the rigid creed that resisted the rush of suicidal feeling. . . . When Religion would have maddened men, Theology kept them sane.

St. Thomas Aquinas, ch. 4

When the journalist says for the thousandth time, "Living religion is not in dull and dusty dogmas, etc." we must . . . say, "There – you go wrong at the very start." If he would condescend to ask what the dogmas are, he would find out that it is precisely the dogmas that are living, that are inspiring, that are intellectually interesting. Zeal and charity and unction are admirable as flowers and fruit; but if you are really interested in the living principle you must be interested in the root or the seed. . . . The dogmas are not dull. Even what are called the fine doctrinal distinctions are not dull. They are like the finest operations of surgery; separating nerve from nerve, but giving life. It is easy enough to flatten out everything around for miles with dynamite, if our object is to give death. But just as the physiologist is dealing with living tissues so the theologian is dealing with living ideas; and if he draws a line between them it is naturally a very fine line.

'What we think about', in *The Thing*

The vice of the modern notion of mental progress is that it is always something concerned with the breaking of bonds, the effacing of boundaries, the casting away of dogmas. But if there be such a thing as mental growth, it must mean the growth into more and more definite convictions, into more and more dogmas. The human brain is a machine for coming to conclusions. . . . Man can be defined as an animal that makes dogmas. As he piles doctrine on doctrine and conclusion on conclusion in the formation of some tremendous scheme of philosophy and religion, he is . . . becoming more and more human. When he drops one doctrine after another, . . . when he says that he has outgrown definitions, when he says that he disbelieves in finality, when, in his own imagination, he sits as God, holding no form of creed but contemplating all, then he is by that very process sinking slowly backwards into the vagueness of the vagrant animals and the unconsciousness of the grass. Trees have no dogmas. Turnips are singularly broad-minded.

Heretics, ch. 20

. . . certainty, or conviction, or dogma, which is the thing that belongs to man only, and which, if you take it from him, will not leave him even a man. For it is the whole business of humanity . . . to deny evolution, to make absolute distinctions, to take a pen and draw round certain actions a line that nature does not recognise; to take a pencil and draw

round the human face a black line that is not there. . . . It is the business
of the divine human reason to deny that evolutionary appearance
whereby all species melt into each other. This is probably what was
meant by Adam naming the animals.

'The Way to the Stars', in *Lunacy and Letters*

The primitive Catholics . . . were ascetic because asceticism was the
only possible purge of the sins of the world; but in the very thunder of
their anathemas they affirmed for ever that their asceticism was not to
be anti-human or anti-natural. . . . If the Church had not insisted on
theology, it would have melted into a mad mythology of the mystics,
removed from reason; . . . and, above all, yet further removed from life
and from the love of life.

The Everlasting Man, Part 2, ch. 4

You say that it is . . . necessary that Religion should exist, but that its essence
is Mysticism; and this does not need to be organised. I should answer that
nothing on earth needs to be organised so much as Mysticism. You say
that man tends naturally to religion; he does indeed; often in the form of
human sacrifice or the temples of Sodom. Almost all extreme evil of that
kind is mystical. The only way of keeping it healthy is to have some rules,
some responsibilities, some definitions of dogma and moral function.

Letter to C.E.M. Joad, 1930, cited Ward, *Gilbert Keith Chesterton*, p. 511

People talk nowadays of getting rid of dogmas and all agreeing like
brethren. But upon what can they all agree except upon a common dogma?
. . . If the dogmas in front of you are false, get rid of them; but do not
say that you are getting rid of dogmas. Say that you are getting rid of lies.
If the dogmas are true, what can you do but try to get men to agree with
them? . . . Men cannot live wholly by instincts. . . . Men must have
theories. . . . A man's philosophy of the cosmos is directly concerned in
every act of his life. Call theories threads of cotton; still the strain of life
is on those threads. Call the metaphysics of free will a mere cob-web;
still in the hour of temptation everything will hang on that cob-web.

Daily News, 13 Feb. 1906

Dogma means the serious satisfaction of the mind. Dogma does not
mean the absence of thought, but the end of thought. . . . A man making
the confession of any creed worth ten minutes' intelligent talk, is always
a man who gains something and gives up something. So long as he does
both he can create: for he is making an outline and a shape.

The Victorian Age in Literature, ch. 1

You cannot develop any ideas except from fixed axioms, which must
not change their meaning.

Letter to *The Nation*, 21 Dec. 1907

So long as there is constancy in ideals, there can be progress towards
. . . ideals. The moment there is change in . . . ideals, the progress, always
difficult, becomes impossible. If there is progress in ideals, there cannot
be progress in anything else.

Daily News, 15 Sept. 1906

Development [of doctrine] is the expansion of all the possibilities and
implications of a doctrine . . . and . . . the enlargement of medieval
theology was simply the full comprehension of that theology. And it is
of primary importance to realise this . . . about the time of [St. Thomas
Aquinas and St. Francis of Assisi] because their tendency, humanistic
and naturalistic in a hundred ways, was truly the development of the
supreme doctrine; which was also the dogma of all dogmas. It is in this
that the popular poetry of St. Francis and the almost rationalistic prose
of St. Thomas appear most vividly as part of the same movement.
They are both great growths of Catholic development, depending upon
external things only as every living and growing thing depends on them;
that is, it digests and transforms them; but continues in its own image
and not in theirs. . . . They were bringing Christianity into Christendom. . . . They both reaffirmed the Incarnation, by bringing God back
to earth.

St. Thomas Aquinas, ch. 1

The great conception which lay at the back of the Hebrew and Christian
scriptures was the conception that to man had been given a certain law,
to champion which was his sole and simple business. 'He hath shown
thee, O man, that which is good' is perhaps of all earthly sayings the
one which has the deepest ring.

The Speaker, 19 Oct. 1901

A dogma is like a flash of lightning – an instantaneous lucidity that
opens across a whole landscape.

George Bernard Shaw (1914), p. 20

There are two things, and two things only, for the human mind, a dogma
and a prejudice. The Middle Ages were a rational epoch, an age of
doctrine. Our age is, at its best, a poetical epoch, an age of prejudice. A
doctrine is a definite point; a prejudice is a direction. . . . A creed is a
collective thing, and even its sins are sociable. A prejudice is a private
thing, and even its tolerance is misanthropic.

What's Wrong with the World, Part 1, sec. 3

A creed is the sword of the spirit; the only tool with which the mind
can fight.

Daily News, 26 June 1909

'Xmas Day'

Good news: but if you ask me what it is, I know not;
It is a track of feet in the snow,
It is a lantern showing a path,
It is a door set open.

Cited Ward, Gilbert Keith Chesterton, p. 62

[Christianity] happened to be the key that could unlock the prison of the whole world. . . . The creed was like a key . . . a key is above all things a thing with a shape. It is a thing that depends entirely upon keeping its shape. The Christian creed is above all things the philosophy of shapes and the enemy of shapelessness. . . . Second, the shape of the key is in itself a rather fantastic shape. A savage who did not know it was a key would have the greatest difficulty in guessing what it could possibly be. And it is fantastic because it is in a sense arbitrary. . . . It either fits the lock or it does not. It is useless for men to stand disputing over it, considered by itself; or reconstructing it on pure principles of geometry or decorative art. . . . And thirdly, as the key is necessarily a thing with a pattern, so this was one having in some ways a rather elaborate pattern. When people complain of the religion being so early complicated with theology and things of the kind, they forget that the world had . . . got into a whole maze of holes and corners. . . . If the faith had faced the world only with the platitudes about peace and simplicity some moralists would confine it to, it would not have had the faintest effect on that luxurious and labyrinthine lunatic asylum. . . . There was undoubtedly much about the key that seemed complex; indeed there was only one thing about it that was simple. It opened the door.

The Everlasting Man, Part 2, ch. 4

The word "heresy" not only means no longer being wrong; it practically means being clear-headed and courageous. The word "orthodoxy" not only no longer means being right; it practically means being wrong. . . . It means that people care less for whether they are philosophically right. For obviously a man ought to confess himself crazy before he confesses himself heretical.

Heretics, ch. 1

Heresy is worse even than sin. An error is more menacing than a crime, for an error begets crimes. . . . I hate modern doubt because it is dangerous.

'The Diabolist', in Tremendous Trifles

[Heresies] always consist of undue concentration upon some one truth or half-truth. Thus it is true to insist upon God's knowledge, but heretical to insist upon it as Calvin did at the expense of his Love. . . . The heretic (who is also the fanatic) is not a man who loves truth too much; no man can love truth too much. The heretic is a man who loves his truth more than truth itself. He prefers the half-truth that he has found to the whole truth which humanity has found. He does not like to see his own precious little paradox merely bound up with twenty truisms into the bundle of the wisdom of the world.

'On Reading', in *The Common Man*

The birth and death of every heresy has been essentially the same. A morbid or unbalanced Catholic takes one idea out of the thousandfold throng of Catholic ideas; and announces that he cares for that Catholic idea more than for Catholicism. He takes it away with him into a wilderness, where the idea becomes an image and the image an idol. Then, after a century or two, he suddenly wakes up and discovers that the idol is an idol; and, shortly after that, that the wilderness is a wilderness. . . . That is what happened to the Calvinistic Scotsman. . . . But he very often becomes an atheist; and the fact that so many of the hard destructive sceptics, from Hume downwards, came from Scotland, was the early and significant evidence of the discovery of the idol and the wilderness.

'The Idols of Scotland', in *The Thing*

THE CHRISTIAN COMMUNITY

Christianity is not a religion; it is a Church. . . . It stands for a combination of things that are nevertheless one thing; and that one thing is really one.

Blackfriars, March 1923

The things that have been founded on the fancy of the Superman have died with the dying civilizations which alone have given them birth. When Christ . . . was establishing His great society, He chose for its corner-stone neither the brilliant Paul nor the mystic John, but a shuffler, a snob, a coward – in a word, a man. And upon this rock He has built His Church, and the gates of Hell have not prevailed against it. All the empires and the kingdoms have failed, because of this inherent and continual weakness, that they were founded by strong men and upon strong men. But . . . the historic Christian Church was founded on a weak man, and for that reason it is indestructible. For no chain is stronger than its weakest link.

Heretics, ch. 4

Christianity says: "See what is the bravest thing the weakest and most cowardly man can do, and build on that. Let us see what is the wisest thing the stupidest man can do, and build on that. Build on the basis, build on the bottom, build on the minimum of human virtue, build, in a word, upon the ordinary man."

'Vox Populi, Vox Dei',
in *Preachers from the Pew*, ed. Rev. W. Henry Hunt (1906)

What puzzles the world . . . about the priests and people of the Catholic Church is that they still behave as if they were messengers. A messenger does not dream about what his message might be, or argue about what it probably would be; he delivers it as it is. It is not a theory or a fancy but a fact. . . . All that is condemned in Catholic tradition, authority, and dogmatism and the refusal to retract and modify, are but the natural human attributes of a man with a message relating to a fact. . . . The religion of the world . . . is divided by the line between the men who are bringing that message and the men who have not yet heard it, or cannot yet believe it.

The Everlasting Man, Part 2, Conclusion

[St. Francis of Assisi] said, "If we had any possessions, we should need weapons and laws to defend them." . . . His argument was this; that the dedicated man might go anywhere among any kind of men, even the worst kind of men, so long as there was nothing by which they could hold him. . . . The difference between a friar and an ordinary man was really that a friar was freer than an ordinary man. . . . For the world catches us mostly by the fringes of our garments, the futile externals of our lives. . . . You could not ruin him and reduce him to beggary, for he was already a beggar. There was a very lukewarm satisfaction even in beating him with a stick, when he only indulged in little leaps and cries of joy because indignity was his only dignity. You could not put his head in a halter without the risk of putting it in a halo.

St. Francis of Assisi, ch. 7

The visionaries are the only practical men, as in that extraordinary thing, the monastery. . . . In the tremendous testament of our religion there are present certain ideals that seem wilder than impieties. . . . The Christian Church had from the first dealt with these visions as being special spiritual adventures which were to the adventurous. She reconciled them with natural human life by calling them specially good, without admitting that the neglect of them was necessarily bad. She took the view that it takes all sorts to make a world, even the religious world; and used the man who chose to go without arms, family or property as a sort of exception that proved the rule. Now the interesting fact is that he really did prove it. This madman who would not mind his own business becomes the business man of the age. The very word "monk" is a revolution, for it means solitude and came to mean community. . . . This communal life became a sort of reserve and refuge behind the individual life; a hospital for every kind of hospitality. . . . Monks and nuns stood to mankind as a sort of sanctified league of aunts and uncles . . . [who] kept the poor from the most distant sight of their modern despair. . . . The abbots were elective. They introduced representative government, . . . in itself a semi-sacramental idea. . . . Mile by mile, and almost man by man, they taught and enriched the land.

A Short History of England, ch. 4

You say that Christ set the example of a self-annihilation which seems to me almost nihilist; but I will never deny that Catholics have saluted that mood as the Imitation of Christ.[1] Lately a friend of mine, young, virile, handsome, happily circumstanced, walked straight off and buried himself in a monastery; never, so to speak, to reappear on earth. Why did he do it? Psychologically, I cannot imagine. Not, certainly, from fear of hell or wish to be "rewarded" by heaven. As an instructed Catholic, he knew as well as I do that he could save his soul by normal living. I can only suppose that there is something in what you say; that Christ and others do accept a violent reversal of all normal things.

Letter to John Middleton Murry, 1932,
cited in Ward, *Gilbert Keith Chesterton*, p. 508

In most communions the ecclesiastical layman is more ecclesiastical than is good for his health, and certainly much more ecclesiastical than the ecclesiastics. My experience is that the amateur is generally much more angry than the professional.

The Catholic Church and Conversion, ch. 3

CHURCH AND SOCIETY

A piece of peculiarly bad advice is constantly given to modern writers, especially to modern theologians: that they should adapt themselves to the spirit of the age. If there is one thing that has made shipwreck of mankind from the beginning it has been the spirit of the age, which always means exaggerating still further something that is grossly exaggerated already. The spirit of the age always means taking the crinolines that are already inconvenient and widening them till they become impossible.

'The Pun', in *Lunacy and Letters*

The Church cannot move with the times; simply because the times are not moving. The Church can only . . . rot and stink with the times. . . . The Church has the same task as it had at the beginning of the Dark Ages; to

---

1. *The Imitation of Christ – De Imitatione Christi –* is a famous manual of Christian spirituality, first circulated in the early fifteenth century, and usually attributed to Thomas à Kempis.

save all the light and liberty that can be saved, to resist the downward drag
of the world, and to wait for better days. . . . It might present its more
human ideal in such abrupt and attractive a contrast to the inhuman trend
of the time as to inspire men suddenly for one of the moral revolutions of
history; so that men now living shall not taste of death until they have seen
justice return. We do not want, as the newspapers say, a Church that will
move with the world. We want a Church that will move the world.

Cited in Ward, *Gilbert Keith Chesterton*, p. 398

The Church is from the first a thing holding its own position and point
of view, quite apart from the accidents and anarchies of its age. That is
why it deals blows impartially right and left, at the pessimism of the
Manichean or the optimism of the Pelagian. It was not a Manichean
movement because it was not a movement at all. It was not an official
fashion because it was not a fashion at all. It was something that could
coincide with movements and fashions, could control them and could
survive them.

The Everlasting Man, Part 2, ch. 4

What a man knows, now [in 1934], is that the whole march of mankind
can turn and tramp backwards in its tracks; that progress can start
progressing . . . in precisely the contrary course from that which has
been called progress for centuries. It can not only lose but fling away all
that its fathers fought for and valued most. . . . There is no way the
world is going. There never was. The world is not going anywhere, in
the sense of the old optimist progressives. . . . The world is what the
saints and the prophets saw it was; it is not merely getting better or
merely getting worse; . . . it wobbles. Left to itself, it does not get
anywhere; though if helped by real reformers of the right religion and
philosophy, it may get better in many respects, and sometimes for
considerable periods. But in itself it is not a progress; it is not even a
process; it is the fashion of the world that passeth away.[1] Life in itself
is not a ladder; it is a see-saw.

Now that is fundamentally what the Church has always said; and for
about four hundred years has been more and more despised for saying. . . .
She did say that we must not count on the certainty even of comforts
becoming more common or cruelties more rare; as if this were an
inevitable social trend towards a sinless humanity; instead of being as it
was a mood of man. . . . We must not trust humanity; in the sense of
trusting a trend in human nature which cannot turn back to bad things.

The Well and the Shallows, ch. 2

---

1. I Cor. 7.31.

The modern world is full of the old Christian virtues gone mad. The virtues have gone mad because they have been isolated from each other and are wandering alone. Thus some scientists care for truth; and their truth is pitiless. Thus some humanitarians only care for pity; and their pity . . . is often untruthful. . . . Humility is in the wrong place. Modesty has moved from the organ of ambition. Modesty has settled upon the organ of conviction; where it was never meant to be. A man was meant to be doubtful about himself, but undoubting about the truth. . . . The old humility made a man doubtful about his efforts, which might make him work harder. But the new humility makes a man doubtful about his aims, which will make him stop working altogether.

Orthodoxy, ch. 3

Modern society must have a morality before it can have a censor of morals. I should say that it must have a religion before it can have a morality.

'On a Censorship for Literature', in *Come to Think of It*

[St. Thomas Aquinas] reconciled religion with reason, . . . expanded it towards experimental science, . . . insisted that the senses were the windows of the soul and that the reason had a divine right to feed upon facts, and that it was the business of the Faith to digest the strong meat of the toughest and most practical of Pagan philosophies. . . . Aquinas was thus fighting for all that is liberal and enlightened.

St. Thomas Aquinas, ch. 1

We have lost our national instincts because we have lost the idea of that Christendom from which the nations came. In freeing ourselves from Christianity we have only freed ourselves from freedom.

'The National Spirit', in *The Glass Walking-Stick*

Only men to whom the family is sacred will ever have a standard or a status by which to criticise the state. They alone can appeal to something more holy than the gods of the city; the gods of the hearth.

The Everlasting Man, Part 1, ch. 7

Capitalism, of course, is at war with the family, for the same reason which has led to its being at war with the Trade Union. . . . Capitalism believes in collectivism for itself and individualism for its enemies. It desires its victims to be individuals, or . . . atoms. . . . If there be any bond, . . . if there be any class loyalty or domestic discipline, by which the poor can help the poor, these emancipators will certainly strive to loosen that bond or lift that discipline in the most liberal fashion. The masters of modern plutocracy know what they are about. . . . A very profound and precise instinct has led them to single out the human household as the chief obstacle to their inhuman progress. Without the family we are helpless before the State.

The Superstition of Divorce (1920), pp. 31-2

It is only by believing in God that we can ever criticise the Government. Once abolish the God, and the Government becomes the God.

Christendom in Dublin (1932), p. 38

The one specially and peculiarly un-Christian idea is the idea of [Thomas] Carlyle – the idea that the man should rule who feels that he can rule. Whatever else is Christian, this is heathen. If our faith comments on government at all, its comment must be this – that the man should rule who does *not* think that he can rule. . . . We have not got to crown the exceptional man who knows he can rule. Rather we must crown the much more exceptional man who knows he can't.

Orthodoxy, ch. 7

The whole modern world is absolutely based on the assumption, not that the rich are necessary (which is tenable), but that the rich are trustworthy, which (for a Christian) is not tenable. . . . The rich man . . . has been bribed already. That is why he is a rich man. The whole case for Christianity is that a man who is dependent upon the luxuries of this life is a corrupt man, spiritually corrupt, politically corrupt, financially corrupt. There is one thing that Christ and all the Christian saints have said with a sort of savage monotony . . . that to be rich is to be in peculiar danger of moral wreck. . . . A Christian may consistently say, "I respect that man's rank, although he takes bribes." But a Christian cannot say . . . "a man of that rank would not take bribes." For it is a part of Christian dogma that any man in any rank may take bribes.

Orthodoxy, ch. 7

[King Alfred the Great, attended by "A great grey woman with scarred face/ And strong and humbled eyes", says:]
"And well may God with the serving-folk
Cast in His dreadful lot;
Is not He too a servant,
And is not He forgot?

Wherefore was God in Golgotha,
Slain as a serf is slain;
And hate He had of prince and peer,
And love He had and made good cheer,
Of them that, like this woman here,
Go powerfully in pain."

From *The Ballad of the White Horse*, Book IV

If the Church exists ten million years hence, amid alien costumes and incredible architecture, I know that it will still put the oppression of the poor among the five sins, crying aloud for vengeance.

The Church Socialist Quarterly, May 1909

These jewels of God, the poor, are still treated as mere stones of the street; but as stones that may sometimes fly. If it please God, you and I may see some of the stones flying again before we see death.

'The Giant', in *Tremendous Trifles*

If we wish to protect the poor we shall be in favour of fixed rules and clear dogmas. The *rules* of a club are occasionally in favour of the poor member. The drift of a club is always in favour of the rich one.

Orthodoxy, ch. 9

Everything in our age has . . . this fundamentally undemocratic quality. . . . The great difference between the mediaeval ethics and ours is that ours concentrate attention on the sins . . . of the ignorant, and practically deny that . . . the sins of the educated are sins at all. We are always talking about the sin of intemperate drinking, because it is quite obvious that the poor have it more than the rich. But we are always denying that there is any such thing as the sin of pride, because it would be quite obvious that the rich have it more than the poor. We are always ready to make a saint or prophet of the educated man who goes into cottages to give a little kindly advice to the uneducated. But the . . . mediaeval saint or prophet was an uneducated man who walked into grand houses to give a little kindly advice to the educated. The old tyrants had enough insolence to despoil the poor, but they had not enough insolence to preach to them. It was the gentleman who oppressed the slums; but it was the slums that admonished the gentleman.

Heretics, ch. 19

Aristocracy is not an institution: aristocracy is a sin; generally a very venial one. It is merely the drift or slide of men into a sort of natural pomposity and praise of the powerful. . . . It is the peculiar honour of Europe since it has been Christian that while it has had aristocracy it has always at the back of its heart treated aristocracy as a weakness. . . . No Christianity, not even the most ignorant or perverse, ever suggested that a baronet was better than a butcher in [the] sacred sense. . . . In Christian society we have always thought the gentleman a sort of joke.

Orthodoxy, ch. 7

Democracy has been steadily disintegrated by doubts; and these political doubts have been contemporary with and often identical with religious doubts. . . . The dogmatic type of Christianity . . . had riveted itself irrevocably to the manhood of all men. . . . It could not gradually dilute democracy, as could a merely sceptical or secular democrat. . . . It is not that it is necessarily at any moment more democratic, it is that its indestructible minimum of democracy really is indestructible. . . . The Declaration of Independence dogmatically bases all rights on the fact that God created all men equal; and that is right; for if they were not created equal, they were certainly evolved unequal.

There is no basis for democracy except in a dogma about the divine origin of man. . . . So far as . . . democracy becomes . . . Christian, . . . democracy will remain democratic. In so far as it does not, it will become wildly and wickedly undemocratic. Its rich will riot with a brutal indifference. . . . Its wage-slaves will either sink into heathen slavery, or seek relief in theories that are destructive. . . . Men will more and more realize that there is no meaning in democracy if there is no meaning in anything; and that there is no meaning in anything if the universe has not a centre of significance and an authority that is the author of our rights.

What I Saw in America, ch. 19

The machinery of voting is profoundly Christian in this practical sense – that it is an attempt to get at the opinion of those who would be too modest to offer it. . . . There is something psychologically Christian about the idea of seeking for the opinion of the obscure rather than taking the obvious course of accepting the opinion of the prominent.

Orthodoxy, ch. 7

When we say that all pennies are equal, we do not mean that they all look exactly the same. We mean that they are absolutely equal in their one absolute character. . . . They are coins of a certain value. . . . It may be put symbolically, and even mystically, by saying that they all bear the image of the King. And . . . it is also the most practical summary of equality that all men bear the image of the King of Kings. . . . This idea had long underlain all Christianity. . . . A dogma of equal duties implies that of equal rights. I know of no Christian authority that would not admit that it is as wicked to murder a poor man as a rich man. . . . The idea of the equality of men is in substance simply the idea of the importance of man.

A Short History of England, ch. 15

We do not . . . agree with those who hold that modern socialism is an exact counterpart or fulfilment of the socialism of Christianity. We find the difference important and profound, despite the common ground of anti-selfish collectivism. The modern socialist regards Communism as a distant panacea for society, the early Christian regarded it as an immediate and difficult regeneration of himself: the modern socialist reviles . . . society for not adopting it, the early Christian concentrated his thoughts on the problem of his own fitness and unfitness to adopt it: to the modern socialist it is a theory, to the early Christian it was a call; modern socialism says, "Elaborate a broad, noble and workable system and submit it to the progressive intellect of society." Early Christianity said, "Sell all thou hast and give to the poor." . . . For three characteristics at least the Galilean programme makes more provision; humility, activity, cheerfulness, the real triad of Christian virtues.

Cited in Ward, *Gilbert Keith Chesterton*, pp. 73-4

Most of us began to realize that Socialism was not inevitable; that it was not really popular; that it was not the only way, or even the right way, of restoring the rights of the poor. We have come to the conclusion that the obvious cure for private property being given to the few is to see that it is given to the many; not to see that it is taken away from everybody or given in trust to the dear good politicians. Then, having discovered that fact as a fact, we look back at Leo XIII and discover in his old and dated document,[1] of which we took no notice at the time, that he was saying then exactly what we are saying now.

The Catholic Church and Conversion, ch. 5

The man who makes an orchard where there has been a field, who owns the orchard and decides to whom it shall descend, does also enjoy the taste of apples. . . . But he is doing something very much grander . . . than merely eating an apple. He is imposing his will upon the world in the manner of the charter given him by the will of God; he is asserting that his soul is his own . . . he is worshipping the fruitfulness of the world. Now the notion of narrowing property merely to *enjoying* money is exactly like the notion of narrowing love merely to *enjoying* sex. In both cases an incidental, isolated, servile and even secretive pleasure is substituted for participation in a great creative process; even in the everlasting Creation of the world.

'Sex and Property', in *The Well and the Shallows*

I realized that for eighteen hundred years the Church Militant had been not a pageant but a riot. . . . There, still living patiently in Hoxton, were the people to whom the tremendous promises had been made. In the face of

1. Leo XIII's encyclical *Rerum novarum* (1891) likened the lot of workers to that of slaves, and suggested that property be more equitably divided amongst them.

that I had to become revolutionary if I was to continue to be religious. In Hoxton one cannot be a conservative without being also an atheist – and a pessimist. Nobody but the devil could want to conserve Hoxton.

Manalive Part 2, ch. 2

The Church from its beginnings, and perhaps especially in its beginnings, was not so much a principality as a revolution against the prince of the world. This sense that the world had been conquered by the great usurper, and was in his possession, has been much . . . derided by those optimists who identify enlightenment with ease. But it was responsible for all that thrill of defiance and a beautiful danger that made the good news seem to be really both good and new. . . . Olympus still occupied the sky . . . philosophy still sat in the high places and even on the thrones of the kings, when Christ was born in the cave and Christianity in the catacombs.

[The Early Church] was resented, because . . . it had declared war. It had risen out of the ground to wreck the heaven and earth of heathenism. It did not try to destroy all that creation of gold and marble; but it contemplated a world without it. . . . Those who charged the Christians with burning down Rome with firebrands were slanderers; but they were at least far nearer to the nature of Christianity than those among the moderns who tell us that the Christians were a sort of ethical society, being martyred . . . for telling men they had a duty to their neighbours. . . . [Christianity] proclaims peace on earth and never forgets why there was war in heaven.

The Everlasting Man, Part 2, ch. 1

Whatever starts wars, the thing that sustains wars is something in the soul; that is something akin to religion. . . . Men fight hardest when they feel that the foe is at once an old enemy and an eternal stranger, that his atmosphere is alien and antagonistic; as the French feel about the Prussian or the Eastern Christians about the Turk. . . . It is a difference about the meaning of life. . . . There is a religious war when two worlds meet; that is, when two visions of the world meet; or in more modern language, when two moral atmospheres meet. What is the one man's breath is the other man's poison.

The Everlasting Man, Part 1, ch. 7

There is indeed in the Moslem character . . . a deep and most dangerous potentiality of fanaticism . . . . [In Jerusalem] the black dress of the Moslem woman and the white dress of the Christian woman are in sober truth as different as black and white. They stand for real principles in a real opposition; and the black and white will not easily disappear in the dull grey of our own compromises.

The New Jerusalem (1920), pp. 28, 99

You cannot have a devotion that is not a boundary. You cannot have a boundary that is not a barricade. If you do not think mankind a sacred brotherhood to be everywhere saluted and saved, then do not say so. But if you do say so, then you must certainly be ready to save it from sharks or tigers, from monsters or from microbes. . . .

I should say that there ought to be no war except religious war. If war is irreligious, it is immoral. No man ought ever to fight at all unless he is prepared to put his quarrel before that invisible Court of Arbitration with which all religion is concerned. Unless he thinks he is vitally, eternally, cosmically in the right, he is wrong to fire off a pocket-pistol. If he does think he is in the right, he is surely justified in praying that the right may prevail. The separation between war and the Church, like the separation between business and the Chapel, would only mean that the religion would grow much too thin, while the cynicism would grow much too fat. It would be a good thing if religion thought a little more about this world – and if politics thought a little more about the other.

'The National Anthem', in *The Glass Walking-Stick*

Part 11

Doctrines

SIN AND EVIL

The Fall is a view of life. It is not only the only enlightening, but the only encouraging view of life. It holds . . . that we have misused a good world, and not merely been entrapped into a bad one. It refers evil back to the wrong use of the will, and thus declares that it can eventually be righted by the right use of the will. Every other creed except that one is some form of surrender to fate. A man who holds this view of life will find it giving light on a thousand things; on which mere evolutionary ethics have not a word to say. For instance, on the colossal contrast between the completeness of man's machines and the continued corruption of his motives; on the fact that no social progress really seems to leave self behind; on the fact that the first and not the last men of any school or revolution are generally the best and purest . . . on that proverb that says: "The price of liberty is eternal vigilance,"[1] which is only what the theologians say of every other virtue, and is itself only a way of stating the truth of original sin; on those extremes of good and evil by which man exceeds all the animals by the measure of heaven and hell; on that sublime sense of loss that is in the very sound of all great poetry . . . : "We look before and after, and pine for what is not";[2] which cries against all prigs and progressives out of the very depths and abysses of the broken heart of man, that happiness is not only a hope, but also in some strange manner a memory; and that we are all kings in exile.

'The Outline of the Fall', in *The Thing*

1. John Philpot Curran (1790): 'The condition upon which God hath given liberty to man is eternal vigilance.'
2. Shelley 'To a Skylark', stanza 18.

The mission of all the prophets from the beginning has not been so much the pointing out of heavens or hells as primarily the pointing out of the earth. Religion has had to provide that longest and strangest telescope – the telescope through which we could see the star upon which we dwelt. . . . The great sin of mankind, the sin typified by the fall of Adam, is the tendency, not towards pride, but towards this weird and horrible humility. This is the great fall, the fall by which the fish forgets the sea, . . . Every man forgets his environment and, in the fullest and most liberal sense, forgets himself. This is the real fall of Adam, and it is a spiritual fall.

'Introduction', in *The Defendant*

While the eye that can perceive what are the wrong things increases in an uncanny and devouring clarity, the eye which sees what things are right is growing mistier and mistier every moment, till it goes almost blind with doubt. If we compare . . . the morality of the "Divine Comedy" with the morality of Ibsen's *Ghosts*, we shall see all that modern ethics have really done. . . . Dante describes three moral instruments – Heaven, Purgatory, and Hell, the vision of perfection, the vision of improvement, and the vision of failure. Ibsen has only one – Hell. . . . The human race, according to religion, fell once, and in falling gained the knowledge of good and of evil. Now we have fallen a second time, and only the knowledge of evil remains to us.

Heretics, ch. 2

In "Paradise Lost" . . . Milton . . . makes all human wickedness originate in an act of . . . romanticism. . . . If we are cads and blackguards (as we are) it is not because our first ancestor behaved like a husband and a gentleman. . . . In the Bible . . . all evil is traced to that ultimate unreasoning insolence which will not accept even the kindest conditions; that profoundly inartistic anarchy that objects to a limit as such. . . . In Eden there was a maximum of liberty and a minimum of veto; but some veto is essential even to the enjoyment of liberty. . . . This Bible idea that all sins and sorrows spring from a certain fever of pride, which cannot enjoy unless it controls, is a much deeper . . . truth than Milton's mere suggestion that a gentleman got entangled by his chivalry to his lady.

'Good Stories Spoilt by Great Authors', in *Lunacy and Letters*

Carlyle objected to the statement that no man could be a hero to his valet[1]. . . . The ultimate psychological truth, the foundation of Christianity, is that no man is a hero to himself. . . . Carlyle said that

---

1. Carlyle, in his *Lectures on Heroes* (Lecture V), is thinking of Montaigne; but the quotation is now attributed to Mme Cornuel (1728).

men were mostly fools.[1] Christianity, with a surer and more reverent realism, says that they are all fools. This doctrine is sometimes called the doctrine of original sin. It may also be described as the doctrine of the equality of men. . . . Whatever primary and far-reaching moral dangers affect any man, affect all men. All men can be criminals, if tempted; all men can be heroes, if inspired. And this doctrine does away altogether with Carlyle's pathetic belief . . . in "the wise few." There are no wise few.

Heretics, ch. 12

The worst things in man are only possible to man. . . . [He] did manufacture out of the old mud and blood of material origins . . . a special and a mortal poison. . . . The poison itself has always been there. Wherefore, . . . it was in the beginning, or, . . . original.

'On Original Sin', in Come to Think of It

The true doctrine of original sin may be stated [as] . . . that moral health is not a thing which will fulfil itself automatically in any complete man like physical health . . . that we all start in a state of war . . . that everything in a cabbage is trying to make a good cabbage, whereas everything in a man is not trying to make what we call a good man.

Daily News, 2 Sept. 1905

If there were to appear in the world a perfectly sane man he would certainly be locked up. The terrible simplicity with which he would walk over our minor morbidities, our sulky vanities and malicious self-righteousness; the elephantine innocence with which he would ignore our fictions of civilization – these would make him a thing more desolating and inscrutable than a thunderbolt or a beast of prey. It may be that the great prophets who appeared to mankind as mad were in reality raving with an impotent sanity.

'Lunacy and Letters', in Lunacy and Letters

The only reason for being a progressive is that things naturally tend to grow worse. The corruption in things is not only the best argument for being progressive; it is also the only argument against being conservative. . . . Christianity . . . [says], "I have always maintained that men were naturally backsliders; that human virtue tended of its own nature to rust or to rot; I have always said that human beings as such go wrong, especially happy human beings, especially proud and prosperous human beings. This eternal revolution . . . you (being a vague modern) call the doctrine of progress. If you were a philosopher you would call it . . . the doctrine of original sin. You may call it the cosmic advance as much as you like; I call it what it is – the Fall."

Orthodoxy, ch. 7

1. *Latter-Day Pamphlets* No. 1 (1850).

The wisest men in the [classical] world set out to be natural. . . . The immediate effect of saluting the sun and the sunny sanity of nature was a perversion spreading like a pestilence. . . . The truth is that people who worship health cannot remain healthy. When Man goes straight he goes crooked. . . . There is a bias in man like the bias in the bowl; and Christianity was the discovery of how to correct the bias and therefore hit the mark. . . . The glad news brought by the Gospel was the news of original sin.

St. Francis of Assisi, ch. 2

Theosophists . . . preach an obviously attractive idea like re-incarnation; but if we wait for its logical results, they are spiritual superciliousness and the cruelty of caste. For if a man is a beggar by his own pre-natal sins, people will tend to despise the beggar. But Christianity preaches an obviously unattractive idea, such as original sin; but when we wait for its results, they are pathos and brotherhood, and a thunder of laughter and pity; for only with original sin can we at once pity the beggar and distrust the king.

Orthodoxy, ch. 9

If we wish to pull down the prosperous oppressor we cannot do it with the new doctrine of human perfectibility; we can do it with the old doctrine of Original Sin.

Orthodoxy, ch. 9

> O God of earth and altar,
> Bow down and hear our cry,
> Our earthly rulers falter,
> Our people drift and die;
> The walls of gold entomb us,
> The swords of scorn divide,
> Take not thy thunder from us,
> But take away our pride.

From 'A Hymn', in *The Collected Poems of G.K. Chesterton*

The most deadly moral danger in my experience of mankind: the danger of egoism and spiritual pride.

'On Preaching', in *Come to Think of It*

. . . sin which is perhaps most horrible to me because it is ingratitude.

Autobiography, ch. 16

All evil began with some attempt at superiority; some moment when . . . the very skies were cracked across like a mirror, because there was a sneer in Heaven. . . . Pride is a poison so very poisonous that it not only poisons the virtues; it even poisons the other vices. . . . A great deal of modern literature and ethics might be meant specially for the encouragement of spiritual pride. Scores of scribes and sages are busy writing about the importance of self-culture and self-realisation; about how every child is to be taught to develop his personality (whatever that may be); about how every man must devote himself to success. . . . The moment the self within is consciously felt as something superior to any of the gifts that can be brought to it, or any of the adventures that it may enjoy, there has appeared a sort of self-devouring fastidiousness and a disenchantment in advance, which fulfils all the Tartarean[1] emblems of thirst and of despair. . . . Pride consists in a man making his personality the only test, instead of making the truth the test. . . . The self as a self is a very small thing and something very like an accident.

'If I had only one sermon to preach', in *The Common Man*

'And what is the one spiritual disease?' asked Flambeau, smiling.
'Oh, thinking one is quite well,' said [Father Brown].

'The Eye of Apollo', in *The Innocence of Father Brown*

Self is the gorgon. Vanity sees it in the mirror of other men and lives. Pride studies it for itself and is turned to stone. . . . Self-consciousness of necessity destroys self-revelation. A man who thinks a great deal about himself will try to be many-sided, attempt a theatrical excellence at all points, will try to be an encyclopaedia of culture, and his own real personality will be lost in that false universalism. Thinking about himself will lead to trying to be the universe; trying to be the universe will lead to ceasing to be anything. If, on the other hand, a man is sensible enough to think only about the universe, he will think about it in his own individual way. He will keep virgin the secret of God; he will see the grass as no other man can see it, and look at a sun that no man has ever known.

Heretics, ch. 9

Ultimate

The vision of a haloed host
That weep around an empty throne;
And, aureoles dark and angels dead,
Man with his own life stands alone.

'I am,' he says his bankrupt creed;
'I am,' and is again a clod:
The sparrow starts, the grasses stir,
For he has said the name of God.[2]

From *The Collected Poems of G.K. Chesterton*

---

1. Tartarus was the place in classical mythology where the wicked were punished, the dungeon of the underworld.
2. Exodus 3.14: 'And God said unto Moses, I AM THAT I AM'.

It will not, I imagine, be disputed that the one black and inexcusable kind of pride is the pride of the man who has something to be proud of. . . . The instinct of the human soul perceives that a fool may be permitted to praise himself, but that a wise man ought to praise God. A man who really has a head with brains in it ought to know that this head has been gratuitously clapped on top of him like a new hat. . . . A man who possesses great powers ought to know that he does not really possess them. . . . The most really health-giving orders of conceit are those that concern something of which a man has no obvious right at all to be conceited, the things over which he exercises no control . . . [such as] the love of country. . . . Far more brutal than these are the people who have in some sort of way deserved their position – the capitalists, the parvenus, the children of the modern mercantile ferocity. Yet they, too, in their way have a silvery thread of graciousness, because they are stupid, and have been, like the aristocrats, the acceptors of some beautiful accident. . . .

The highest thing in the world is goodness. It is so high that, fortunately, the great majority of people who have it are horribly frightened of it, and keep their own virtue as they would keep some sort of wild horse or griffin. But every now and then there do appear people who are good and who know they are good, and who are proud of being good. . . . These were the people whom Jesus Christ could hardly forbear to scourge.

This is . . . the whole subtlety of the sin of pride; all other sins attack men when they are weak and weary; but this attacks when men are happy and valuable and nearer to all the virtues. And when it attacks most easily the results are vilest. The whole difference between the religion of Christianity and such a religion, for instance, as that of Brahmanism, is merely this. The castes of Christian Europe are insolent, abominable, unendurable things, which have been endured . . . for centuries; but they have one great virtue, they are irreligious. But in Brahminism the castes are religious things; it is a virtue to be aristocratic. And against any people who claim to rule me by spiritual superiority, I will everlastingly and happily rebel, conscious of that image of deity which equalises us all.

'The True Vanity of Vanities',
in G.K. Chesterton: The Apostle and the Wild Ducks

Christendom . . . has insisted on . . . theological free-will. . . . This is the real objection to . . . modern talk about treating crime as a disease, about making a prison merely a hygienic environment like a hospital, of healing sin by slow scientific methods. The fallacy of the whole thing is that evil is a matter of active choice, whereas disease is not. . . . The whole point

... is perfectly expressed in the very word which we use for a man in hospital; "patient" is in the passive mood; "sinner" is in the active. . . . All moral reform must start in the active not the passive will.

Orthodoxy, ch. 8

The worst result of popular evolutionism has been this. It has substituted the Beast for the Devil. It has made us think that our enemy is what they call our 'lower nature', which means our mere lusts and appetites, things entirely innocent in themselves. . . . Tennyson . . . spoke of moral improvements as 'moving upward, working out the brute' . . . The thing that is wrong in us is not, as evolutionists say, the brute [but] . . . the devil, the austere, intellectual virgin devil of the medieval story. He will suffer for evil. He will perform heroic acts for evil. . . . The worst sins of all are the purely human sins. You may move upwards, working out the brute, and not work them out in the least. Nay, you may work them in. The less beastly you grow, the more bad you may grow.

Daily News, 3 Feb. 1906

In one way . . . ancient [sexual] sin was infinitely superior . . . to the modern sin. . . . It was the cult of Fruitfulness. . . . It was at least on the side of Life. It has been left to the last Christians . . . to invent a new kind of worship of Sex, which is not even a worship of Life. It has been left to the very latest Modernists to proclaim an erotic religion which at once exalts lust and forbids fertility. . . . The priests of Priapus[1] . . . go into the kingdom of heaven before them.

'Sex and Property', in *The Well and the Shallows*

There is, as a ruling element in modern life, in all life, this blind and asinine appetite for mere power. There is a spirit abroad among the nations of the earth which drives men incessantly on to destroy what they cannot understand, and to capture what they cannot enjoy.

G.F. Watts (1920), p. 110

[Charles Dickens's] revolt was simply and solely the eternal revolt; it was the revolt of the weak against the strong. . . . He disliked oppression. He disliked a certain look on the face of a man when he looks down on another man. And that look on the face is, indeed, the only thing in the world that we have really to fight between here and the fires of hell. . . . He saw that under many forms there was one fact, the tyranny of man over man.

'Oliver Twist',
in *Appreciations and Criticisms of the Works of Charles Dickens*

---

1. The ancient Greek god of fertility and reproduction.

What is the matter with the cult of Service is that, like so many modern notions, it is an idolatry of the intermediate to the oblivion of the ultimate. . . . The sin of Service is the sin of Satan: that of trying to be first where it can only be second. . . . There is a sense in serving God, and an even more disputed sense in serving man; but there is no sense in serving Service. To serve God is at least to serve an ideal being. . . . There arises the horrible idea that industry, reliability, punctuality, and business activity are good things; that mere readiness to serve the powers of this world is a Christian virtue.

'The Sceptic as Critic', in *The Thing*

Madness is a preference for the symbol over that which it represents. The most obvious example is the religious maniac, in whom the worship of Christianity involves the negation of all those ideas of integrity and mercy for which Christianity stands. . . . This is the great sin of idolatry, against which religion has so constantly warned us. . . . Idolatry exists wherever the thing which originally gave us happiness becomes at last more important than happiness itself. . . . This is idolatry: the preference for the incidental good over the eternal good which it symbolises. It is the employment of one example of the everlasting goodness to confound the validity of a thousand other examples. It is the elementary mathematical and moral heresy that the part is greater than the whole.

'Lunacy and Letters', in *Lunacy and Letters*

Extreme evil . . . is . . . the unpardonable sin of not wishing to be pardoned.

Autobiography, ch. 4

Men may keep a sort of level of good, but no man has ever been able to keep on one level of evil. That road goes down and down. The kind man drinks and turns cruel; the frank man kills and lies about it.

'The Flying Stars', in *The Innocence of Father Brown*

The popular tales about bad magic are specially full of the idea that evil alters and destroys the personality. . . . In all such instinctive literature the denial of identity is the very signature of Satan. In that sense it is true that the true God is the God of things as they are – or, at least, as they were meant to be.

'Wishes', in *The Uses of Diversity*

. . . they think [*The Strange Case of Dr Jekyll and Mr Hyde*] means that man can be cloven into two creatures, good and evil. The whole stab of the story is that man *can't*: because while evil does not care for good, good must care for evil. Or, in other words, man cannot escape from God, because good is the God in man; and insists on omniscience.

The Victorian Age in Literature, ch. 4

[In *The Strange Case of Dr Jekyll and Mr Hyde*] Jekyll is the ordinary mixed, moderately humane man, whose character has begun to suffer from some evil drug or passion. Now, that . . . is the habit of being Hyde. . . . So far from preaching that man can be successfully divided into two men, good and evil, [Robert Louis Stevenson] specifically preached that man cannot be so divided; . . . that . . . the good is still dragged down by the mere existence of the bad. . . . Hyde is the innocence of evil. He stands for the truth . . . that there is in evil, though not in good, this power of self-isolation, this hardening of the whole exterior, so that a man becomes blind to moral beauties or deaf to pathetic appeals. . . . Precisely because Jekyll, with all his faults, possesses goodness, he possesses also the consciousness of sin, humility. He knows all about Hyde, as angels know about devils. . . . Virtue has the heavy burden of knowledge; sin has often something of the levity of sinlessness.

'Tricks of Memory', in *The Glass Walking-Stick*

'I am a man,' answered Father Brown gravely; 'and therefore have all devils in my heart.'

'The Hammer of God', in *The Innocence of Father Brown*

If most of [Jesus's] words mean anything they do mean that there is at our very feet, like a chasm concealed among the flowers, an unfathomable evil. . . . [Sodom and Gomorrah] are the foundations of a fallen world, and a sea below the seas on which men sail. . . . In all our brains . . . were buried things as bad as any buried under that bitter sea, and if [Jesus] did not come to do battle with them, even in the darkness of the brain of man, I know not why He came. . . . The more truly we can see life as a fairy-tale, the more clearly the tale resolves itself into war with the dragon who is wasting fairyland.

The New Jerusalem (1920), pp. 185-8

Why do men entertain this queer idea that what is sordid must always overthrow what is magnanimous; that there is some dim connection between brains and brutality, or that it does not matter if a man is dull so long as he is also mean? Why do they vaguely think of all chivalry as sentiment and all sentiment as weakness? They do it because they are, like all men, primarily inspired by religion. For them, as for all men, the first fact is their notion of the nature of things. . . . And it is their faith that the only ultimate thing is fear and therefore that the very heart of the world is evil. They believe that death is stronger than life, and therefore dead things must be stronger than living things; whether those dead things are gold and iron and machinery or rocks and rivers and forces of nature. It may sound fanciful to say that men we meet at tea-tables or talk to at garden-parties are secretly worshippers of Baal or Moloch. But this sort of commercial mind has its own cosmic vision and it is the vision of Carthage.[1] The Punic power fell, because there is in this materialism a mad indifference to real thought. By disbelieving in the soul, it comes to disbelieving in the mind.

The Everlasting Man, Part 1, ch. 7

We all know the story of how Herod, alarmed at some rumour of a mysterious rival, . . . ordered a massacre. . . . The demons also, in that first festival of Christmas, feasted after their own fashion. Unless we understand the presence of that Enemy, we shall not only miss the point of Christianity, but . . . the point of Christmas. . . . By the very nature of the story the rejoicings in the cavern [at Bethlehem] were rejoicings in a fortress or an outlaw's den; . . . they were rejoicings in a dug-out. . . . There is in that image a true idea of an outpost, of a piercing through the rock and an entrance into an enemy territory. There is in this buried divinity an idea of *undermining* the world; of shaking the towers and palaces from below; even as Herod the great king felt that earthquake under him.

The Everlasting Man, Part 2, ch. 1

[As they watch the flying red sparks of an outdoor fire at night, Chesterton speaks with an evil man, who asks him, 'why do you care about morality?' Chesterton replies:]

"Give me those few red specks and I will deduce Christian morality. Once I thought like you, that one's pleasure in a flying spark was a thing that could come and go with that spark. Once I thought that the delight was as free as the fire. Once I thought that red star we see was alone in space. But now I know that the red star is only on the apex of an invisible pyramid of virtues. That red fire is only the flower on a stalk of living habits, which you cannot see. Only because your mother made you say 'Thank you' for a bun are you now able to thank Nature or chaos for those red stars of an instant or for the white stars[2] of all time. Only because you were humble before fireworks on the fifth of November do you now enjoy any fireworks that you chance to see. You only like them being red because you were told about the blood of the martyrs; you only like them being bright because brightness is a glory. That flame flowered out of virtues, and it will fade with virtues. Seduce

1. Baal and Moloch were dark Phoenician gods, and Carthage was a Phoenician ('Punic') power.
2. Perhaps alluding to Matthew Arnold's lines in 'Stanzas from the Grande Chartreuse': 'For rigorous teachers seized my youth,/ And purged its faith, and trimmed its fire,/ Showed me the high, white star of Truth,/ There bade me gaze, and there aspire.'

a woman, and that spark will be less bright. Shed blood, and that spark will be less red. Be really bad, and they will be to you like the spots on a wall-paper."

He only said, " But shall I not find in evil a life of its own?. . . . What you call evil I call good."

'The Diabolist', in *Tremendous Trifles*

CHRIST AND SALVATION

Tie in a living tether
The prince and priest and thrall,
Bind all our lives together,
Smite us and save us all.

From 'A Hymn', in *The Collected Poems of G.K. Chesterton*

As compared with a Jew, a Moslem, a Buddhist, a Deist, or most obvious alternatives, a Christian *means* a man who believes that deity or sanctity has attached to matter or entered the world of the senses. . . . St. Thomas [Aquinas] wanted to recover what was in essence the body of Christ itself; the sanctified body of the Son of Man which has become a miraculous medium between heaven and earth. And he wanted the body, and all its senses, because he believed, rightly or wrongly, that it was a Christian thing.

St. Thomas Aquinas, ch. 1

The Body was no longer what it was when Plato and Porphyry and the old mystics had left it for dead. It had hung upon a gibbet. It had risen from the tomb. It was no longer possible for the soul to despise the senses, which had been the organs of something that was more than man. Plato might despise the flesh; but God had not despised it. The senses had truly become sanctified; as they are blessed one by one at a Catholic baptism. "Seeing is believing" was no longer the platitude of a mere idiot, or common individual, as in Plato's world; it was mixed up with real conditions of real belief. Those revolving mirrors that send messages to the brain of man . . . had truly revealed to God himself the path to Bethany or the light on the high rock of Jerusalem. . . . After the Incarnation had become the idea that is central in our civilisation, it was inevitable that there should be a return to materialism; in the sense of the serious value of matter and the making of the body.

St. Thomas Aquinas, ch. 4

There is in all good things a perpetual desire for expression and concrete embodiment. . . . The trend of good is always towards Incarnation.

'The Mystagogue', in A Miscellany of Men

Man has been made more sacred than any superman or super-monkey; . . . his very limitations have already become holy and like a home; because of that sunken chamber in the rocks, where God became very small.

Autobiography, ch. 10

[With the birth of Christ] the whole universe had been turned inside out. . . . All the eyes of wonder and worship which had been turned outwards to the largest thing were now turned inward to the smallest. . . . God who had been only a circumference was seen as a centre; and a centre is infinitely small. . . . The spiritual spiral henceforward works inwards instead of outwards, and in that sense is centripetal and not centrifugal. The faith becomes, in more ways than one, a religion of little things. . . . It is the paradox of that group in the cave [at Bethlehem], that while our emotions about it are of childish simplicity, our thoughts about it can branch with a never-ending complexity.

The Everlasting Man, Part 2, ch. 1

Any agnostic or atheist whose childhood has known a real Christmas has ever afterwards . . . an association in his mind between two ideas that most of mankind must regard as remote from each other; the idea of a baby and the idea of unknown strength that sustains the stars. . . . For him there will always be some savour of religion about the mere picture of a mother and a baby; some hint of mercy and softening about the mere mention of the dreadful name of God. . . . We are psychological Christians even when we are not theological ones. . . . It would be vain to attempt to say anything adequate . . . about the change which this conception of a deity born like an outcast or even an outlaw had upon the whole conception of law and its duties to the poor and outcast. It is profoundly true to say that after that moment there could be no slaves.

The Everlasting Man, Part 2, ch. 1

If a man is much in the habit of reflecting that God was once a little baby, . . . he will not in fact be able to keep up the practice of a pure religion of Fear. He will not be able to think of the Lord as merely rigid and ruthless; and the particular sort of sternness and grimness which Puritanism valued will certainly pass out of his creed.

G.K.'s Weekly, 21 Dec. 1929

A Child in a foul stable,
Where the beasts feed and foam;
Only where He was homeless
Are you and I at home.
. . . . . .
To an open house in the evening
Home shall men come,
To an older place than Eden
And a taller town than Rome.
To the end of the way of the wandering star,
To the things that cannot be and that are,
To the place where God was homeless
And all men are at home.

From 'The House of Christmas',
in *The Collected Poems of G.K. Chesterton*

We often hear of Jesus of Nazareth as a wandering teacher; and there is a vital truth in that view in so far as it emphasises an attitude towards luxury and convention which most respectable people would still regard as that of a vagabond. It is expressed in his own great saying about the holes of the foxes and the nests of the birds[1]. . . . He is . . . a stranger upon the earth. . . . He shared the drifting life of the most homeless and hopeless of the poor.

The Everlasting Man, Part 2, ch. 3

That Christ was and is the most merciful of judges and the most sympathetic of friends is a fact of considerably more importance in our own private lives than in anybody's historical speculations. . . . Christ was indeed human; but more human than a human being was then likely to be.

The Everlasting Man, Part 2, ch. 3

If the divinity [of Christ] is true it is certainly terribly revolutionary. That a good man may have his back to the wall is no more than we knew already; but that God could have his back to the wall is a boast for all insurgents for ever. Christianity is the only religion on earth that has felt that omnipotence made God incomplete. Christianity alone has felt that God, to be wholly God, must have been a rebel as well as a king. Alone of all creeds, Christianity has added courage to the virtues of the Creator. For the only courage worth calling courage must necessarily mean that the soul passes a breaking point – and does not break. . . . In . . . the Passion there is a . . . suggestion that the author of all things . . . went not only through agony, but through doubt. It is written, "Thou shalt

1. Mat. 8.20.

not tempt the Lord thy God." No; but the Lord thy God may tempt Himself; and it seems as if this was what happened in Gethsemane. In a garden Satan tempted man: and in a garden God tempted God. He passed in some superhuman manner through our human horror of pessimism. When the world shook and the sun was wiped out of heaven, it was not at the crucifixion, but at the cry from the cross: the cry which confessed that God was forsaken of God. And now let the revolutionists choose a creed from all the creeds and a god from all the gods of the world, carefully weighing all the gods of inevitable recurrence and of unalterable power. They will not find another god who has himself been in revolt. . . . Let the atheists themselves choose a god. They will find only one divinity who ever uttered their isolation; only one religion in which God seemed for an instant to be an atheist.

Orthodoxy, ch. 8

Nothing short of the extreme . . . and startling doctrine of the divinity of Christ will give that particular effect that can truly stir the popular sense like a trumpet; the idea of the king himself serving in the ranks like a common soldier. By making that figure merely human we make that story much less human. We take away the point of the story which actually pierces humanity; the point of the story which was quite literally the point of a spear. . . . Any knowledge of human nature will tell us that no sufferings of the sons of men, or even of the servants of God, strike the same note as the notion of the master suffering instead of his servants.

The Everlasting Man, Part 2, ch. 5

If we wish to exalt the outcast and the crucified, we shall rather wish to think that a veritable God was crucified, rather than a mere sage or hero.

Orthodoxy, ch. 9

In every century, in this century, in the next century, the Passion is what it was in the first century, when it occurred; a thing stared at by a crowd. It remains a tragedy of the people; a crime of the people; a consolation of the people; but never merely a thing of the period. And its vitality comes from the very things that its foes find a scandal and a stumbling-block; from its dogmatism and from its dreadfulness. It lives, because it involves the staggering story of the Creator truly groaning and travailing with his Creation; and the highest thing thinkable passing through some nadir of the lowest curve of the cosmos. And it lives, because the very blast from this black cloud of death comes upon the world as a wind of everlasting life; by which all things wake and are alive.

The Way of the Cross (1935), p. 23

LOVE

. . . The paradox of Faith — the absolutely necessary and wildly unreasonable maxim which says to every mother with a child or to every patriot with a country, 'You must love the thing first and make it lovable afterwards.'

The World, 27 Sept. 1904

One must somehow find a way of loving the world without trusting it; somehow one must love the world without being worldly.

Orthodoxy, ch. 5

Love is a noble thing; but love is not union. Nay, it is rather a vivid sense of separation and identity. . . . All the greatest saints have felt their lowness, not their highness, in the moment of ecstasy. . . . Division and variety are essential to praise.

T.P.'s Weekly, Christmas Number, 1910

I want to love my neighbour not because he is I, but precisely because he is not I. I want to adore the world, not as one likes a looking-glass, because it is one's self, but as one loves a woman, because she is entirely different. If souls are separate love is possible. If souls are united love is obviously impossible. . . . Love desires personality; therefore love desires division. It is the instinct of Christianity to be glad that God has broken the universe into little pieces, because they are living pieces. . . . Christianity is a sword which separates and sets free. No other philosophy makes God actually rejoice in the separation of the universe into living souls. But according to orthodox Christianity this separation between God and man is sacred, because this is eternal. That a man may love God it is necessary that there should be not only a God to be loved, but a man to love him.

Orthodoxy, ch. 8

We make our friends; we make our enemies; but God makes our next-door neighbour. Hence he comes to us clad in all the careless terrors of nature; he is as strange as the stars, as reckless and indifferent as the rain. He is Man, the most terrible of the beasts. That is why . . . the old scriptural language showed so sharp a wisdom when [it] spoke, not of one's duty towards humanity, but one's duty towards one's neighbour. The duty towards humanity may often take the form of some choice which is personal or even pleasurable. . . . But we have to love our neighbour because he is *there*. . . . He is the sample of humanity which is actually given us. Precisely because he may be anybody he is everybody.

Heretics, ch. 14

The love of those whom we do not know is quite as eternal a sentiment as the love of those whom we do know. In our friends the richness of life is proved to us by what we have gained; in the faces in the street the richness of life is proved to us by the hint of what we have lost. And this feeling for strange faces and strange lives, when it is felt keenly by a young man, almost always expresses itself in a desire after a kind of vagabond beneficence, a desire to go through the world scattering goodness like a capricious god. It is destined that mankind should hunt in vain for its best friend as it would hunt for a criminal; that he should be an anonymous Saviour, an unrecorded Christ.

Robert Browning (1903), p. 43

Charity means pardoning what is unpardonable, or it is no virtue at all. . . . Charity is the power of defending that which we know to be indefensible. . . . Charity to the deserving is not charity at all, but justice. It is the undeserving who require it, and the ideal either does not exist at all, or exists wholly for them. . . . Charity is a reverent agnosticism towards the complexity of the soul.

Heretics, ch. 12

Love is not blind. . . . Love is bound; and the more it is bound the less it is blind.

Orthodoxy, ch. 5

We ought to see far enough into a hypocrite to see even his sincerity. We ought to be interested in that darkest and most real part of a man in which dwell not the vices that he does not display, but the virtues that he cannot. And the more we approach the problems of human history with this keen and piercing charity, the smaller and smaller space we shall allow to pure hypocrisy of any kind. The hypocrites shall not deceive us into thinking them saints; but neither shall they deceive us into thinking them hypocrites.

Heretics, ch. 5

If there is one question which the enlightened and liberal have the habit of deriding and holding up as a dreadful example of barren dogma and senseless sectarian strife, it is this Athanasian question of the Co-Eternity of the Divine Son. On the other hand, if there is one thing that the same liberals always offer us as a piece of pure and simple Christianity, untroubled by doctrinal disputes, it is the single sentence, 'God is Love.' Yet the two statements are almost identical; at least one is very nearly nonsense without the other. The barren dogma is only the logical way of stating the beautiful sentiment. For if there be a being without beginning, existing before all things, was He loving when there was nothing to be loved? If through that unthinkable eternity He is lonely, what is the meaning of saying He is love? The only justification of such a mystery is the mystical conception that in His own nature there was something analogous to self-expression; something of what begets and beholds what it has begotten. . . . It was emphatically [St. Athanasius][1] who really was fighting for a God of Love against a God of colourless and remote cosmic control; the God of the stoics and the agnostics. It was emphatically he who was fighting for the Holy Child against the grey deity of the Pharisees and the Sadducees. He was fighting for that very balance of beautiful interdependence and intimacy, in the very Trinity of the Divine Nature, that draws our hearts to the Trinity of the Holy Family. His dogma . . . turns even God into a Holy Family.

The Everlasting Man, Part 2, ch. 4

MORALITY

We awake at our birth staring at a very funny place. After serious examination of it we receive two fairly definite impressions; the first, delight and the second fear. The first leads us to dance and kick about in the sunlight; the second leads us not to do it too much for fear we should get sunstroke. The first leads us, that is to say, to institute festivals and so create art. The second leads us to institute rules and so create morality. One tells us that the praise of the Lord is the beginning of art; the other, that the fear of the Lord is the beginning of wisdom.[2] And in the days of religion, . . . these two things, however exaggerated in one direction or another, were still parts of a whole.

Daily News, 1 Aug. 1903

Visionary religion is . . . more wholesome than our modern and reasonable morality. . . . It can contemplate the idea of success or triumph in the hopeless fight towards the ethical ideal. . . . A modern morality, on the other hand, can only point with absolute conviction to the horrors that follow breaches of law; its only certainty is a certainty of ill. It can only point to imperfection. It has no perfection to point to. But the monk meditating upon Christ or Buddha has in his mind an image of perfect health. . . . It is wholeness and happiness that he is contemplating.

Heretics, ch. 2

1. St Athanasius (c.296-373), Bishop of Alexandria, successfully defended the doctrine of the Son being of one substance with the Father, and of the deity of the Holy Spirit
2. Psalm 111.10.

Virtue is not the absence of vices or the avoidance of moral dangers; virtue is a vivid and separate thing, like pain or a particular smell. Mercy does not mean not being cruel or sparing people revenge or punishment; it means a plain and positive thing like the sun, which one has either seen or not seen. Chastity does not mean abstention from sexual wrong; it means something flaming, like Joan of Arc.

'A Piece of Chalk', in *Tremendous Trifles*

[St. Thomas Aquinas] did want to distinguish Man from God. . . . Its upshot was . . . Free Will, or [the] moral responsibility of Man. . . . Upon this sublime and perilous liberty hang heaven and hell, and all the mysterious drama of the soul.

St. Thomas Aquinas, ch. 1

There is no such thing as a condition of complete emancipation. . . . In moral matters . . . there is no lawlessness, there is only a free choice between limitations.

Daily News, 21 Dec. 1905

About sex especially men are born unbalanced; we might almost say men are born mad. They scarcely reach sanity till they reach sanctity.

The Everlasting Man, Part 1, ch. 6

Sex cannot be admitted to a mere equality among elementary emotions or experiences like eating and sleeping. The moment sex ceases to be a servant it becomes a tyrant. . . . The modern talk about sex being free like any other sense, about the body being beautiful like any tree or flower, is either a description of the Garden of Eden or a piece of thoroughly bad psychology.

St. Francis of Assisi, ch. 2

Pride makes man a devil; but lust makes him a machine.

Daily News, 19 Feb. 1910

MAN AND GOD

I might convince a man that Matter as the origin of Mind is quite meaningless, if he and I were very fond of each other and fought each other every night for forty years. But long before he was convinced on his deathbed, a thousand other materialists would have been born, and nobody can explain everything to everybody. St. Thomas [Aquinas] . . . asks how all these people are possibly to find time for the amount of reasoning that is needed to find truth. . . . His argument for Revelation is not an argument against Reason. . . . The *conclusion* he draws from it is that men must receive the highest moral truths in a miraculous manner; or most men would not receive them at all.

St. Thomas Aquinas, ch. 1

St. Thomas [Aquinas emphasized] that Man is to be studied in his whole manhood; that a man is not a man without his body, just as he is not a man without his soul. . . . It is specially connected with the most startling sort of dogma, which the Modernist can least accept; the Resurrection of the Body.

St. Thomas Aquinas, ch. 1

There was . . . a more subtle danger in Augustine the Platonist than even in Augustine the Manichee. There came from it a mood which unconsciously committed the heresy of dividing the substance of the Trinity. It thought of God too exclusively as a Spirit who purifies or a Saviour who redeems; and too little as a Creator who creates. That is why men like Aquinas thought it right to correct Plato by an appeal to Aristotle: Aristotle who took things as he found them, just as Aquinas accepted things as God created them. . . . Humanly speaking, it was [Aquinas] who saved the human element in Christian theology.

St. Thomas Aquinas, ch. 3

The *heart* of humanity . . . is . . . satisfied by the strange hints and symbols that gather round the Trinitarian idea, the image of a council at which mercy pleads as well as justice, the conception of a sort of liberty and variety existing even in the inmost chamber of the world. For Western religion has always felt keenly the idea "it is not well for man to be alone." The social instinct asserted itself everywhere. . . . If this love of a living complexity be our test, it is certainly healthier to have the Trinitarian religion than the Unitarian. For to us Trinitarians . . . God Himself is a society. . . . Out of the desert . . . come the cruel children of the lonely God; the real Unitarians who with scimitar in hand have laid waste the world. For it is not well for God to be alone.

Orthodoxy, ch. 8

To say that all will be well anyhow . . . cannot be called the blast of a trumpet. . . . To a Christian existence is a *story*, which may end up in any way. In a thrilling novel . . . the hero is not eaten by cannibals; but it is essential to the existence of the thrill that he *might* be. . . . So Christian morals have always said to man, not that he would lose his soul, but that he must take care that he didn't. In Christian morals . . . it is wicked to call a man "damned": but it is strictly religious and philosophic to call him damnable.

Orthodoxy, ch. 8

'The Beatific Vision'

Through what fierce incarnations, furled
  In fire and darkness, did I go,
Ere I was worthy in the world
  To see a dandelion grow?

Well, if in any woes or wars
  I bought my naked right to be,
Grew worthy of the grass, nor gave
  The wren, my brother, shame for me.

But what shall God not ask of him
  In the last time when all is told,
Who saw her stand beside the hearth,
  The firelight garbing her in gold?

From *The Collected Poems of G.K. Chesterton*

The wise man will follow a star, low and large and fierce in the heavens; but the nearer he comes to it the smaller and smaller it will grow, till he finds it the humble lantern over some little inn or stable. Not till we know the high things shall we know how lowly they are. Meanwhile, the modern superior transcendentalist will find the facts of eternity incredible because they are so solid; he will not recognise heaven because it is so like the earth.

William Blake (1920), p.210

Whatever it is that we are all looking for, I fancy that it is really quite close. . . . Always the Kingdom of Heaven is "at hand". . . . So I for one should never be astonished if the next twist of a street led me to the heart of that maze in which all the mystics are lost.

'A Glimpse of My Country', in *Tremendous Trifles*

Books by
G.K. Chesterton

Referred to in the Text

Alarms and Discursions, Methuen, 1910

All I Survey, Methuen, 1933

All is Grist, Methuen, 1931

All Things Considered, Methuen, 1908

Appreciations and Criticisms of the Works of Charles Dickens, Dent, 1911

Autobiography, Hutchinson, 1936

Avowals and Denials, Methuen, 1934

The Catholic Church and Conversion, Burns, Oates & Washbourne, 1927

Charles Dickens, Methuen, 1906

Chaucer, Faber & Faber, 1932

Christendom in Dublin, Sheed & Ward, 1932

The Collected Poems of G.K. Chesterton, Cecil Palmer, 1927

The Coloured Lands, Sheed & Ward, 1938

Come to Think of It, Methuen, 1930

The Common Man, Sheed & Ward, 1950

The Defendant, Brimley Johnson, 1901

The Everlasting Man, Hodder & Stoughton, 1925

Fancies Versus Fads, Methuen, 1923

Generally Speaking, Methuen, 1928

George Bernard Shaw, John Lane, the Bodley Head, 1909

G.F. Watts, Duckworth, 1904

G.K. Chesterton: The Apostle and the Wild Ducks, Paul Elek, 1975, essays ed. Dorothy Collins

G.K.C. As M.C., Methuen, 1929, essays selected J.P. de Fonseka

The Glass Walking-Stick, Methuen, 1955, essays ed. Dorothy Collins, Preface Arthur Bryant

A Handful of Authors, Sheed & Ward, 1953, essays ed. Dorothy Collins

Heretics, John Lane, the Bodley Head, 1905

The Innocence of Father Brown, Cassell, 1911

Irish Impressions, Collins Sons, 1919

Leo Tolstoy, Hodder & Stoughton, 1903; other authors: G.H. Perris, Edward Garnett

Lunacy and Letters, Sheed & Ward, 1958, essays ed. Dorothy Collins

The Man Who Was Orthodox, Dennis Dobson, 1963, uncollected writings introd. A.L. Maycock

Manalive, Nelson, 1912

A Miscellany of Men, Methuen, 1912

The New Jerusalem, Hodder & Stoughton, 1920

Orthodoxy, John Lane, the Bodley Head, 1908

An Outline of Christianity, ed. A.S. Peake, vol. 3 (of 5), Waverley Book Co., 1926, – other contributors

Preachers from the Pew, ed. Rev Henry Hunt, 1906, – other contributors

The Queen of Seven Swords, Sheed & Ward, 1926

The Resurrection of Rome, Hodder & Stoughton, 1930

Robert Browning, Macmillan, 1903

Robert Louis Stevenson, Hodder & Stoughton, 1927

St. Francis of Assisi, Hodder & Stoughton, 1923

St. Thomas Aquinas, Hodder & Stoughton, 1933

A Short History of England, Chatto & Windus, 1917

Sidelights on New London and Newer York, Sheed & Ward, 1932

The Spice of Life, Darwen Finlayson, Beaconsfield, 1964, essays ed. Dorothy Collins

The Superstition of Divorce, Chatto & Windus, 1920

The Thing, Sheed & Ward, 1929

Tremendous Trifles, Methuen, 1909

Twelve Modern Apostles and Their Creeds, Duffield, New York, 1926, introd. Dean Inge – other contributors

Twelve Types, Arthur L. Humphreys, 1902

The Uses of Diversity, Methuen, 1920

Utopia of Usurers, Boni & Liver-Right, New York, 1917

The Victorian Age in Literature, Williams & Norgate, 1913

The Way of the Cross, Hodder & Stoughton, 1935, with Frank Brangwyn

The Well and the Shallows, Sheed & Ward, 1935

What I Saw in America, Hodder & Stoughton, 1922

What's Wrong With the World, Cassell, 1910

William Blake, Duckworth, 1910

Index

Printed in the United Kingdom
by Lightning Source UK Ltd.
116343UKS00001B/178-420